THE NORTH CAROLINA SYMPHONY

THE NORTH CAROLINA SYMPHONY

A History

Joe A. Mobley *and*
John W. Lambert

Foreword by Roy C. Dicks

McFarland & Company, Inc., Publishers
Jefferson, North Carolina

ISBN (print) 978-1-4766-7062-1
ISBN (ebook) 978-1-4766-3601-

LIBRARY OF CONGRESS AND BRITISH LIBRARY
CATALOGUING DATA ARE AVAILABLE

LIBRARY OF CONGRESS CONTROL NUMBER: 2019942446

Front cover image: the orchestra performs in Meymandi Concert Hall
(photograph by Michael Zirkle, courtesy North Carolina Symphony)

Manufactured in the United States of America

McFarland & Company, Inc., Publishers
Box 611, Jefferson, North Carolina 28640
www.mcfarlandpub.com

To all the musicians of the
North Carolina Symphony Orchestra,
past and present

Table of Contents

Foreword
by Roy C. Dicks

The North Carolina Symphony's long-standing mission of bringing classical music to towns and schools around the state has sparked many a child's wonder at the powerful magic an orchestral concert can evoke, often instilling in him or her a lifelong love of music.

I think I can rightly claim to be a poster child for the organization's admirable goals, because I attended my first North Carolina Symphony concert at around age eight and was hooked right away. Now, more than six decades later, I look back fondly on many of its fine concerts I attended, first as student, later as adult fan, and then as music critic.

My initial experiences with the North Carolina Symphony came in my hometown of Fayetteville. My first live concert was a children's program my mother took me to in the mid–1950s at Fort Bragg, where she worked as a civilian. My memory of it is now rather dim, but I distinctly recall one piece—Leroy Anderson's "Typewriter." I sat there mesmerized, not only by the unique "instrument" being played but also by the sound of the full ensemble filling the hall.

Later, while I was a student at Alexander Graham Junior High School, the orchestra visited several times for assemblies. Again, I don't have much memory of the details except for a performance of Stravinsky's *Firebird* Suite. I can still hear the frightening fortissimo chord that begins the spooky "Infernal Dance of Kastchei's Subjects" and the ensuing frenzied rhythms.

By the time I was in senior high school, I was eagerly attending full evening programs of the North Carolina Symphony on its yearly tours to Fayetteville (and was the proud possessor of annual membership cards). The programs I saved from those concerts remind me that, besides hearing works by familiar composers such as Mozart, Beethoven, and Brahms, I also was exposed to rather sophisticated fare by Howard Hanson, Hunter Johnson, and Carl Nielsen.

In those high school years, I'd begun collecting classical music LPs to explore the vast standard repertoire as performed by world-class orchestras and legendary conductors. Yet I was equally thrilled by hearing North Carolina Symphony concerts live. I went backstage once to meet conductor Benjamin Swalin, whom I naïvely asked why the orchestra had not made any recordings. He patiently explained the costs, contracts, and competition involved but thanked me for my interest. (Although I had to wait well into the twenty-first century, I now happily have multiple commercial CDs on my shelf recorded by the orchestra on the BIS, Telarc, and Steinway labels.)

My four years at East Carolina University furthered my classical music education through live performances in the campus arts series, including the Czech Philharmonic and the Detroit Symphony Orchestra. Also, during that time, I had opportunities to attend Friends of the College concerts in Raleigh, including those by the Vienna Philharmonic and the Pittsburgh Symphony Orchestra. Although I did not hear the North Carolina Symphony during those years, the exposure to such notable ensembles gave me grounding to appreciate what we had in our homegrown one.

After settling in Raleigh in 1970 to begin a career as a reference librarian, I was able to resume attending North Carolina Symphony concerts, as time and funds permitted. By then I had become a serious opera fan, so most of the performances I witnessed in the 1970s with conductor John Gosling were vocal. It still amazes me that I was able to hear world-class singers, such as Eileen Farrell, Mattiwilda Dobbs, James McCracken, and Roberta Peters, right in my own backyard. I heard choral masterpieces as well, including Mahler's massive, rarely performed Symphony No. 8 (a particular obsession of mine), which was performed in the prestigious Friends of the College series.

My toe in the water as a classical music critic came unexpectedly in November 1978 when the *Spectator*, a fledgling weekly alternative paper in Raleigh, put out a call for arts reviewers. Although my eight-year stint with that publication ultimately concentrated on theater and dance, my very first review was of a North Carolina Symphony concert conducted by Gosling. Violinist Pinchas Zukerman and his wife, flutist Eugenia Zukerman, played concertos by Bach, Ibert, and Bruch, and the program ended with a performance of Respighi's *Fountains of Rome*. The concert was of such high quality that it made my first professional review an easy task.

For the next twenty years or so, I attended the orchestra's concerts on an irregular basis, depending on my disposable income and the programming. But I have fond memories of several during that period that fed my soul, all conducted by Gerhardt Zimmermann. There were a glorious 1984 Verdi *Requiem*; a gala concert in 1987 of works by North Carolina–based Pulitzer Prize–winner Robert Ward, in honor of his seventieth birthday; and an unexpected return of Mahler's Symphony No. 8 in 1989, again for the Friends of the College series.

My relationship with the North Carolina Symphony took a major shift in 1997. I had just retired from my library career when an offer came from the *News and Observer*, Raleigh's daily newspaper. The features editor asked if I would be interested in reviewing classical music performances, prompted in part by letters I had written to the paper about its classical coverage. I protested at first that I was not a degreed musician and my experience was only avocational, but the editors convinced me they wanted reviews for the general public, not for musicians or academics. I accepted the challenge, writing reviews of the North Carolina Symphony, among other area music ensembles, for the next two decades. My first review was of a concert in Memorial Auditorium conducted by Gerhardt Zimmermann, which offered the familiar (Mendelssohn's Piano Concerto No. 1 and Schubert's Symphony No. 4) and the new (Hilary Tann's *Here, the Cliffs*, a world premiere commission for violin and orchestra).

One troubling aspect in my first few years of reviewing the orchestra was the deadening acoustic of Memorial Auditorium. I was particularly glad, therefore, to witness the orchestra's well-deserved move into the new Meymandi Concert Hall in February 2001. In its permanent home, the North Carolina Symphony could finally be experienced in an appropriate local venue. At the opening night gala, Zimmermann conducted Stravinsky's *Firebird* Suite, instantly taking me back to the thrill I had experienced at that junior high concert four decades earlier. This time, however, there were the exhilaration of hearing solo woodwinds clearly spotlighted and the marvel of listening to the strings playing the most delicate passages with the merest touch of their bows.

An unexpected opportunity to further observe the orchestra's worthiness arose the next season when the search for a new music director began. It was a revelation to hear the musicians expertly adjust to the styles and personalities of eleven guest conductors between September 2002 and October 2003.

Welshman Grant Llewellyn ultimately received the nod and quickly began shaping the orchestra into its finest form, which, combined with the new concert hall, made North Carolina Symphony concerts very exciting events. Llewellyn's interpretations have often made me hear familiar works in new ways, especially those that have been given hard-driven and overblown performances in the past. His Beethoven, Brahms, and Mahler have been particularly revelatory. The concerts by resident conductor William Henry Curry and a handful of guest conductors each season have also added to my enjoyment and learning.

It's not an exaggeration to say that the North Carolina Symphony has been a significant influence on my cultural life through six decades of attending its concerts. I look forward to many more engaging evenings listening to standard repertory as well as new works. I can only hope that all the young people who continue to attend the orchestra's programs will get the spark of wonder and excitement that I did so many years ago.

The orchestra's history, so well documented in this fine book, should be an eye-opener on what it takes to keep such a valuable cultural institution in existence and how important it is to keep it alive for generations to come.

Music, theater, and dance critic Roy C. Dicks lives in Raleigh.

Preface

Throughout the decades, many North Carolinians, natives and new-comers alike, have shown an appreciation for the classical music repertoire. The story of the North Carolina Symphony—the population's major orchestra and the oldest continuously state-supported symphony in the nation—reveals much about that appreciation and about musical traditions in the South. A number of articles, reviews, and other writings have dealt with aspects of the symphony and its growth. A 1971 doctoral dissertation by Howard Turner Pearsall examined the first thirty years of the orchestra's development. In 1987 former longtime conductor Dr. Benjamin Swalin published *Hard Circus Road*, an excellent book-length account of the symphony and his experiences as its leader. But no systematic study heretofore has addressed the history of the orchestra in the context of North Carolina's cultural milieu. Therefore that history—from the Old North State's earliest experiences with classical music to the present day—is the subject of the chapters that follow.

In the 1940s, the symphony took as its motto "This Is Your Music"—a fitting title for its story. That and the other quotations herein are rendered verbatim, with emendations in square brackets.

A number of people deserve acknowledgment for their assistance in the preparation of this book. William Henry Curry, Jimmy Gilmore, Paul Gorski, Richard Hoffert, the late Dr. Albert Jenkins, Susan Jenkins, Sandi Macdonald, the late Thomas McGuire, James Ogle, Hugh Partridge, Irvin and Ann Pearce, Vincent Simonetti, Ronald Weddle, and David Worters participated in interviews with the authors and/or shared materials from their personal collections. Longtime music and theater critic Roy C. Dicks was kind enough to write the foreword and make available information and sources from his files. Thanks are due to Sue Guenther, Meredith Laing, and Deborah Nelson of the North Carolina Symphony office, as well as Liza Beth of Chorus America, Suzanne Bolt and Karen Dabson of the Durham Symphony, and Christine Kastner of the Fayetteville Symphony. The authors are indebted to the staffs of the Southern Historical Collection and the North Carolina Collection in Wilson Library at the University of North Carolina at Chapel Hill, particularly Jason Tomberlin, head of Research and Instructional Services (Special Collections). The staff of the State Archives of North Carolina were most helpful, especially Kim Andersen, head of the Audiovisual Materials Unit. Special recognition must be given to the authors' wives, Nancy Lambert and Kathleen Wyche, for their copyediting and proofreading help.

Introduction

When Americans think about the musical traditions and tastes of the South, they often have certain common—even stereotypical—images in mind. According to those ideas, southerners have appreciated and performed mostly music that springs from their unique social and economic circumstances and experiences, which until recent decades were largely rural. When one reflects on the South's love of and contributions to music over time, one immediately thinks of country, folk, spirituals, gospel, jazz, blues, rhythm and blues, and even the evolution of rock and roll.

But since the colonial era, the classical repertoire has been part of the musical tradition in the South. Of course, in the North American colonies, early performances were few and limited mostly to the upper class of society. In the earliest days of the Republic, orchestral performances of classical works remained rare. "In comparison with European music," writes authority John H. Mueller, "the beginnings of the American orchestra were … pathetically meagre. For in this country there were no luxurious courts or castles which could sustain a Haydn, nor a landed nobility which could pension a Beethoven, nor yet the rich tradition in which whole nations take pride, and are thereby automatically impelled to nurture the arts and set standards for emulation."[1]

By the first half of the nineteenth century, however, classical music was reaching a growing, if still limited, audience through individual and group performances. In North Carolina, it found its most accomplished voice in the culture of the Moravians, who brought with them to the New World the sophisticated musical traditions of Europe. And classical music was being heard to a recognizable extent in some homes, academies, and public events throughout the state, especially in the urban areas. Eventually it was being played by what might be termed symphony orchestras.

Symphony orchestras are generally considered to be musical ensembles of a certain size, type, and quality—composed of wind, string, brass, and percussion instruments—that play symphonic, classical works. Orchestras are led by conductors, also known as music directors. (This book refers to each North Carolina Symphony conductor as a conductor, a music director, a music director/conductor, or an artistic director/conductor, according to the symphony's usage at the time.) Of course classical music is also performed in ways other than by a symphony orchestra—for example, by a chamber orchestra, which is a smaller ensemble that plays in a smaller space.

Historian of American music John Warthen Struble gives a good summary of what exactly constitutes classical music. "Frequently," he writes, "it is easier to say what it is not. For instance, folksong which serves a utilitarian purpose—such as maintaining the rhythm of some repetitive job that it accompanies—or tunes used for communal singing and dancing are not themselves 'classical music,' though they may serve as a basis for later classical works. Music used in religious services or music intended to serve as background for conversation and social occasions generally is not thought of as 'classical' when it is created but may become so with the passage of time, or when it is presented in an exclusively concert format." Classical music, therefore, might arise from "vernacular foundations," but when it is composed formally and played in concert, it reaches another, more sophisticated plane.[2]

Opera (or grand opera) is customarily considered a part of the classical genre. It is drama set to music, with the actors singing various roles. Most often symphony orchestras play the instrumental music that accompanies the singers and perform overtures and interludes as well. In "pure" opera, all the parts are sung. A more lighthearted version called opéra comique contains spoken dialogue. Both forms were heard in North Carolina before the Civil War and gained popularity in public auditoriums and so-called opera houses in the late nineteenth and early twentieth centuries. Ballet is also considered classical, as a form of dance usually set to a classical composition and accompanied by an orchestra. Its development, however, seems to have come more slowly in North Carolina than did the popularity of concerts and opera.

During the late nineteenth and early twentieth centuries, North Carolinians' interest in classical music began to grow substantially as local orchestras were established and traveling music companies called in the state's towns in burgeoning numbers. This interest was part of a post–Civil War regional transformation known as the advent of the "New South," whereby North Carolina and the other southern states underwent large-scale industrialization, accompanied by a growth in towns and cities and a rising urban middle class whose education, leisure time, and contact with the outside world led to enthusiasm for cultural activities.

Around 1900 a new fervor for reform in politics and social and economic life in North Carolina led to the ascendancy in state government of a progressive wing of the Democratic Party. Progressives, as they were called, instigated such reforms as improved public education, public health, roads and highways, child labor regulations, tax and election laws, and prison conditions; the prohibition of alcohol; and women's suffrage. The Progressives' programs did not include substantial benefits for African Americans, who still suffered under the injustices of segregation (through "Jim Crow" laws), disfranchisement, and racial violence by white supremacy groups. Nevertheless, the new breed of Democrats, who believed that government should play a large role in addressing the problems of society, or at least white society, brought about significant improvements in North Carolina.

The wave of political progressivism that swept through the state in the first two decades of the twentieth century spawned a cultural progressivism that sprang from the same ideology of improving or perfecting society. This cultural "revolution" included the establishment of private and public programs and agencies for the support of literature, art, folklore, history, and historic preservation. And a large part of this rising cultural progressivism was an enthusiastic promotion of classical music by a sizable and influential portion of the state's upper- and rising-middle-class population. Women especially were active in the formation of music clubs in various towns and cities to bring and support classical music in their communities. From the statewide North Carolina Federation of Music Clubs after World War I came the first call for the creation of a North Carolina symphony orchestra.

That call was answered for the first time in 1932, ironically when the state and nation lay in the depths of the Great Depression. At that time, native North Carolinian Lamar Stringfield, an accomplished musician, conductor, and composer with the experience of forming an orchestra in Asheville, led an effort to develop a state orchestra. Stringfield worked from the Institute of Folk Music at the University of North Carolina (UNC) at Chapel Hill. With the backing of a number of prominent supporters, the governor's office, and newly created local Symphony Society clubs, the first orchestra, consisting of volunteer musicians, gave a number of concerts throughout the state. Stringfield managed to arrange the appearances of a few well-known guest artists.

As the symphony, like the rest of the state and nation, struggled with the financial hardships of the Depression, it received a substantial boost from President Franklin D. Roosevelt's New Deal program. The Federal Emergency Relief Administration (FERA), directed in North Carolina by Annie Land O'Berry, provided $45,000 to help finance operations, pay out-of-work musicians, and set the orchestra on the path to self-sustainability. The orchestra continued to expand its range and number of concerts as the FERA worked hand-in-hand with the Symphony Society. But the initial success did not last.

Stringfield, at times controversial, resigned as music director to take a position with another New Deal agency, the Works Progress Administration

(WPA), in Atlanta. The WPA took over control of the orchestra from the FERA and set new guidelines, which included denying pay to musicians who were not eligible for relief and excluding the Symphony Society from decision making. As a result, the symphony dwindled almost to extinction.

It would, however, be saved and rejuvenated by newlyweds Benjamin Franklin Swalin and Maxine McMahon Swalin, who arrived in North Carolina in the 1930s, and whose names will forever be associated with the history of the North Carolina Symphony. Through tireless effort and commitment, the Swalins built the orchestra into a cultural institution that performed in communities and schools throughout North Carolina from the 1940s to the 1970s, exposing a large segment of the state's population to classical music, often for the first time. A significant portion of this book is devoted to their story.

Although the North Carolina Symphony remains North Carolina's premier *state* orchestra, the public's appetite for classical music has given rise over the years to a proliferation of various local orchestras, chamber music ensembles, choral societies, and opera and ballet groups. These have included orchestras and other music organizations in such cities as Asheville, Charlotte, Fayetteville, Greensboro, Hickory, Raleigh, Salisbury, Wilmington, and Winston-Salem, as well as the Brevard Music Center, college and university music departments, and the School of the Arts in Winston-Salem, presently part of the UNC system. In 1948 Raleigh's Alfred Johnson Fletcher and his wife, Elizabeth Utley Fletcher, established the Grass Roots Opera (later called the National Opera Company), which toured towns with grand and light opera using few costumes and little scenery. In 2010 North Carolina Opera sprang from a merger of the Opera Company of North Carolina and Capitol Opera Raleigh. The best-known ballet companies are Carolina Ballet and Charlotte Ballet. Carolina Ballet arose in 1997 from the Raleigh Dance Theatre, established in 1984. The Charlotte company originated as the North Carolina Dance Theatre in 1970 and took its present name in 2014.

1

Classical Music
from "Poor Carolina"
to "The Sahara of the Bozart"

Classical music had a definite presence in the colonial South, even though its appreciation and performance were limited largely to the upper-class gentry. According to historians of southern music Bill C. Malone and David Stricklin, "During the colonial era the southern upper classes did not yet possess a cultural sense of mission that encouraged inculcating musical appreciation among the lower classes."[1] William Byrd (1674–1744) of Westover plantation in Virginia possessed a large library that included English and Italian operas. In his *Histories of the* [1728] *Dividing Line betwixt Virginia and North Carolina*, he alluded to the "Marvellous Power of Music" to inspire persons, as well as to promote psychological and physical health.[2]

In Williamsburg, the colonial capital of Virginia, the royal Governor's Palace began holding weekly amateur concerts following Peter Pelham's recitals there in 1752. Pelham was the organist at Bruton Parish Church and also gave private lessons. Eventually he supplemented his income as keeper of the Public Gaol in the town. He reportedly provided condemned prisoners a final opportunity to hear good music as he transported them to church in shackles prior to their executions. The amateur musicians at the palace concerts included the governor himself, Francis Fauquier, and members of the local planter aristocracy. The first violinist was John Randolph, a large landowner, lawyer, and author. The governor's good friend and councillor Robert Carter probably played the harpsichord and the German flute. Carter had an organ built in London and placed in his house, which stood beside the palace. John Page of Rosewood plantation most likely played with the group, too.

The best known of these amateur performers was Thomas Jefferson, who played the violin and might even have attempted the cello. In addition, he hired Pelham to play for him privately. He later stated that in the twelve years prior to the Revolution, he devoted three hours a day to practicing the violin. According to Jefferson's biographer, "There was a musical accompaniment to many of Jefferson's most intimate associations throughout the first half of his life, and it was probably during these years at Williamsburg that music became the 'favorite passion' of his soul."[3] That passion continued throughout his career and life. While serving as minister to France after the Revolution, Jefferson collected and shipped home boxes of musical scores. His vast library at Monticello contained works by such composers as Corelli, Bach, Handel, and Haydn.[4]

The port of Charleston, South Carolina, acquired the largest reputation as a center of musical sophistication in the colonial South. The first classical concert in the city was performed by John Salter, a church organist, in 1752. Soon afterward *Flora; or, Hob in the Well*, the first ballad opera in North America, was staged in Charleston's courtroom. Then in 1762, a group of 120 prominent South Carolinians established the St. Cecilia Society, the first musical society founded in what would become the United States. The society's paid orchestra gave annual concerts and recitals and at times featured foreign artists. Maria Storer, perhaps the best-known vocalist to appear in colonial America, sang there in February 1774. However, as Malone and Stricklin write, the society "was above all a socially exclusive club of gentlemen. There is no reason to believe that the 'lower orders' ever heard any of the concerts sponsored by the organization." (The St. Cecilia Society survived until 1912, but by then its paid musicians constituted only a quintet.)[5]

Even among its gentry, colonial North Carolina did not enjoy the same musical reputation as did its neighbors Virginia and South Carolina. In fact, because of its slowly developing economy, early North Carolina was overshadowed in all areas of development by the colonies immediately to its north and south. A number of elements contributed to a weak economy in "poor Carolina": the lack of a large and profitable staple crop, a primitive transportation system, a shortage of labor and hard currency, and perhaps most of all a coastal geography—marked by the barrier sand islands known as the Outer Banks—that created shallow sounds and dangerous inlets and capes and that denied the colony deepwater harbors, essential for a thriving maritime commerce.[6] As historian William S. Price, Jr., has written, "A small-scale economy, a dearth of educational institutions, and a social and political leadership bent on making money fast meant that North Carolina ... did [not] have a cosmopolitan city like Charleston, with its sophisticated cultural life."[7] Yet classical music did play a part in social and cultural life on the plantations and in the towns, primarily among the upper class. Governor William Tryon's wife, Margaret Wake, for example, apparently was a fairly accomplished musician who loved social events and played the organ and the clavichord, including on visits to Williamsburg and Salem, North Carolina.[8]

Margaret Wake Tryon, wife of Governor William Tryon, played the organ and the clavichord in colonial North Carolina. The governor and his family lived at Tryon Palace in New Bern (courtesy State Archives of North Carolina).

The Revolutionary War inhibited social and cultural activity, including music, in the nation struggling for its independence. In June 1778, Jefferson wrote to an acquaintance in Italy, Giovanni Fabbroni, that "If there is a gratification which I envy any people in this world, it is to your country its music. This is the favorite passion of my soul, & fortune has cast my lot in a country where it is in a state of deplorable barbarism." He realized that musicians from the Old World were not likely to find a profitable career in music in the United States. But perhaps Italian skilled workers and craftsmen who were also musicians might be enticed to immigrate to America and fill both economic and cultural needs. "The bounds of an American fortune will not admit the indulgence of a domestic band of musicians," he declared, "yet I have thought that a passion for music might be reconciled with that economy which we are obliged to observe." He noted that on his own plantation, he would like to have employees such as a gardener, weaver, cabinetmaker, stonecutter, and winemaker who could also perform music. He observed to Fabbroni that "In a country where like yours music is cultivated and practised by every class of men I suppose there might be found persons of those trades who could perform on the French horn, clarinet or hautboy & bassoon, so that one might have a band of two French horns, two clarinets, & hautboys & a bassoon, without enlarging their domestic expenses. A certainty of employment for a half dozen years, and at the end of that time to find them if they choose a conveyance to their own country might induce them to come here on reasonable wages." He suggested to his Italian friend that "perhaps it might be practicable for you in [your] ordinary intercourse with your people, to find out such men disposed to come to America." Of course,

Jefferson's scheme for importing worker musicians never became reality in the South.[9]

But the late eighteenth and early nineteenth centuries did witness a growth in musical interest, although at first professional instructors, instruments, and performances were few. In Raleigh, North Carolina, in 1804, New Englander Francis Maurice—who taught piano, violin, dancing, and French—arrived and began giving lessons with his "Grand Piano Forte." Three years later, the family of Thomas Sambourne came to the state capital to teach both vocal and instrumental music, as well as drawing and French. The Sambournes were permitted to place their piano in one of the rooms of the State House to give instruction to both youths and adults. Local newspaper editor Joseph Gales observed that "till lately, a Piano had scarcely been seen." His bookstore offered published guides for playing the violin and flute.[10]

During the antebellum era, private academies featured a large portion of formal musical education, and such instruction was usually for young women. Of the nearly three hundred academies founded in North Carolina between 1820 and 1860, many were exclusively female, and music inevitably made up part of the course of study. Accomplishment at the piano or harp or in singing was considered a requirement for young ladies of the upper and middle classes, who largely made up the student body in those institutions. Their training included the classical repertoire, although they frequently preferred popular songs of the day. In 1823 the prominent banker and legislator William Polk instructed his daughter Mary, a student at Salem Academy, to "not neglect her piano or harp." Mary Blount Bryan of New Bern was concerned that her daughter Charlotte, in school in Pennsylvania, was neglecting her music. She reminded Charlotte that her "musical education was acquired by a great deal of application & money."[11] At the Young Ladies' Boarding School in Warrenton, the instructor of music charged twenty-five dollars per quarter to teach "Music, vocal and instrumental, treble, tenor, counter bass and thorough bass for the Piano Forte, and Dancing." At the Charlotte Female Academy, the fee "for music on the piano" was twenty dollars. Tuition at LaVallee Female Seminary in Halifax County included "$15 for Music on the piano forte, $30 for music on the harp, $10 for music on the guitar."[12] After Thomas Sambourne died suddenly in Raleigh, his widow remained in the town for a number of years, teaching music at the Raleigh Academy as head of the young ladies' department as well as giving private lessons. In 1813 the native German pianist John F. Goneke came to Raleigh via New Bern and Washington, North Carolina. He installed two or three pianos in his house near the academy and for the next ten years provided lessons for the students and the public. He then constructed a concert hall, theater, and shop on Fayetteville Street, where he continued to give instruction. Several other music teachers appeared in the state capital in the 1820s and 1830s.[13]

At St. Mary's School for young women in Raleigh, musical instruction always had a high priority, and voice, piano, harp, and guitar were taught. The head of the music department, the Frenchman Gustav Blessner (1808–1888), was a violinist, pianist, and composer. He published his compositions, a number of which were dedicated to his students. His wife, also a music teacher as well as an organist and artist, designed the cover of the publication. Shortly after he arrived at St. Mary's in the 1840s, Blessner performed on the piano at a party given by Governor John M. Morehead. Locals enjoyed the regular musical soirees given by Blessner and his students, which featured piano, harp, violin, and vocalists. One attendee commended the "rich feast of music ... served up by the Department over which Mr. Blessner presides."[14] For the commencement exercises at UNC in 1844, Blessner composed "The Grand March of the University of North Carolina."[15] Among his more than twenty-six compositions, some that gained national attention were "The Faustina Polka"; "Les Belles de L'Amerique," a quadrille; "La Romana," a waltz; and "La belle Savoyarde," a polka.[16] While at St. Mary's, he owned "a fine double-action Harp, made by Erard, of Paris," and two "excellent Guitars, of Martin's manufactory, in New York," which he offered for sale to the public.[17] After the Civil War, Blessner lived for a time in Canandaigua, New York, taught music at the Ontario Female Seminary there, and eventually became the head of the Department of Music at the Pittsburgh Female College in Pennsylvania.[18]

Music lessons in the antebellum South remained largely a female pursuit. Upper-class young men generally were not encouraged to take lessons or play an instrument, especially the piano, such an activity not being considered manly for a southern gentleman. Maunsel White, a large planter and merchant of New Orleans, denied his son's request for piano lessons, admonishing him not to waste time "drumming" on the instrument. Georgia's Bishop Atticus G. Haywood expressed embarrassment at his son's desire to study piano in Boston.[19]

Although music instruction was available in nineteenth-century North Carolina for those who could afford it, it was not always of the best quality. Nor were the students necessarily adept when exhibiting their knowledge and skill. The wealthy North Carolina planter Ebenezer Pettigrew, of Bonarva plantation near Lake Phelps, admired the musical accomplishment of his future wife, Ann (Nancy). But he found the piano rendition by another lady hard to bear. "On my way home," he recalled to a relative about a recent trip, "I was introduced to a room where there was a Piano, The Lady (she was a marryed one) seemed disposed to entertain me.... I am fond of music, but mercy defend me! The contrast, The Person, with her great hand hammering down on the keys, by which a rattling was produced more like an empty cart in quick motion with all the boards loose, than that delightful music which

I had been hearing all the week from the fair hand of the lovely Nancy. Thinks I to myself, what mortifications must we endure! I sought for my bed as soon as good manners would permit. This comparison of sounds must go very little farther. I would not wound the fealings of the Lady for any consideration."[20]

By the second decade of the nineteenth century, pianos were becoming common sources of entertainment in the more affluent parlors throughout North Carolina. In homes statewide, afternoon teas, evening parties, and other social gatherings frequently included piano playing and group singing.[21] The young future governor and university president David L. Swain observed that pianos were "About as numerous as silver spoons" in Buncombe County. Young single women presumably were encouraged to learn to play the instrument in an effort to impress potential husbands. According to one Raleigh critic, however, brides usually ceased to play "in less than a year after wedlock."[22]

Appearances in North Carolina by traveling professional musical artists were few in the first third of the nineteenth century. But the number grew in the two decades prior to the Civil War. In the 1850s, Wilmington, the state's largest town at the time, enjoyed at least ten concerts each year. In 1850 Jenny Lind, the "Swedish Nightingale" who sang before large audiences throughout the South, traveled through Wilmington en route to Charleston. However, her manager, P. T. Barnum, declined to allow her to sing in Wilmington because the town did not have a theater or hall large enough for profitable ticket sales. But three years later, the renowned Norwegian violinist Ole Bull, who also toured the South, drew a sizable audience. In 1857 Miss M. M. Gibbs, "the Jenny Lind of the South," entertained the port's inhabitants. The next year, the famous pianist Sigismund Thalberg gave a concert.[23] Like Wilmington, Raleigh did not host Jenny Lind because the town did not have a concert hall of sufficient size. But the local newspapers faithfully followed her tour through the South, and music stores offered "the whole series of the Lind songs, published in New York ... with emblematic vignettes finely executed by lithograph."[24]

Jenny Lind and Ole Bull appeared before large audiences in such southern cities as Richmond, Charleston, New Orleans, Natchez, and Memphis.[25] Also making frequent appearances was "the South's first great classical musician and composer, and the nation's first musical matinee idol." Louis Moreau Gottschalk was born in New Orleans in 1829. As a child prodigy, he was tutored by François Letellier, organist and choirmaster at St. Louis Cathedral in New Orleans. When he was only twelve years old, he traveled to Europe to study with leading teachers. His tours in Europe won him recognition and praise, including by Frederic Chopin, who heard him in concert. Recognizing the popularity and success of Jenny Lind, Gottschalk returned to America in

1853 and began concertizing in southern cities. "Like most crowd-pleasers in American musical history," write Malone and Stricklin, "Gottschalk achieved fame with more than just splendid musicianship. Dramatic stage presence, dark good looks, and an exotic Latin charm all contributed to the charisma that earned Gottschalk his international reputation."[26]

The type of showmanship exhibited by Gottschalk and Jenny Lind, as well as Bull and other musicians, had popular appeal for North Carolinians, although neither of the first two ever performed in the Old North State. Huge audiences turned out to hear traveling classical artists. But as Malone and Stricklin further note, "Whether the reception of such musicians indicates a genuine hunger for, or appreciation of, high culture among southerners is open to question. In the days before phonograph records, radio, or television, many audiences starved for entertainment thronged to whatever was available. They could alternate easily between a melodrama and a Shakespearean tragedy, a minstrel show and a concert by Jenny Lind."[27]

In the antebellum era, New Orleans surpassed Charleston as the South's center of music, particularly staging French and Italian operas. At least as early as the turn of the nineteenth century, operas had been performed in the Crescent City's St. Peter Street Theater, with André Grétry's *Sylvain* possibly being the first. Also heard at the theater were compositions by Boieldieu, Méhul, Dalayrac, and Monsigny, all of whom were known in Paris. The Théâtre d'Orléans became the main cultural hall when it was built in 1809. After burning in 1813, it was soon reconstructed. It began hosting artists from the Paris Opera House and featuring works by Rossini, Mozart, Gluck, Cherubini, and other European composers. Meyerbeer's *Les Huguenots* and Donizetti's *Lucia di Lammermoor* were sung in French there. At the Anglo-American Theater in 1835, Meyerbeer's *Robert le Diable* made its American debut. In the next year, the nation's premiere of Bellini's *Il Pirata* was presented in New Orleans by an Italian troupe. When the French Opera House arose as the main musical center on the eve of the Civil War, soprano Adelina Patti sang in its second season. Prior to the war, the Frenchman Antoine Jullien often conducted concerts in New Orleans.[28]

Several opera companies performed in North Carolina's main port city, Wilmington, in the decade before the Civil War. Dutch soprano Madame Rosa de Vries of the Italian Opera Company appeared in 1855. Three years later, construction of the town's Thalian Hall, a combination opera house and city hall, facilitated operas including those by the Excelsior Opera Troupe. The French Opera Comique denied its audience the pleasure of the full opera experience when its orchestra did not show up. The Cooper English Opera Troupe encountered a restless audience when only part of the company appeared on opening night and, furthermore, was late arriving. The locals were assuaged, however, when the full company finally assembled and gave

three contracted full performances, as well as a special Saturday "Grand Operatic Matinee" for the ladies of the town. "We are a music loving people,"
declared a local newspaper, "and can appreciate good playing and music."[29]

Musicians with a degree of classical skill also called at Raleigh. Probably
the best known was the English soprano Madame Anna Bishop, who sang at
the Yarborough Hotel in 1851 and 1853, accompanied by a ballad singer, a pianist, and a harpist. She was followed at the same hall in 1854 by flutist Madame
Amelia Siminski.

The inability of North Carolina's towns to attract more traveling classical
companies resulted in large part from the lack of concert halls big enough
to ensure sufficient ticket profits for the artists. Wilmington's problem was
partly alleviated by the building of Thalian Hall. In Raleigh the Capitol, the
county courthouse, and the town hall were often used, as were various commercial buildings, including the Yarborough House and other hotels. None,
however, proved adequate for accommodating sizable audiences. In 1853 an

Classical musicians and traveling opera companies performed in Wilmington's
Thalian Hall, constructed in the 1850s. The building also served as city offices (courtesy State Archives of North Carolina).

editor lamented that Raleigh was without "a public hall in this city sufficiently large to induce the troupes of travelling musicians, and other artists of the day, to pay us a visit."[30]

The composition of classical music in eighteenth- and nineteenth-century North Carolina reached its highest level in the culture of the Moravians (*Unitas Fratrum,* or Unity of Brethren), who settled in the region of Wachovia, where they founded the communities of Bethabara, Bethania, Salem, and Friedland in present-day Forsyth County and Friedburg in Davidson County. The Moravian church first arose in Germany. In America it initially established itself in Pennsylvania and then founded a settlement on the Wachovia tract in North Carolina.[31]

Moravian music was primarily sacred, although a small element was secular. Customarily an integral part of worship services, which featured congregational singing, it was also performed on special occasions and at anniversary events. Compositions included vocal and choral as well as instrumental works. Accomplished Moravian musicians, many of whom were ministers, usually became the composers. Three composers of particular note resided in Salem. Johannes Herbst (1735–1812) migrated to Pennsylvania from Germany and England in 1786, bringing more than a thousand choral and vocal compositions, three hundred of which were written by him. He died only eight months after coming to Salem to be its minister, but he left his library and legacy of musical works. Johann Friedrich Peter (1746–1813) settled in Pennsylvania in 1770 and then "served as pastor in Salem from 1780 to 1790, where he composed, in addition to many anthems and solo songs, six string quintets which are the earliest known chamber music written in America." Edward William Leinbach (1823–1901) was born in Salem and was "one of the relatively rare professional musicians among the Moravian composers." He received formal training in Boston and then returned to Salem to become "church organist, choirmaster, and teacher in the Salem Female Academy, in the course of which he composed a number of anthems and hymn tunes."[32]

The quality of Moravian musical culture was heavily influenced by the development and sophistication of music in Europe. According to John A. Hutcheson, Jr., the Moravians' music sprang from "some of the most musically fertile parts of Europe" and "drew on both the rich musical heritage of German Protestantism and the proximity of many prominent composers of the late baroque, classical, and early romantic eras." Consequently, "the inhabitants of Salem in the revolutionary and early national eras sang, played, and sometimes wrote music similar to what might have been heard or written at the same time in Vienna, Prague, Leipzig, or London."[33] Another authority, Donald M. McCorkle, sees special elements of the baroque surviving in the Moravians' music. "Two remnants in particular," he writes, "the *Collegium musicum* and the trombone choir, were woven into their musical fabric both in Bethlehem, Pennsylvania, and in Salem, North Carolina, and to some extent in several of the smaller settlements as well. Each of these performance-media had a distinguished, but unchronicled, existence in America; and each doubtless made a contribution to American music."[34] On July 4, 1829, Salem musicians and vocalists performed Haydn's *Creation* at the local female academy.[35]

Unfortunately, Moravian music in North Carolina was not heard extensively outside the Moravian community. And by the time of Leinbach's death, much of it had faded away, as the Moravian culture was increasingly absorbed into mainstream society. Nevertheless, a number of compositions survived in the Moravian archives at Bethlehem, Pennsylvania, and Salem.[36]

Whether in North Carolina's concert halls or private parlors, classical music generally did not appeal to the taste of most of the population. As explained, that genre was taught, composed, and performed for appreciative students and audiences. But the larger public usually gravitated toward popular tunes, band concerts, and minstrel shows.

Despite the appearances of classical concerts and operas in Wilmington, "Minstrel shows proved the most popular entertainment for the masses during the late antebellum years." Some of the traveling minstrel troupes that visited the port city were J. Morris's Concert and Olio Company of New York; the Plantations Melodists; Julien's Minstrels and Burlesque Opera Troupe; Kunkel's Nightingale Opera Troupe; the New Orleans Opera Troupe; Geo. Christy's Minstrels; and Buckley's Minstrels. So popular was this type of musical and comedy entertainment that the people of Wilmington formed their own minstrel company, the Sound Serenaders.[37]

These boisterous blackface stage shows featured singing, dancing, and joking high jinks. The white actors blackened their faces with burnt cork and "presented caricatures of black slaves, portraying them as superstitious, happy-go-lucky 'dancing darkies.'" Two of the most popular characters were Jim Crow and Zip Coon. According to authority Bill Barlow, "From its inception, minstrelsy's characterization of black people was stereotyped. Plantation slaves were depicted as contented, comical, and childlike, while urban house servants were portrayed as dandies and dummies who aped white mannerisms and longed to be white themselves. Most of the popular figures in antebellum minstrel entertainment were from the South and had some knowledge of African American folklore prior to putting on burnt cork." Ironically, as Barlow points out, "the song and dance performed by the white minstrels laid the groundwork for a better appreciation of authentic African American music and humor by white Americans."[38]

The musical tradition derived from the southern African American experience had a direct impact on the nature of classical music, most especially in the works of American composers. That tradition dated back to the earliest days of American slavery and sprang—via the European slave trade—from the "folksong" of West Africa. Although "It is impossible to describe with certainty exactly what the music of the first slaves was like," by the early nineteenth century there had occurred a "substantial mixing of African and Anglo-American elements in the music of southern slaves." The Christian hymns that became part of slave culture in the South "gave rise to the mournful religious song type known as the 'Negro spiritual,' perhaps as early as 1800."[39] The influence of the African American musical tradition, with its black folklore melodies and spirituals, would eventually be manifested in such classical compositions as Dvořák's *New World* Symphony, Henry F. Gilbert's *Dance in Place Congo* and *Comedy Overture on Negro Themes*, John Powell's *Rhapsodie Negre*, William Grant Still's *Afro-American* Symphony, and George Gershwin's *Porgy and Bess*.[40]

Along with minstrel shows, professional musicians and companies of various genres, reputations, and talents called at Raleigh. Among them were Thomas Hamblin's Operatic Serenaders; two companies of Swiss bell ringers; the Singing Orphean Family from the Banks of the Kennebec; a Scottish piper; a Madame Lovarny, "who sang in several foreign languages"; and a certain Herr Stoepel, who played a type of "Wood and Straw Instrument" at the town hall.[41]

Band music, with its martial airs, was always a favorite with nineteenth-century North Carolinians. According to North Carolina historian Guion Griffis Johnson,

> Nearly every town of more than five hundred inhabitants had at least one band; and, if an academy was located in the community, it might even have a music club. All who owned and could play a musical instrument were usually eligible for membership. The band master was frequently a local music teacher. Occasionally, such an organization evinced its modesty by choosing such a name as the Amateur's Band; but, after faithful practice and especially after uniforms were obtained, it became "the City Brass Band."
>
> The band appeared on all important occasions. If students were to be examined at the local academy, the band enlivened the occasion by a few selections. If the Fourth of July was to be celebrated, the band led the parade; a criminal to be hanged, the band cheered the crowds with flare of trumpets and beating of drums.[42]

When Chester H. Oakes, a Boston musician, arrived in Raleigh in 1845 to teach instruments and tune pianos, local amateurs enlisted him to give them instruction in martial band music. In addition to providing instruction in piano, guitar, and violin, H. I. I. Solomons taught "the brass Instruments usually employed in a Band." He organized the City Band, which played some of his own compositions, among them "The City of Oaks Grand Quick March." The band played on Independence Day and "during the beautiful moonlit evenings."[43] At first band music had a largely military tone. However, "By the middle of the nineteenth century," writes music historian Richard

Crawford, "bands in America were serving functions that had nothing to do with the military." Often their "music served as an adjunct to some other purpose," as they played for all sorts of public and private events, and varied concerts increasingly became regular features. As they broadened their programs, they performed more selections from the classical repertoire.[44] Visiting New Bern in 1848, young Mary Bryan noted that the town could boast of two fine bands, the City Brass Band and an African American band.

Some towns had glee clubs or harmonic societies. In Raleigh Goneke directed a concert at the State House that featured his music students and the local Harmonic Society. In Greensboro in the 1850s, Heinrich Schneider, music director at Edgeworth Female Seminary, led a glee club. But such organizations were few and generally did not last long.[45]

A good deal of the amateur and professional music in antebellum North Carolina might not have been of the "better sort." Nevertheless, it would be an exaggeration to say that the general population never heard and appreciated—even from the popular bands, singers, and instrumentalists—some versions or renditions from the classical repertoire. Often a traveling company or artist would include among the lighter fare a particular melody from an orchestral piece or an operatic aria. A party gathered for an evening around a parlor piano might hear a version of a classical movement along with current popular songs and tunes.

By the outbreak of the Civil War, Americans had developed strong regional traditions in folk music, which later would influence American composers of classical music. American music historian John Warthen Struble has observed that "At times these regional styles pulled against each other.... At times they merged to influence each other reciprocally and to form new subgenres, as in the case of southern hymnody and the music of the plantations. Other groups, like the Moravians and some Appalachian communities, remained insular and devoted exclusively to the musical traditions of their ancestors. But, during the decades immediately preceding the Civil War, a clear kind of 'American' sound began to emerge in the South, especially reflected in southern hymns, the ballads of Stephen Foster and some of the songs of the minstrel troupes active at the time."[46]

During the Civil War, the public's passion for music surged throughout the Confederate states, including North Carolina. Such was the appetite for music that publishers in the South printed more than 648 pieces of sheet music and a number of songbooks. Music provided considerable relief from the anguish of war for both soldiers in the field and the folks at home.

Classical music had a following in the Confederacy, mostly among the educated populace. Classical works were heard at parties, receptions, concerts, and special events where members of that class assembled. But few amateur musicians approached the level of Georgia poet, author, lawyer, and accomplished flutist Sidney Lanier. His interest in the flute began at an early age, and he maintained a knowledge and love of classical music and a skill with the instrument throughout his life. During the war, some female academies continued to attempt to instruct their students in the classical repertoire. Catherine Hopley, from England, struggled to teach her students at a Baptist academy near Warrenton, Virginia, about classical music. But her pupils, like most wartime Southerners, preferred popular, patriotic, and sentimental tunes.

The South's piano virtuoso Louis Gottschalk remained loyal to the Union after secession and departed the Confederacy when the war broke out. Still, some of his romantic compositions, such as "Serenade," "The Last Hope," and "The Dying Poet," continued to have appeal in the Confederate states. After his death in Rio de Janeiro, Brazil, in 1869, many of Gottschalk's works were forgotten. But others, such as his Symphony No. 1 (*A Night in the Tropics*), were not.[47]

Most of the wartime music played and sung on the home front was patriotic and saccharine, usually enjoyed at group gatherings in homes where there was a piano or other musical instrument or at small community gatherings. Some of the favorite songs were "Dixie" (which became the "anthem" of the Confederacy), "The Bonnie Blue Flag," "Maryland, My Maryland," "Beauregard's March," "The Yellow Rose of Texas," and the sad and sentimental "Somebody's Darling," "Lorena," and "When This Cruel War Is Over."[48]

The war virtually halted the influx of Northern traveling troupes that might have staged classical productions. Most concerts were provided by local amateurs and given for the benefit of charities. But a few professional performers did appear in the towns. In Raleigh, for example, the Confederate Minstrels showed up to give a number of performances, one for the aid of "the sick soldiers." A group of musical troubadours known as the Sloman family stayed in town for an extra night to raise money for a soldier blinded in the fighting. In 1864 one performer calling himself the Blind Refugee gave a concert in the town hall and charged two dollars for admission.[49]

For North Carolina's soldiers serving in the Confederate army, music was an integral part of their experience, providing them with diversion and bolstering their morale. According to historian Bell Irvin Wiley, "Perhaps the favorite recreation of the Confederate Army was music. In camp and on the march Johnny Reb found comfort in the sentimental melodies of the time…. Vocalizing in small groups seems to have been the general thing, but now and then mass singings on such scale as to be called 'musical sprees' or 'jubilees' were staged. Once in a while song fests acquired additional zest by combination with convivial drinking." As with the civilian population, much music was available from the many publishers of sheet music and songbooks. These works "consisted of the reissuing of favorites, old and new; but a considerable quantity of fly-by-night trash came forth under the guise of patriotic melodies—items that frequently had more patriotism than melody." Among the sentimental songs, "Home Sweet Home" was probably the favorite of the soldiers. But it was closely followed by "Lorena" and "All Quiet along the Potomac Tonight." Some regiments had glee clubs, usually short lived. Occasionally musicians, some of whom might have had an element of classical training, packed along their violins or flutes and serenaded their comrades.[50]

At least one of North Carolina's Confederate generals appreciated and played classical music. James Johnston Pettigrew, from the family plantation Bonarva, was the most intellectual and cultured of the Tar Heel State's generals, and he epitomized the idealized and romanticized image of the chivalrous Confederate officer. A child prodigy and well educated, he had a keen grasp of mathematics and was proficient in four languages. He admired the civilizations of the Spanish and Italians and taught himself Hebrew and Arabic. While traveling and studying in Europe before the war, writes Pettigrew's biographer, the young Carolinian discovered "music of a quantity and quality unheard of in America." In Berlin, for example, he "spent many afternoons

in the winter gardens listening to the orchestra performances that were free for the purchase of a little refreshment. In his diary he kept a detailed record of the operas and symphonies which he heard and described the atmosphere and circumstances of Berlin performances." Later, when living among family and practicing law in Charleston, "he installed a pianoforte in his lodgings and took music lessons," achieving a certain level of skill.[51]

Regimental bands supplied the music for marches and parades. At times they also gave night concerts, which sometimes included civilian guests. The most popular patriotic song performed by

North Carolina's intellectual Confederate general James Johnston Pettigrew had a passion for classical music (courtesy State Archives of North Carolina).

the bands was "Dixie." But the bands' selections ran all the way from "Maryland, My Maryland" to "Pop Goes the Weasel." Wiley notes that the "Difficulty of procuring instruments, scarcity of cultivated talent, and the stringencies of campaigning prevented the maintenance of high-class bands. European visitors to Southern camps were shocked by the 'discordant braying' of some of the musical organizations, and there can be little doubt that the majority were of inferior rating."[52]

North Carolina's Moravians constituted the best of the regimental bands, and they served in several of them. The most famous was the band of the Twenty-sixth Regiment North Carolina Troops, made up of Moravian musicians from Salem. The band joined the regiment just before the Battle of New Bern, North Carolina, in March 1862. On the march during the eastern campaign, the band at times played lively tunes as the regiment stepped along— often rendering the soldiers' favorite, "Get out the Wilderness." In the evenings, it might serenade the troops, and occasionally civilians who came into camp to listen. The diarist Julius Augustus Leinbach was a musician in the band. His brother, the classically trained Edward Leinbach, composed "Governor Vance's Inauguration March," which the band played at the gubernatorial inauguration of its former colonel Zebulon B. Vance in Raleigh in 1862.[53]

Although the main musical emphasis in North Carolina and the other Confederate states was not on the classical, the war nonetheless had an impact on the rise of classical music, with a specific American flavor, in the South. As Struble has written, "When the cataclysm that was the Civil War finally came, it uprooted untold thousands of people from every region of the country, mingled them together and often left them transplanted on 'alien' cultural ground. Traumatic as this process was, it provided the crucible needed to forge a characteristically American style of folk music, which later became the partial basis of a serious attempt at a national classical style."[54]

In the postwar era, too, North Carolinians found comfort and pleasure in music amid difficult times. Southern historian E. Merton Coulter has written that "Music helped Southerners to forget their defeat and their continuing troubles during the Reconstruction, and many a household and community found this forgetfulness around the organ or piano and the village brass band.... Music lovers organized their Mozart Clubs within their social circles, and many country villages as well as the larger cities organized brass bands. Contests for musical supremacy were sometimes held at which, according to some critics, more noise than music was made."[55]

In the late nineteenth century, virtually every county in rural North Carolina had at least one band that played at public concerts, picnics, holidays, and other events. The music might not have been of the highest quality and inevitably focused on the popular taste. But it was not unusual for the audience to hear at least one familiar strain from the classics. In one "contest for musical supremacy" in remote Pamlico County in May 1883, for example, two bands—the Bayboro Band and the Pamlico Band—played at a large picnic in the county seat. A local newspaper reporter observed, "The Bayboro band possibly can play seventeen or thirty respectable pieces, and the Pamlico band half as many more…. Bayboro leads off with—what? Ah! 'Tis Wagner's 'Score of Parsifal[.]' Pamlico follows in hot pursuit with 'Don't be angry with me Darling.'"[56]

The female academies that opened or returned to their prewar enrollments were once again making musical training part of their curricula. As during the antebellum period, classical music was taught and performed. But frequently more pedestrian and currently popular instrumentals and vocals had preference among the young women and even their instructors. At the recently opened Peace Institute in Raleigh, student Kate Lewis Scales, adopted daughter of general, governor, and congressman Alfred M. Scales, was praised for her talent as a singer. She received regular voice lessons at the school and performed in a number of public concerts as a soloist and in duets, trios, and choruses. "We are to have a grand concert here next Tuesday night," she wrote to her father in February 1877, "and I am to sing a solo; it is to be given for the benefit of the church and the choir are to take part; it is to be divided into two separate parts—one old tunes and the latter part is to consist of the modern music."[57] The "modern music" featured at her concerts meant new, predominantly saccharine songs that she seemed to prefer, such as "Will Thou Love Me Fairest Maiden" and "Come! The Lark Is Moving!" One of her favorites was composed by her music instructor at Peace. She wrote to her mother that it was "a duett for Miss Polly and me. It is the 'Parting Kiss' and is beautiful. The words are by Byron."[58]

Although much of the late–nineteenth-century public entertainment featured traveling minstrels, actors, singers, bands, and popular tunes, the public's enthusiasm for classical music and opera was growing. That interest, to be sure, was relative in a largely rural state recovering from the Civil War. Nonetheless, communities began forming small orchestras in the late nineteenth century. A number of Raleigh's young men in early 1889 formed the Euterpean Orchestra and began "practicing two and three nights per week." The Raleigh *News and Observer* called on the public to support the group.[59] In April the newspaper was pleased to announce that "On the evening of the 22d inst. the Euterpean orchestra and the Governor's Guard will give a combination entertainment of musical and spectacular specialties. The proceeds will go toward defraying the expense of the Guard to the Washington Centennial. The programme will include a number of orchestral renditions, also duets, quartettes, &c."[60] On October 25 the paper informed its readers that the Euterpean Orchestra was "now practicing regularly every night for the purpose of giving a series of five concerts in Metropolitan Hall beginning about November 15th. Season tickets for the whole five entertainments will be issued at one dollar each. Those concerts will consist of solos, duets, quartets full orchestra selections, etc, and the music will be of a very high grade.... The concerts will be under the direction of Prof. J. H. Wilhelmi who is a musician of rare taste and experience."[61]

These orchestras, however short lived, were generally small groups of musicians organized to perform ensemble music, and they included string players. For example, in May 1889 the Raleigh Orchestra, led by R. H. Haywood, featured five musicians. Haywood was first violin, John Haywood was second violin, and George Haywood played bass violin. Clarence Alston performed with the cornet, and Ed. Black the piccolo. According to one report, the orchestra "has given several evening concerts at the Yarboro House recently, and the guests have been struck with the excellence of their music."[62]

From the 1870s until World War I, a number of buildings known as opera

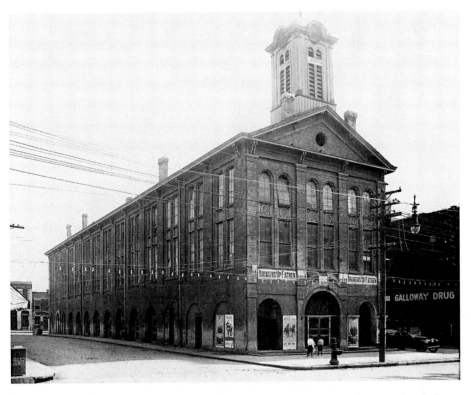

Orchestras and opera companies performed in the auditorium on the upper level of Raleigh's Metropolitan Hall (built ca. 1870), also known as the Old City Market. The market operated on the ground level (photograph from 1914, courtesy State Archives of North Carolina).

houses appeared in North Carolina towns. Most of those entertainment halls were created from space in the upper levels of existing buildings. Tucker Hall in Raleigh and Williams Hall in Fayetteville, for instance, were established in commercial structures. Benbow Hall in Greensboro and Jarrell's Hall in High Point were converted from space in hotels. Many of the opera houses were located in municipal buildings or town halls. Wilmington's Thalian Hall was the best known of those facilities. But others existed in such towns as Apex, Belhaven, Dunn, Kings Mountain, Oxford, Randleman, Smithfield, Tarboro, Warrenton, and Washington. Usually the manager of an opera house was a local businessman. If the venue was affiliated with a lodge hall or a militia, that organization provided the management. If it was in a municipal building, a town official was responsible for its administration.

Theater ruled as the main attraction in the "houses." Wilmington's Simeon Archibald Schloss became the state's best-known theater manager. Beginning with Thalian Hall in 1895, he obtained leases "on opera houses in Raleigh (1898), Greensboro (1901), Charlotte (1903), Winston-Salem (1905), Asheville (Grand Opera House, 1906), and Monroe (1907); Tarboro, Goldsboro, and Wilson (1908); Concord (1909); and again in Asheville (the Asheville Auditorium, 1910). At the height of its success, the Schloss Theatres Circuit controlled 14 opera houses in North Carolina, South Carolina, and Virginia."

Many towns in North Carolina had opera houses, where operas and other musical entertainment played. Shown is an opera house built in 1916 in the town of Hamlet (courtesy State Archives of North Carolina).

Schloss and other managers booked their attractions through the New York Theatrical Syndicate. According to one authority, Paul F. Wilson, "The term 'attraction' was used to cover a wide variety of presentations, including plays, musicals, minstrel shows, vaudeville, motion pictures, lectures, or concerts. A company that produced a single play or musical comedy (a recent New York success), carried its own star, supporting cast, and scenery, and played one-night stands was called a combination company. Troupes that played a week in each town (six nights with two matinees, no Sundays), had a selection of plays (nonroyalty plays or old chestnuts that had long since lost their value to the combination companies), and used the stock scenery provided by each opera house were called repertoire companies."

Minstrel shows enjoyed the height of their appeal in the 1870s and then began to decline in popularity. But they were performed by repertory companies at some opera houses as late as the 1920s. By that time, however, they had been largely replaced by vaudeville, which had derived from the minstrels. Motion pictures appeared in North Carolina around the turn of the twentieth century and were shown at the opera houses, originally accompanied by a vaudeville act. In the years after World War I, motion pictures became the public's choice for entertainment, and opera houses became almost exclusively venues for showing films. A few of them continued to provide live entertainment in the 1920s, but for the most part, the age of the so-called opera house had ended.[63]

During their existence, however, the opera houses did in fact feature grand opera. In 1870 the company of Isabella McCulloch and P. Brignoli presented Verdi's *Il Trovatore* in Wilmington's Thalian Hall and Raleigh's Tucker Hall, which opened in 1867. The lower level of Tucker Hall was a dry goods store, and the upper-level auditorium hosted concerts and theater productions.[64] In 1870 Raleigh's Metropolitan Hall was completed and began offering musical events in its auditorium on a level above the city market and fire and police departments, which occupied the ground floor.[65] A number of touring opera companies appeared there. On March 6, 1889, the Emma Juch Operatic and Concert Company gave a performance that featured various artists rendering selections from such composers as Scarlatti, Mendelssohn, Liszt, and Wagner. The company performed the entire second act of Gounod's opera *Faust*, with Emma Juch appearing as Marguerite.[66] Among the performers was "Mr. Victor Herbert, violoncello and musical director, solo violoncellist of the Theodore Thomas orchestra and assistant conductor of the Seidi [*sic*] concerts in the Metropolitan Opera House, New York."[67] Herbert (1859–1924) frequently toured as a cello soloist, as well as serving as first cellist for several orchestras, among them the Metropolitan Opera. He also was a guest conductor at the New York Philharmonic and music director of the Pittsburgh Symphony. He composed several operettas and two grand operas. His Cello

Concerto in D became his most popular concert piece. Subsequently he was portrayed in two motion pictures, in 1939 and 1946.[68]

Other artists on stage at the Raleigh production of March 6 included tenor "Wm. J. Lavin, who made his debut at the Royal Albert Hall concerts in London two years ago," as well as Joseph Lyne [sic], "a famous young English baritone," the contralto "Miss Rosa Linde," and "Miss Adele Aus der Ohe, pianiste, the famous protege of Von Bulow and Liszt."[69] The *News and Observer* published a complimentary review the next day.

> The Emma Juch Company drew one of the largest and most refined audiences last night ever assembled in Metropolitan Hall. Much was expected of the distinguished artists all of whom came with the very highest recommendations, but it is perfectly safe to say that everybody was more than delighted at the brilliant success of the performance, from beginning to end.
>
> Miss Juch possesses a voice which at times thrills the audience by its beautiful *diminuendo* sweetness, then calls for storms of applause by its full, rich and melodious volume.
>
> Raleigh has never been favored with a pianist who has given such general satisfaction as Miss Aus Der Ohe. She executes passages that for technique are perfect. She is void of harsh execution, giving expression to the most difficult passages, at times making the piano sound like an Æolean Harp. The whole troupe was made up of artists of the most superior type.
>
> The rendition of the selection from Faust was entirely successfull and won high applause.[70]

Appearing at Metropolitan Hall on November 29, 1889, was the Boston Symphony Orchestral Club, which in that autumn was on its fourth annual tour. Former musicians of the Theodore Thomas Orchestra and the Boston Symphony Orchestra made up the touring company.[71] A review on the following day declared that "no more superb music was ever heard in Raleigh. The selections were classical and scientific, yet brilliant and showy and brought forth rounds of applause from the appreciative audience. Miss Augusta Ohrstrom was inimitable in her vocal selections and warbled like a veritable nightingale. She received *en core* after *en core*. Mons. Alfred De Seve's violin solo work won storms of applause. The concert was altogether one of the most perfect ever rendered here."[72] Also in Metropolitan Hall in November 1889, the MacCollin Opera Company presented Edward Jacobowski's comic opera *Erminie*, with a twelve-piece orchestra. Raleigh's Euterpean Orchestra followed with its own concert in the hall.[73]

Traveling troupes and local musical clubs continued to perform in the dual-purpose opera houses in North Carolina. But such facilities were limited in seating and often proved less than commodious for a concert or opera. Regarding Raleigh's Metropolitan Hall, the *State Chronicle* noted on December 16, 1890, that "It is being sureptitiously whispered about that the gabbling of geese marred the beautiful chords and musical symphonies of the Boston

Orchestra last Friday night. The geese were cooped up in the market below. We must have a new opera house."[74]

North Carolina's towns and cities grew commercially and culturally as part of the urbanization and industrialization sweeping the "New South" in the late nineteenth and early twentieth centuries. The term *new* implied a South that left slavery behind, that adopted modern agriculture and embraced industrialization, urbanization, and progressive ideas. With the development of its cigarette, textile, and furniture industries, North Carolina became the leading industrial state in the South and witnessed the expansion of a largely urban middle class, as well as an industrial working class.[75] Amid this new "progress," civic promoters encouraged the establishment of opera houses or auditoriums for theatrical and musical events as a means of drawing visitors and investors and increasing business in their towns. In the state capital, for example, "local boosters began agitating for a first-rate opera house, citing the fact that Raleigh's new north-south rail connections were bringing through many theatrical companies who 'will stop if they can get a good theatrical hall.'"[76]

Constructed by W. B. Baum of Norfolk, Virginia, Raleigh's new Academy of Music opened on the corner of Salisbury and Martin Streets in 1893. Under the management of Sherwood Upchurch, the academy's seats were filled by audiences eager to see and hear a traveling production of a recent Broadway play, often with an original cast. Famous actors such as Ethel and John Barrymore made appearances. The academy also became the venue for oratorios and an Artist Concert of opera arias by guest soloists from New York. In 1902 the famed John Philip Sousa and his band gave a well-attended concert there. Sousa (1854–1932) had been director of the United States Marine Band from 1880 to 1892, and his subsequent touring band brought him international fame. In addition to writing more than a hundred marches, he composed light operas such as *El Capitan* and *The Queen of Hearts* and a number of orchestral suites.

In 1907 the Raleigh Choral Society began the North Carolina Music Festival, which continued for several years. At the festival in 1908, a hundred singers performed Handel's *Messiah*, and 350 schoolchildren gave a concert. The recently formed, forty-piece Raleigh Philharmonic Orchestra, conducted by Gustav Hagedorn, accompanied both performances. In the following year, a touring company named the Pittsburgh Festival Orchestra, with twenty-five musicians conducted by Carl Bernthaler, accompanied the chorus.[77]

Beginning around 1900, a new wave of "progressivism," which was rising throughout the nation, entered North Carolina politics and simultaneously the state's cultural development. This tide of change would have a significant impact on the lives of North Carolinians in the coming decades. At the time, the traditionally conservative Democratic Party gave rise to a new wing of

A number of musical and theatrical stars appeared at Raleigh's Academy of Music, constructed in 1893 (courtesy State Archives of North Carolina).

reform-minded leaders known as Progressives, who believed that government should play a large role in addressing the problems and ills of society. These Progressives bolstered or initiated such programs as public education, public health, child labor laws, prison reform, prohibition of alcohol, fair elections (at least for white voters), and "good roads." A few, like Chief Justice Walter Clark, supported voting rights for women. But the Progressives' agenda did not include desegregation and voting rights for African Americans, who had fallen victim to racial violence, Jim Crow segregation, and the loss of their voting rights in the state Suffrage Amendment of 1900. Yet—with the very serious caveat of a nonprogressive acceptance of white supremacy—the Progressives of the first two decades of the twentieth century enacted a significant program of government-supported public reforms that set North Carolina on the path to a reputation as the South's most progressive state. North Carolina women joined the progressive surge with the establishment of the Federation of Women's Clubs, the Women's Christian Temperance Union, and the Equal Suffrage League (later the League of Women Voters), which campaigned for women's rights, education, and ratification of the Nineteenth Amendment to the United States Constitution, giving the vote to women.[78] The political, economic, and social progressivism characteristic of the first two decades of the twentieth century was accompanied by a cultural progressivism that sprang from the same ideology of the perfectibility of society. Appreciation and promotion of classical music were elements of this progressive trend.

The rising tide of cultural progressivism spawned a surge in literature, with a number of North Carolina writers gaining national recognition for the first time. Among the acclaimed authors were novelists James Boyd, Charles Chesnutt, and Thomas Wolfe; short story writer William Sydney Porter (O. Henry); and dramatist Paul Green, winner of the Pulitzer Prize.[79] To promote literature and the study of history, a group of culture-minded North Carolinians in 1900 founded the North Carolina Literary and Historical Association, which became the "lobbyist and drumbeater for historical and literary interests both in the legislature and among the public." Early in its career, the organization began presenting awards for the best books of fiction and nonfiction published by North Carolina writers each year. In the following decades, the association expanded its activities, including increasing the number of awards it presented at annual meetings to authors and promoters of literature and history. It also gave birth to such cultural groups as the North Carolina Folklore Society. Classical music received a boost when "Lit and Hist" supported the creation of the North Carolina Federation of Music Clubs in 1917.[80]

In the 1920s, the North Carolina Literary and Historical Association helped establish the North Carolina State Art Society, the predecessor of the North Carolina Museum of Art. The Art Society began as a private organization created in 1924 as a branch of Lit and Hist committed to fostering the cultural heritage of the state. Publisher John F. Blair became the founding president. Clarence H. Poe, editor of the *Progressive Farmer* and a leading activist for agricultural and other public causes and projects, presided as chair of the executive committee. In the following year, the society supported its first art exhibit and convened its first board meeting. In his 1927 will, Robert F. Phifer, a New York industrialist from North Carolina who died in 1928, contributed his private art collection and a sizable endowment to be held in trust. The legislature soon chartered the North Carolina State Art Society and authorized a board of directors but no government funding. Public support for the visual arts had begun.[81]

A "progressive" interest in the cultural life of North Carolinians was also manifested in a historic preservation movement in the state. Although "in the early twentieth century there was no organized statewide preservation organization to undertake a systematic effort such as existed in Virginia," a significant public and private movement nevertheless arose to preserve historic sites and structures as part of North Carolina's cultural heritage. The movement began as early as 1896 with the founding of the private, nonprofit Roanoke Colony Memorial Association, which purchased for preservation the Roanoke Island site of the first English colony in North America. In 1907 the state legislature assigned to the new North Carolina Historical Commission responsibility for the "preservation of battlefields, houses, and other places celebrated in the history of the state." Various women's groups—such as the Colonial Dames, Daughters of the American Revolution, and United Daughters of the Confederacy—joined the state's efforts and launched major campaigns to save and preserve the historic buildings and landscapes of North Carolina. Their success ultimately led in 1939 to the creation of a major private historic preservation organization, the North Carolina Society for the Preservation of Antiquities (later the Historic Preservation Society of North Carolina, then the Historic Preservation Foundation of North Carolina, also known as Preservation North Carolina).[82]

The public's desire for preserving North Carolina's historical culture had led to the establishment of a state office known as the North Carolina Historical Commission in 1903. That agency eventually evolved into the present-day North Carolina Office of Archives and History as it developed the landmark State Archives for the collection of state documents, as well as programs in historic sites, historic preservation and archaeology, and historical publications, along with a museum of history.[83]

A component of this rising cultural progressivism was an enthusiasm for the promotion of classical music, and women were in the vanguard of a movement to disseminate and encourage appreciation of the genre. In 1907 Salem Academy and College held the Winston-Salem Music Festival to celebrate the opening of Alumnae Memorial Hall, which its promoters maintained "embodied the very latest and most approved architectural ideas for a Conservatory of Music and Auditorium. We do not hesitate," they boasted, "to claim that the auditorium is the finest music hall in the South in all its appointments. Ventilation and lighting have received special attention, and there is not a poor seat in this hall."

The festival featured an orchestra of twenty-eight musicians and a chorus of one hundred voices. The orchestra was a revival of the Salem orchestra established in the early 1890s. The program comprised three days of concerts. On May 18, the first segment was Dvořák's *Te Deum*, divided into four sections and written for an orchestra and chorus and soprano and bass soloists. According to the Salem sponsors, "This work is among the more recent of the larger works of Dvorak, and belongs to his American period, the score having been published in 1896 ... but we have been unable to find any record of a performance since that time in the United States." The second segment of the concert "will consist of solos by Mr. [Eugene H.] Storer and Mrs. [Grace

Bonner] Williams; the Sextette from 'Lucia,' and Gounod's 'By Babylon's Wave' for chorus and orchestra." The May 19 performance was Haydn's *Creation*, to commemorate the 1829 presentation in Salem and "deemed the fitting oratorio to be rendered at the opening of the new building." The final concert, on May 20, highlighted the new organ for the auditorium. The organist was H. A. Shirley. The published program announced that "His choice of selections will range from Bach and Handel to modern composers. The chorus and orchestra, under Mr. Storer's direction, will give numbers from the 'Messiah' and Gounod's 'Unfold, Ye Portals,' from the 'Redemption.' Haydn's 'Farewell' Symphony will close the evening." All North Carolinians were invited to attend the festival, and the hosts suggested hotels and applied for special railroad fares.[84]

Women's clubs throughout the state began forming organizations to establish and foster classical music in their communities. The Greensboro Coney Club (subsequently named the Euterpe Club) was founded in 1889, and the women of Wilmington sponsored the Reineke Club in 1892. The Saturday Club appeared in Asheville around 1898. Other musical clubs followed in Chapel Hill, Hickory, and Gastonia. In 1914 Raleigh had the St. Cecilia Choral Society and Winston-Salem the Thursday Morning Club. As the state grew in the aftermath of World War I, women's organizations, especially the North Carolina Federation of Music Clubs, led in statewide efforts to promote "classical music by staging performances, training future musicians, and financing research projects." In 1927 Estelle Walker Harper (Mrs. W. A. Harper), the federation's president, first suggested the creation of a North Carolina symphony orchestra.[85]

But not everyone acknowledged the emphasis on the cultural arts that was growing in the South. In 1917 the influential and sarcastic essayist and critic H. L. Mencken denigrated southern culture in the New York *Evening Mail* in an article titled "The Sahara of the Bozart." The widely read essay appeared again in his book *Prejudices, Second Series* in 1920. In it Mencken condemned the post–Civil War South as a "gargantuan paradise of the fourth-rate," which was "almost as sterile, artistically, intellectually, culturally, as the Sahara Desert." He maintained that the pinnacle of American civilization had been reached in the antebellum South, especially in Virginia. That civilization and its culture of literature, art, and music had collapsed after the Civil War, as the region became dominated by poor whites. "It is," he wrote, "as if the Civil War stamped out every last bearer of the torch, and left only a mob of peasants on the field." To him, "The old aristocracy went down the red gullet of war; the poor white trash are now in the saddle." In addition, he blamed a large part of the South's cultural backwardness on the religious puritanism of the ordinary folk, "the Baptist and Methodist barbarism that reigns down there now." Throughout the entire postwar South, he saw "not a single picture gallery worth going into, or a single orchestra capable of playing the nine symphonies of Beethoven, or a single opera-house, or a single theater devoted to decent plays, or a single public monument ... that is worth looking at, or a single workshop devoted to the making of beautiful things." In regard specifically to classical music, "One would find it difficult to unearth a second-rate city between the Ohio and the Pacific that isn't struggling to establish an orchestra." But "You will find no such impulse in the South. There are no committees down there cadging subscriptions for orchestras; if a string quartet is ever heard there, the news of it has never come out; an opera troupe, when it roves the land, is a nine days' wonder."[86]

There was an element of truth in Mencken's observations about the post–Civil War South. No resident professional orchestra appeared in the region until well after 1900.[87] But Mencken's demeaning and sarcastic remarks about the Southland in the late nineteenth and early twentieth centuries were the hallmark of the exaggeration and social venom that characterized his commentary on a variety of national topics. Certainly, his portrait of an antebellum southern civilization dominated by a social and economic elite whose sophisticated culture of art and music vanished with Confederate defeat was more myth than reality. Some members of the upper class appreciated and even performed classical music, but their numbers were few. And not all the gentry shared their tastes.

Nor did a significant segment of the common folk have exposure to classical music. "Little is known," write historians Malone and Stricklin, "concerning the extent to which the southern lower classes were exposed to the fine arts during the colonial period or even during the nineteenth century. While some formal education was available for the children of the poor, only rarely did they gain admission to musical conservatories. Plain folk sometimes attended concerts given by such musical luminaries as Jenny Lind and Ole Bull, but opportunities for them to have heard concerts or recitals of high-art music ... would have been uncommon."[88] But as the North Carolina experience reveals, that situation began changing in the postbellum South, as public interest in classical music grew along with the new industrialization and urbanization transforming the state and region.

Thus despite Mencken's exaggerated portrait of the post–Civil War South, North Carolina was no cultural wasteland. Instead, from Reconstruction through the 1920s, the state's citizens increasingly sought out and supported literature, visual arts, history, historic preservation, and of course classical music. In that era, they sowed the seeds of cultural development in North Carolina. Those seeds would spring forth and bear fruit as North Carolinians' enthusiasm grew in the coming decades, when the state and nation acquired a new focus in the political, social, economic, and cultural life of the people, and classical music experienced a major awakening in the Old North State.

2

Lamar Stringfield, the New Deal, and the Founding of the Orchestra

Lamar Stringfield was born near Raleigh in 1897, the sixth of seven children of the Rev. Oliver Larkin Stringfield and Ellie Beckwith Stringfield. Oliver Stringfield, a Baptist minister, had once been principal of Wakefield Academy in eastern Wake County, and he became a trustee and major fundraiser for the Baptist Female University (later known as Meredith College), which opened in downtown Raleigh in 1899. He advocated for and campaigned to finance higher education for women in North Carolina, South Carolina, and Kentucky. Stringfield Dormitory on the present Meredith College campus is dedicated to him. In 1968 the college named a room in the dormitory for his wife.

The Stringfield family resided for a time on North Person Street in the state capital before moving to the North Carolina mountains in 1902. Lamar's early years spent in the mountains had a significant impact on his later musical compositions as well as the state's musical traditions and the establishment of its first symphony orchestra. Oliver Stringfield presided as pastor for churches in Barnardsville, Burnsville, and Asheville for short periods before he finally settled the family at Mars Hill, where two of his children served on the faculty at Mars Hill College. Like his siblings, Lamar was homeschooled for his early education by his mother and older sisters. He then entered Mars Hill College but had little academic success and attended for only three semesters. However, he developed an early and lasting passion for music, which had always been a part of the family's domestic routine. At age six, he received his first formal music instruction from his eldest sister. After a few years of practice, he achieved a degree of proficiency with the piano and began to show an interest in other instruments, especially the cornet. When the family lived for a while at the Baptist Assembly at Ridgecrest, Lamar took up the banjo and played with some local musicians at a nearby railway station. This experience probably inspired his interest in the mountain folk music for which he would later become so well known.[1]

Stringfield gained significant musical experience when he joined the army in 1916. He saw duty on the Mexican border, and after the United States entered World War I in Europe, he served in France and Belgium and on the Hindenburg Line as a member of the band of the 105th Engineer Regiment in the famed Thirtieth ("Old Hickory") Division. Members of the band also worked as litter bearers for the wounded. Originally Stringfield's preferred instrument had been the cornet, but he abandoned it for the flute. He practiced that instrument rigorously, receiving instruction in flute playing from Harold Clark, serving from Knoxville, Tennessee, and in music theory from the bandmaster Joseph DeNardo, who would remain a friend for years after the war. "I gave Lamar his first music theory lesson in Belgium while we were preparing to go to the front," DeNardo later recalled. "We were under shell fire but we kept on with our music whenever we got a breathing spell."

Following the armistice in 1918, Stringfield's unit withdrew into France for reorganization. While there he began to compose seriously, with the idea of blending the mountain folk music with which he was so familiar and the classical motif. He once asked DeNardo, "If you take mountain music, would it be all right to put it in art song and make music peculiar to the mountains, yet in a kind of refined way?" Because of his growing talent with the flute, the band selected Stringfield as one of five men to receive musical training in Paris after the war ended. Apparently at that time, he received instruction from the famed teacher Nadia Boulanger.[2]

Upon being discharged from the army in April 1919, Stringfield returned to Asheville and began taking further instruction in music theory from DeNardo, who had moved to that city. He also took lessons in flute from Emil Medicus, a local music teacher, and began composing his first significant works. His compositions included *Lost* for piano in 1919 and, in the following year, *In Lindy's Cabin* for violin and piano, *Polka Dot Polka* for cornet, and three smaller works. Around the same time, he left North Carolina for New York, where he enrolled in the Institute of Musical Art (later known as Juilliard School of Music). There Georges Barrère instructed him in the flute. He also studied composition under Percy Goetschius, Franklin Robinson, and George Wedge, and conducting with Chalmers Clifton and Henry Hadley. During his studies, Stringfield won a cash prize for *Indian Legend*, "a symphonic poem based on folk materials and Cherokee Indian themes." In 1923 *Mountain Sketches*, which he wrote for flute, violoncello, and piano, premiered at the school. He graduated in 1924 with a degree in flute.[3]

Stringfield then embarked on a career as a flutist, conductor, and composer. He performed as guest director for the Baltimore Symphony, the New

York Civic Orchestra, the Philadelphia Civic Orchestra, and several other musical groups. He played the flute with the Chamber Music Art Society and the New York Chamber Music Society for a number of seasons. In 1927–1928 he was a guest conductor for the National Opera Association in Washington, D.C. For his accomplishment as a musician and conductor, Stringfield received an award from the American Orchestral Society. In 1928 the Joseph Pulitzer Scholarship Prize, a traveling fellowship, was presented to him for *From the Southern Mountains*. He spent August and September of that year in Europe, where he found his return to Paris disappointing because of postwar changes, particularly the traffic and noise. By the end of the year, his interests increasingly focused on founding and directing musical organizations, with both private and public support.[4]

By the summer of 1926, Stringfield had returned to his mountain roots to give a number of band concerts in Asheville. Their success led him to propose to the music committee of the Asheville Chamber of Commerce a plan for creating an Asheville Symphony Orchestra, promoted by the Asheville Symphony Society.[5] "I had a wild dream," he said, "of a symphony orchestra for Asheville, North Carolina."[6]

In his plan for concerts in the summer of 1927, Stringfield proposed to bring to Asheville between twenty and thirty New York musicians to serve as the basis of the orchestra; they would be supplemented by local players. He intended to have string, woodwind, brass, and percussion sections and to use guest vocal and instrumental soloists and conductors. He asked soprano Marie Tiffany of the Metropolitan Opera Company to appear, as well as conductors Henry Hadley, his former teacher and associate director of the New York Philharmonic Orchestra, and Josiah Zuro from the New York Sunday Symphony Orchestra. For the first season, he called for a budget of $18,000, primarily to pay the musicians; it did not provide for guest soloists or conductors. He hoped that local groups and bands would employ the symphony players to perform at dances in order to bolster their salaries. The chamber of commerce approved the plan, and the symphony's first concert took place at the Plaza Theatre on June 5, 1927. It included selections from Beethoven, Schubert, and Liszt, as well as Stringfield's own "Mountain Song." The audience for each of the first season's concerts numbered from 1,200 to 1,600. But the orchestra did not meet expenses and finished the season with a $560 deficit. Nevertheless, Stringfield wanted to continue the series the next year. However, the Asheville Symphony Society's board of directors declined his request.[7]

In 1930 Stringfield returned from New York to North Carolina to reside permanently, except for out-of-state interludes as a lecturer at Juilliard, as a guest conductor, or for other work. He wrote a score for playwright Paul Green, an old army acquaintance. Green's play *Tread the Green Grass* premiered at

Lamar Stringfield was the founder and first music director of the North Carolina Symphony (1932–1938) (photograph from the 1930s, courtesy State Archives of North Carolina).

the University Theater at the University of Iowa. Ever since his efforts to establish an Asheville orchestra, Stringfield had been formulating plans for creating a statewide symphony for North Carolina. A number of North Carolina newspapers, including the *Asheville Citizen-Times,* the *Winston-Salem Journal,* and the *Twin-City Sentinel,* had been calling for city orchestras or a state symphony. In the fall of 1930, Stringfield, along with supporters Baxter Durham and Willie Horton, met in Raleigh with Governor O. Max Gardner to ask for his help in obtaining state funds to finance a state symphony orchestra. Although Gardner was sympathetic to the idea, he—amid the financial stringency of the Great Depression—did not call for government funding. Josephus Daniels, the influential editor of the Raleigh *News and Observer,* encouraged Stringfield to discuss his plans with Harry Chase, president of UNC.[8]

Stringfield then took his ideas to Chapel Hill, where his concept for a state orchestra was viewed initially with some skepticism. Local editor Louis Graves recalled that "before we had been acquainted with him fifteen minutes we all knew he was loony," because "any sane person would have seen it was impossible to create a creditable symphony orchestra in North Carolina."[9] But President Chase endorsed the concept of a state orchestra and suggested that Stringfield meet with Harold Dyer, head of the university's Department of Music, and Howard Odom, head of the Department of Sociology. Joined by Frederick H. Koch, director of the Carolina Playmakers theater company, the men founded UNC's Institute of Folk Music, with Stringfield as research associate. Paul Green had advocated for the creation of a university position for his friend. The Institute of Folk Music had as its mission to train young musicians in the arts of performing, conducting, and composing. The organization created three small orchestras that held rehearsals three times per week and gave forty to fifty concerts each year. Stringfield set out his plans for the institute in a document titled "Research in Musical Composition." It was from Stringfield's institute and its musicians that the first North Carolina Symphony Orchestra eventually would be born.

With the institute underway on the university campus, Stringfield's dream and the demand for a statewide orchestra continued to grow, and the establishment of an orchestra became part of a general plan by Governor Gardner's office to help North Carolina recover from the economic hardships of the Great Depression. The North Carolina Ten Year Plan was established in 1931 to increase revenue by promoting tourism in the state through the development of its recreational and cultural resources, including the founding of a state symphony. Tyre C. Taylor, executive secretary to Gardner, became director of the plan. With his and Stringfield's urging, a meeting took place in the office of UNC president Frank Porter Graham on February 19, 1932. In addition to Graham, Taylor, and Stringfield, several interested supporters attended and, after hearing Stringfield's ideas, approved Taylor's proposal to launch the North Carolina Symphony Society to guide and support the establishment of a North Carolina Symphony Orchestra. The people present at the meeting formed a steering committee to organize the society.[10] Stringfield later recalled that "it took me three years of talking the plan, and the simplicity of its working, before I could get twelve people together to discuss it. Even then, the University of North Carolina would not allow me to commit it to such a crazy idea."[11]

The steering committee reported to seventy-five members of the newly created society at the Carolina Inn on the university campus on March 21, 1932. A salon ensemble played for the group prior to the committee report. Then Stringfield outlined his plan for a state orchestra, and the society's role in making it a success. He pointed out that the symphony would give jobs to out-of-work musicians. He anticipated having fifty or more players, who would be chosen from professional, amateur, and student musicians. He wanted the orchestra to have its headquarters in the state's eastern and Piedmont regions in the winter and in the mountains in the summer. He called for two demonstration concerts, one of which would take place in Chapel Hill. He hoped that the symphony could become an entirely professional group by 1935. The North Carolina Symphony Society's initial role was to secure the support of 20,000 members, who would pay an annual membership fee of one dollar each. Patrons would be solicited for additional funds. Stringfield projected that the orchestra's financial requirements for the next two years would total $25,000.

After his report, the society elected Colonel Joseph Hyde Pratt (1870–1942) as president. Pratt soon publicly announced the orchestra's creation, claiming it to be the first state orchestra in the nation. Pratt was a chemist and mineralogist with a doctoral degree from Yale who had moved to North Carolina in 1897, when he became assistant manager for a mining company and served as mineralogist for the North Carolina Geological Survey. He began teaching economic geology at UNC in 1899 and published widely in his scientific field. In 1906 he received appointment as the state geologist. During World War I, Pratt saw action with the Thirtieth Division, attaining the rank of colonel and receiving the Distinguished Service Cross. In addition to his interest and leadership in the early days of the North Carolina Symphony Society, he was active in the Red Cross and the federal public relief agencies of the New Deal in the 1930s. He also applied his knowledge, influence, and zeal to conservation, forestry, and historic preservation organizations, as well as the Good Roads Association.[12]

Stringfield began soliciting popular support for the orchestra by encouraging local communities and organizations to form North Carolina Symphony Clubs to bolster the Symphony Society's efforts. The first such club was organized in Hickory, after Stringfield appealed to Mrs. Alex Shuford, who enlisted twenty-five members. Mayor George Lyerly became the first president. Stringfield next called at Asheville, where the chamber of commerce agreed with plans to organize a symphony club.

Stringfield and the Symphony Society then set about preparing for the orchestra's first demonstration concert, slated for May 14, 1932. The overall plan fell to the society's music committee, which instructed Stringfield to find a sufficient number of qualified musicians who would agree to play for future concerts on a volunteer basis. He traveled throughout North Carolina and secured agreements from seventy players to perform at various times. In Hill Music Hall on the UNC campus on May 13, Stringfield assembled more than forty musicians for rehearsals for the next day's

Joseph Hyde Pratt served as the first president of the North Carolina Symphony Society (engraving from 1906 courtesy State Archives of North Carolina).

concert. The performers came from cities and towns as far away as Wilmington in the east and Asheville in the west. They included members of the short-lived Asheville Symphony Orchestra of 1927; the Musical Arts Society of Asheville; the public schools of Durham, Greensboro, and Winston-Salem; and the Institute of Folk Music at the university. The full orchestra went through three rehearsals, and the strings had a separate rehearsal, followed by a final rehearsal for the full orchestra. For the program on May 14, Stringfield chose compositions by Wagner, Beethoven, Stoessel, Borodin, and Tchaikovsky. At the intermission, President Pratt spoke to the audience about the mission of the Symphony Society.

The orchestra's next performance took place at a junior high school in Durham on December 1 and was sponsored by the city's Charity League. The concert featured pianist, composer, and conductor Percy Grainger, who was invited by Stringfield to appear. The program included Humperdinck's *Hansel and Gretel* Overture, Beethoven's Symphony No. 1 in C Major, Grainger's own *Danish Folk Song* Suite, and Tchaikovsky's *1812* Overture. On the following day, the orchestra presented another concert as part of the Student Entertainment Series in Memorial Hall at UNC. It also featured Grainger, and the

In May 1932, the North Carolina Symphony gave its first public concert in Hill Hall on the campus of the University of North Carolina in Chapel Hill (North Carolina Collection, Wilson Library, University of North Carolina at Chapel Hill).

program consisted of Mozart's *Marriage of Figaro* Overture, Grieg's *Peer Gynt* Suite No. 1, three compositions by Grainger, and Stringfield's own *Legend of John Henry*.[13]

Prior to the UNC concert, the *Greensboro Daily News* had announced that it would be the first time Stringfield's composition had been performed publicly. Correspondent Guy A. Cardwell, Jr., noted that "few people in Chapel Hill are unfamiliar with the John Henry story, particularly since the publication by the University of North Carolina press in 1929 of a detailed study of the legend by Dr. Guy B. Johnson, a [UNC] professor. For this reason, it seems peculiarly fitting that the people of Chapel Hill should be the first to hear Mr. Stringfield's symphonic elaboration of several of the John Henry themes. This is, it is believed, the first time that a composer of ability has taken an epic of the American negro and woven from thoroughly indigenous material a major composition." According to the newspaper, Stringfield wrote *The Legend of John Henry* in three weeks, after "several months of preparation." The composer himself declared that "This subject is the largest and most emotional which I have approached. From the many available melodies and verses I had to make a selection of those which best carried the spirit of the John Henry legend, which best suggested the towering form

THE NORTH CAROLINA SYMPHONY SOCIETY
Presents Its
First Symphony Concert
LAMAR STRINGFIELD, *Conducting*

———o———

PROGRAM

I. REINZI OVERTURE...*Richard Wagner*

II. SYMPHONY NO. I IN C MAJOR.................*Ludwig van Beethoven*

(Intermission 10 Minutes)

"WHAT IS THE SYMPHONY SOCIETY?".....................*Joseph Hyde Pratt*

III. LA MEDIA NOCHE (from "Hispania" Suite).......*Albert Stoessel*

IV. ON THE STEPPES OF CENTRAL ASIA.............*Alexander Borodin*

V. MARCHE SLAVE......................................*Peter Tschaikowsky*

The program of the first public concert played by the North Carolina Symphony, in 1932 (courtesy State Archives of North Carolina).

and supple muscles of the hero, and which were most suitable for elaboration."[14]

The *Daily Tar Heel*, UNC's student newspaper, publicized both the Durham and UNC concerts and urged students to attend, noting that "Admission to either concert is one dollar, but students will be admitted to both concerts for half price. A student entertainment book is not needed for this reduced admission." The *Tar Heel* made special mention that the university was to be the site for the premiere of a major symphonic work. It reported that when Stringfield had recently appeared with the National Symphony Orchestra in Washington, D.C., to conduct his *Southern Mountains* Suite, music director Hans Kindler, who had read the score of *The Legend of John Henry*, asked him to perform it there. But Stringfield declined, reserving his latest work for the Chapel Hill event.[15]

The *Greensboro Daily News* editorialized about UNC's support for the establishment of the orchestra and the promotion of classical music in North Carolina. "Forces associated with the University of North Carolina are supporting the Symphony society in publicity," it observed, "whereby interest in the state is being enlisted, to take the practical form of attendance upon the concerts. The orchestra is in no sense a university project, or indeed an official project at all; but it is an enterprise that is going the university's way." Even the student newspaper, declared the Greensboro editorialist, "takes note of a tide in musical attention, a recession of interest in cultural music within the decade, with a turn lately in the other direction, away from freak music which is called music for want of a better convenient term, and towards classicism."[16]

The local *Chapel Hill Weekly* sang Stringfield's praises for his efforts in forming the orchestra.

> For the last year he has devoted his energies chiefly to the organization and development of the North Carolina Symphony Orchestra. Discouragements (the chief of which is the lack of money) have failed to thwart him. Going back and forth through the state, he has enlisted the cooperation of musicians and music lovers, and has fired them with his enthusiasm. And so he has built up an organization which, considering its lack of resources and the fact that its members dwell in widely separated communities, has been amazingly successful.[17]

Percy Aldridge Grainger, the well-known guest conductor and performer at the first concerts, was born George Percy Grainger in Brighton, Victoria, Australia, in 1882. He took his early instruction in music in Melbourne. As an adolescent, he received classical training in Frankfurt, Germany, and then performed in London and on tour in Europe as a pianist prior to coming to the United States in 1914. When the nation joined World War I, Grainger served as an army bandsman. He acquired American citizenship in 1918. Like Stringfield he had a strong interest in folk music, particularly for him British and Scandinavian melodies. He was also influenced by the poetry of Rudyard Kipling and Walt Whitman. Innovative and unusual in his approach to music, Grainger experimented with various mechanical and electronic musical devices, which he anticipated would produce a higher "free music" than the human art. He was also eccentric, or "avant-garde," in his personal and sexual practices, and "on matters of race Grainger was an avowed proponent of Anglo-Saxonism and Nordicism moving from a more racial intent in writings of the 1910s and 1920s to a more openly racist frame of mind in writings of the 1930s and 1940s." Although he lived most of his life in the United States, he traveled extensively in Europe and Australia, where he established the

Grainger Museum at the University of Melbourne. Late in his career, he continued to appear in concerts, teach at music camps, and make new arrangements and revisions to his own and other compositions. In his lifetime, Grainger composed more than four hundred works, "either original compositions or folk-music settings." He died in White Plains, New York, in 1961.[18]

As 1932 came to an end, the North Carolina Symphony Society had met its financial obligations and retained a slight profit. On January 3, 1933, the society was incorporated as a nonprofit organization with the overall mission "to foster culture and education." At that time, it had 653 charter members.[19]

Stringfield's efforts to establish a statewide symphony orchestra had met with some initial success. But he sought to expand the reach of classical music to the state's small communities, which in the depths of the Great Depression of the 1930s could ill afford to sponsor performances by the full orchestra. Consequently, with the cooperation of the faculty and students of the Institute of Folk Music, of which he remained associate director, Stringfield organized the North Carolina Little Symphony Orchestra, which began its 1933 season with a concert at the Carolina Playmakers Theater at UNC on January 20. The program emphasized native folklore and included compositions by North Carolina composers. Earl Slocum presided as guest conductor. The Little Symphony played again on March 4 at Southern Pines. Among the musical selections was Stringfield's own "Cripple Creek" from his *Mountain* Suite. To

An early concert featured Lamar Stringfield *(center)* and the first North Carolina Symphony (courtesy North Carolina Symphony).

reach folks in the hinterland, Stringfield also created the North Carolina Symphony Trio. The initial members were Adeline McCall, pianist; Stringfield, flutist; and Ralph Weatherford, cellist. The trio gave its first performance in the small town of Ellerbe on May 12. In addition to compositions by Rameau, Barrère, Debussy, Roussel, and Cui, the group played Stringfield's *Mountain Sketches*.

With the support of the Junior League, the full orchestra gave its next concert on May 29 at Memorial Auditorium in Raleigh. Stringfield conducted compositions by Mozart, Beethoven, Borodin, and Tchaikovsky, as well as his own *Legend of John Henry*. That was followed by another concert in Memorial Hall in Chapel Hill on June 10. Then on December 9, the symphony performed again in Raleigh's Memorial Auditorium in a concert to honor Governor J. C. B. Ehringhaus. Stringfield conducted, and the guest artist was John Powell, a pianist, composer, and member of the executive committee of the Symphony Society. On the program were selections from Beethoven, Dvořák, and Wagner, as well as a performance of Powell's *Rhapsodie Negre*.[20]

Guest artist John Powell was born in Richmond, Virginia, in 1882. He studied music with his musical family and then piano and harmony with F. C. Hahr, who reportedly had been a student of Liszt. After graduating from the University of Virginia, Powell received instruction from Theodor Leschetizky and Karel Navrátil in Vienna. He debuted with the piano in 1907 in Berlin and then toured for four years in Europe before coming back to the United States. In the coming years, he performed as a pianist, including some of his own compositions, throughout the United States and Europe. His works comprised orchestral compositions, choral settings, three piano sonatas, one violin concerto, two piano concertos, and an opera. Like Stringfield he had a keen interest in folk music, especially from the American South. This was reflected in his compositions such as *Rhapsodie Negre* (for piano and orchestra) and *Sonata Virginianesque*—both influenced by African American culture—and in his fascination with Anglo-American folk heritage. In fact, "One of Powell's most important achievements lies in the area of ethnomusicology," writes music historian L. Moody Sims, Jr. "A methodical collector of the South's rural songs, he was the founder of the Virginia State Choral Festival and the moving spirit behind the annual White Top Mountain Folk Music Festival." Sims further notes that "For the most part southerners have contented themselves with inherited music, folk songs, and contemporary tunes. Apart from Powell, southern composers have remained virtually unknown except to other musicians. During the first half of the 20th century, however, Powell received national recognition and acclaim not only as a virtuoso performer of the classical repertoire at home and abroad but also as a composer of distinctively American music."[21]

Another major artist (and native North Carolinian) who performed in

Memorial Auditorium in 1934 was not accompanied by the new North Carolina Symphony Orchestra, although she probably would have been except for the color of her skin. Caterina Jarboro was born in Wilmington in 1903. Her father, a barber, was African American, and her mother was American Indian. She was christened Katherine Lee Yarborough at St. Thomas Catholic Church in the Port City but later changed her name when she began her career as an operatic soprano. She obtained her early education at Wilmington's St. Thomas Catholic School, where she received musical instruction from the Franciscan sisters. When her parents died in 1916, Jarboro moved to Brooklyn, New York, where she received musical training and began appearing in theater productions. Like most black musical performers, Jarboro found her opportunities for concerts and stage roles limited amid the racial inequality of the era. She therefore traveled to the more racially tolerant Paris, where she sought further training, and then studied in Italy and made her operatic debut singing the title role in Verdi's *Aida* at the Puccini Opera House in Milan in 1930.

She returned to the United States in 1932 and in the following year accepted an offer to sing Aida with the Chicago Civic Opera at the New York Hippodrome Theater. Jarboro thus became the first African American opera singer to perform a leading part with a major opera company in the United States. Although widely renowned for her operatic concert voice, the famed Marian Anderson did not debut in a full opera production until she sang the role of Ulrica the sorceress in Verdi's *Un Ballo in Maschera* at New York's Metropolitan Opera House in 1955. Until that time, the Metropolitan's board had adhered to a policy of not hiring black singers, but other accomplished African Americans had sung with smaller companies such as the National Negro Opera Company and the New York City Opera Company, which began featuring black principal singers in 1946.[22]

A *New York Times* critic gave Jarboro a glowing review for her rendition of Aida at the Hippodrome on July 22, 1933.

> Caterina Jarboro, Negro soprano, made her New York début as Aida last night in the Chicago Opera Company's presentation of Verdi's opera at the New York Hippodrome. She scored an immediate popular success. After her "Ritorna vincitor" in the first act, she was three times recalled by enthusiastic applause.
>
> The young soprano, who made her operatic début in this rôle at the Puccini Theatre in Milan in 1930, brought to its presentation last night some admirable attributes—a vivid dramatic sense that kept her impersonation vital without recourse to over-acting; an Italian diction remarkably pure and distinct, a musicianly feeling for phrase and line, and a voice whose characteristically racial timbre, husky and darkly rich, endowed the music with an individual effectiveness.[23]

She gave the same performance on July 24 and was joined by another accomplished black operatic voice, Jules Bledsoe, a baritone who sang the role of Amonasro.[24]

But after her concert in Raleigh's Memorial Auditorium in November 1934, Jarboro received only a brief mention in the *News and Observer*. The paper noted that "her work has been praised highly by critics," and that "Her performance last night, composed mostly of numbers taken from outstanding operas, was well received by the audience. The singer favored Shaw University students [African Americans] with several requested compositions. [African American pianist] Carl Diton was the accompanist." The African American Guild of St. Ambrose Episcopal Church sponsored the event.[25] That Jarboro's Raleigh debut took place before a largely black audience with no orchestral accompaniment and little public attention or praise is not surprising given the racism prevalent in the Jim Crow South at the time. It would be many years before the North Carolina Symphony Orchestra accompanied a black visiting artist or had an African American musician among its players.

After her *Aida* appearance in New York, Jarboro performed in other major opera roles in the United States and Europe and also sang at concerts and benefit events at Carnegie Hall and Town Hall in New York. The New York Metropolitan Opera Association at one time invited her to become a member but withdrew the offer when it learned that she was African American. She later declined a second invitation. Jarboro retired from singing in 1955. Her hometown of Wilmington honored her in a ceremony in its Thalian Hall in 1975 and with a star on its Walk of Fame in 1999. She died in New York City in 1986.[26]

As the North Carolina Symphony, like the rest of the state and nation, struggled with the financial hardship of the Great Depression, it received a significant boost from President Franklin D. Roosevelt's New Deal, an innovative national system of federally funded economic and social welfare recovery programs intended to end the Depression. Among the programs was the Federal Emergency Relief Administration, one of the first "to direct federal involvement in unemployment relief" as well as other forms of aid to the states.[27] The director of the FERA in North Carolina was Annie Land O'Berry, who prior to her appointment had been active in Democratic Party politics, including the role of women, and public welfare. Through her efforts, North Carolina received nearly $40 million in relief funds, most of which she managed to dispense without regard for political patronage.[28] As part of the federal recovery program, her agency awarded $45,000 to the North Carolina Symphony Orchestra.

"The Federal Government went into the music business in this State last week when Mrs. Thomas [O'Berry], Federal relief administrator for North Carolina, approved an appropriation of $45,000 for the maintenance of the North Carolina Symphony Orchestra," wrote a Chapel Hill correspondent for the *New York Times* on May 17, 1934. He further noted that North Carolina "is the fourth State to obtain government money for such a purpose," and that Stringfield hoped the federal grant would help make the orchestra "permanently self supporting."[29]

The FERA made the appropriation "Because many musicians in North Carolina are in distressing circumstances.... This action was part of a general plan for musicians throughout the country, whose economic condition had been seriously impaired" by the Depression, as well as by the advent of recorded music and motion pictures with sound. Both O'Berry's agency and the directors of the North Carolina Symphony Society hoped "that this movement can be made into a permanent self-sustaining project so that the members of the orchestra's personnel will become self-supporting, and so that North Carolina may retain this State-wide orchestra as a focal point for the efforts of its musicians."[30]

Ironically, it was the hard times of the Great Depression, which spawned the revolutionary programs of the New Deal, that introduced the first major governmental and public support for a state symphony orchestra for North Carolina. As music historians Bill C. Malone and David Stricklin have written, "The Great Depression was a cultural as well as an economic event. Along with the distress it brought to virtually every segment of the U.S. economy, including the entertainment industry, it also wrought serious changes in the nature and structure of the various forms of commercialized southern folk music."[31] A similar claim could be made for the public performance of classical music in the South, inasmuch as it was the economic decline of the Depression, along with the federal government's response to it, that led to the beginnings of state symphony orchestras in the region. As was the case during the horror and tumult of the Civil War, when Southerners sought out the diversionary comfort of musical and theatrical entertainment, the difficult circumstances in the Depression-era South stimulated a public yearning for the diversions of theater, motion pictures, and folk, country, gospel, band, jazz, blues, ragtime, and symphonic music. The increasing availability of radio and recordings intensified this musical escape and comfort.[32]

With federal money in hand, the Symphony Society set about making plans for the orchestra for 1934 and 1935. The members projected one hundred concerts performed by both the full orchestra and the Little Symphony. The orchestra would have fifty or more musicians, who would rehearse for thirty hours per week. Professionals would be paid $21 per week, and semiprofessionals would receive $15. The music director's salary was $23. The society also set a concert admission fee, usually fifty cents, with teachers and students admitted at half price. Admission fees were collected to pay for transportation, rental of auditoriums, and other expenses not provided for in the federal grant. The orchestra first resided for several weeks in Chapel Hill to give a series of concerts on the UNC campus. On July 10, it played at a concert in Greensboro, where Stringfield and American composer and conductor Robert

Russell Bennett appeared on the podium. The program included works from Brahms, Beethoven, and Sibelius, as well as Bennett's composition *Abraham Lincoln: A Likeness in Symphony Form.*

Bennett (1894–1981) was well known to theatergoers as well as devotees of classical music. In addition to his classical compositions—which included orchestral, chamber music, and keyboard works—he became famous for his arrangements and orchestrations of Broadway and Hollywood musicals for such composers as Richard Rodgers, Cole Porter, George Gershwin, Irving Berlin, and Jerome Kern. Bennett received a Guggenheim music fellowship and the RCA Victor award for his *Abraham Lincoln.* He journeyed from New York to Greensboro at Stringfield's request to perform his symphony and was impressed with the orchestra's skill. Apparently Stringfield had been one of the flutists who premiered Bennett's Rondo Capriccioso for four flutes at the New York Flute Club in 1922.[33]

After the Greensboro concert, the orchestra traveled to western North Carolina, where it planned to give a series of concerts for the summer season. The *Asheville Advocate* announced the orchestra's arrival on July 20.

> The first of a series of eight concerts to be presented in Asheville during the ensuing six weeks by the North Carolina Symphony Orchestra, under the direction of Lamar Stringfield, will be given at the McDowell Auditorium tonight, starting at 8:30 o'clock.
>
> The 60 musicians composing the orchestra, representing outstanding artists of the state, are expected to arrive in the city today, coming by bus from Chapel Hill, their permanent headquarters.
>
> The orchestra will make its summer headquarters in this city, playing a total of 18 concerts during the local engagement. Ten of these will be presented in other cities and towns of Western North Carolina, and possibly in South Carolina and Tennessee.

The newspaper further noted that ticket sales for the previous day indicated that a large audience would attend the first concert, and that bus service from Pack Square to the McDowell Street School auditorium would be provided for persons without cars. It also pointed out that eight members of the orchestra, with its summer headquarters in the city Arcade Building, would be from Asheville. The others "will be billeted in various homes and hotels in the City." Season tickets for the eight Asheville concerts sold for $2.50 for adults and $1.25 for children. Prices for individual concerts were 50 cents for adults and 25 cents for children. The low costs, the *Advocate* declared, "are made possible by reason of the fact that salaries of the orchestra members are being defrayed through a special appropriation by the Federal Emergency Relief Administration." It reassured residents who might be intimidated by the prospect of classical music that "While the background of the concerts will be made up of the finest symphonic composition of the great masters, there will be a sufficient interpretation of lighter numbers to provide variety to the program and appeal to all musical tastes."[34]

At a concert on Friday evening, August 3, in the McDowell Street School auditorium, the orchestra played selections by Mozart, Franck, Rimsky-Korsakov, Saint-Saëns, and Tchaikovsky. But "as representative of American masterpieces," Stringfield also included works by composer and conductor Henry Hadley, one of his instructors at Juilliard, and the New York composer Emerson Whitborne. The musicians performed Hadley's "Angelus" from his Third Symphony. According to the *Advocate*, "Hadly [*sic*] is well known to Asheville through his classical compositions as well as by reason of the fact that he appeared in Asheville a few years ago as director of the New York Philharmonic orchestra at the biennial convention of the National Federation of Music Clubs. The Angelous is said to be inspired by the ringing of the vesper chimes in Milan." The orchestra played Whitborne's "Pell Street," a musical depiction of a night in New York's Chinatown from his *New York Days and Nights*.[35] The following Sunday afternoon, the orchestra performed Hadley's *The Enchanted Castle*, as well as selections from Debussy, Johann Strauss, and Wagner. Hundreds of people attended the concert. On August 7, the symphony played in Hendersonville. On that program were compositions by Brahms, Dvořák, and Tchaikovsky, as well as the specially featured *Natchez on the Hill* by John Powell. In Asheville three days later, the selections were compositions by Humperdinck, Beethoven, Borodin, and the "Danse Barbare" from ragtime pianist and songwriter William J. Donaldson's *Congo Sketches*. "Danse Barbare" had been arranged by the famed African American arranger, composer, conductor, and oboist William Grant Still of Mississippi. Also on the program was *Old Joe Clark Steps Out*, a composition by Charles G. Vardell, director of the Department of Music at Salem College, who attended the concert to hear the orchestra play his work based on the folksong "Old Joe Clark."[36] When the orchestra performed again in Asheville on August 24, it played the entire *Abraham Lincoln* by Bennett. "Two movements from this symphony were played in the city by the orchestra a few weeks ago," announced the *Advocate*. "This will be the third time that the orchestra has played the composition in its entirety, and it is the only group that has played it more than once."[37] On the afternoon of August 26, the symphony rendered a "popular" concert that included "Circassian Beauty" from John Powell's *At the Fair*.[38]

To end its season in western North Carolina, the orchestra gave its last concert in Hendersonville on September 17, 1934. During the mountain tour, the symphony had given eleven concerts in the McDowell Street School auditorium in Asheville and twelve performances in surrounding towns. The Little Symphony had played three concerts in Asheville. On the eve of the orchestra's departure, Stringfield publicly declared: "I want to express my appreciation to the music lovers of Western North Carolina for their enthusiasm and sympathy toward our efforts.... We have endeavored to include in our programs the works of all of the old masters and at the same time to acquaint the public with the fine music of our new American composers. I think our Western North Carolina season has been an artistic success."[39]

As the summer season concluded, the symphony moved its headquarters to Winston-Salem, where it performed twelve concerts in the fall and early winter of 1934, appearing at the Reynolds and Salem College auditoriums. During the same period, it performed in Durham; Greensboro; Raleigh; Danville, Virginia; Richmond, Virginia; Washington, D.C.; Atlanta, Georgia; Spartanburg, South Carolina; Chattanooga, Tennessee; and Knoxville, Tennessee.[40]

In December 1934, the orchestra concluded the year and its eightieth concert with a weeklong musical festival in Winston-Salem. Quinto Maganini, a composer and flutist with the San Francisco Symphony and the New York Philharmonic, appeared as guest conductor, and Marie Maher as soloist. In early November, the orchestra had played two of Maganini's compositions. Thus by the end of its first major year, with the determination and leadership of Stringfield, the support of the Symphony Society, and federal funding, the North Carolina Symphony Orchestra had established itself on a sound basis, performed throughout North Carolina and in other states, and acquired a degree of national musical reputation, along with the neighboring state of Virginia. The *New York Times* of December 23, 1934, observed that despite the Depression, North Carolina and Virginia had created successful symphony orchestras. Richmond correspondent and editor Virginius Dabney declared that "Those who picture the average Southerner as a lackadaisical individual with little initiative or energy, and a decided preference for remaining in a state of inertia, may have to revise their ideas, in view of what has happened during the depression in Virginia and North Carolina. Both States have successfully launched symphony orchestras." The national circumstances of financial stress and skepticism made their achievement even more remarkable. "In neither State," noted Dabney, "did the effort begin until after the great crash of 1929. In both instances the constant deepening of the depression led numerous Cassandras to prophesy failure. Yet both efforts have been successful, and it would appear that the Richmond Symphony and the North Carolina Symphony are firmly on their feet and destined for many years of usefulness."[41]

Soon after the new year, the North Carolina Symphony Orchestra moved its headquarters to Raleigh, where it presented its first concert of 1935. That performance was followed by a children's program at Hugh Morson High School in the capital. The orchestra next presented concerts in a number of cities and towns in the state. From March 11 to March 13, it performed at the North Carolina Symphony Festival in Durham, including a children's concert on March 12 at Central Junior High School. That same month, the orchestra broadcast on radio stations WPTF in Raleigh and WDNC in Durham. Under the FERA, the symphony gave several other radio concerts: four over Raleigh's WPTF in January and February 1935; three over Charlotte's WBT in April and May 1935; and one over NBC from Asheville's WWNC in August 1935—the first broadcast by a southern symphony on that network.

In late April, the symphony moved its headquarters to Charlotte, where the full orchestra and the smaller one each gave eight concerts. Season tickets went on sale. Those for the full orchestra's eight concerts cost $3.00 for adults and $1.50 for students, and those for the little orchestra's series cost $2.50 for adults and $1.25 for students. Adults who purchased tickets for both series paid $5.00, and students paid $2.50.[42]

In June the orchestra launched another summer season in western North Carolina, beginning with concerts in Asheville. The performances coincided with other tourist events in the mountains. "The first of a series of Summer concerts by the North Carolina Symphony Orchestra and the annual golf tournament at the municipal links are events of the next two weeks," reported the *New York Times* from Asheville on June 16. "The symphony Orchestra, which maintains Summer headquarters here and each year gives a series of concerts will play its first program on Tuesday. Lamar Stringfield is director of the orchestra. At least five concerts will be given here and others are scheduled at Blowing Rock, Lake Junaluska and other near-by resort points."[43] The audiences for the Asheville concerts totaled more than 7,200 persons. Additional performances were given at Cullowhee, Hendersonville, Marion, Montreat, Morganton, and Spruce Pine. During this time, Stringfield convinced Thor Johnson, a charter member of the symphony, to return to North Carolina from the University of Michigan to be assistant director for the orchestra. A number of the musicians formed a band and, conducted by Stringfield and Johnson, played free afternoon concerts in Asheville's parks and Hendersonville's school playgrounds.

Of the 210 works performed in the summer of 1935, sixty were by American composers, including North Carolinians Stringfield and Vardell. Soloists included John Powell, pianist; Stringfield, flutist; Kay Rickert, violinist; and William Zimmerman, pianist. The most-performed major compositions were by Beethoven, Brahms, and Dvořák. Other works included those of Mozart, Schubert, Sibelius, and Wagner. The mountain season ended on September 8. The series concluded with a special concert, conducted by Stringfield, "depicting the racial and cultural history of North Carolina." It featured compositions by Stringfield that demonstrated the musical influences of American Indians and African Americans. According to Howard Turner Pearsall's history of the North Carolina Symphony Orchestra, "This was the first concert in which Stringfield was able to use his works to show through music the cultural contributions made to the state of North Carolina by minority groups."

But Stringfield's days with the orchestra were numbered. He soon resigned as musical director. Some members of the Symphony Society had already noted his dissatisfaction with the "musical standards" and "instability of the orchestral personnel."[44] His relationship with the society members and the musicians grew increasingly adversarial. "He had his enemies," as well as "his faults," the *Durham Herald* remarked. Stringfield gained a reputation as a taskmaster in rehearsals and "expected his musicians to 'put out.'" His temperamental "frankness" also hindered his dealings with the Symphony Society.[45] Shortly after the last concert, he moved with his family to Oxford, North Carolina, and in October 1935, he accepted a position in Atlanta as the regional director of the Federal Music Project, a division of another New Deal agency, the Works Progress Administration.

For many of the Great Depression's unemployed, the WPA provided jobs and salaries in public works projects such as buildings, roads, bridges, and other construction. The agency also hired out-of-work writers, actors, artists, historians, and musicians. The WPA, as part of its Federal Music Project, assumed direct control of the North Carolina Symphony Orchestra in September 1935, and the FERA ceased providing funds for its support.

The WPA then reorganized the orchestra in Asheville under the supervision of Ralph Weatherford. He was one of the symphony's charter members and one of its 1933 trio. Weatherford held auditions for the reorganized orchestra. Those musicians hired were required to teach music at various venues as well as perform in concerts.[46] A correspondent for the *New York Times* reported on November 14 that "Joseph De Nardo of Asheville was today appointed permanent director of the North Carolina Symphony Orchestra, now a Works Progress Administration project, following a conference here of State and Federal music project officials. G. O. Shepherd of Asheville was appointed business manager of the orchestra under the Federal set-up."[47] As mentioned earlier, DeNardo, the orchestra's new director, had been one of Stringfield's instructors and a music teacher, band leader, and assistant director of the Asheville orchestra of 1927. He had helped Stringfield recruit musicians for the original orchestra, and in the coming weeks, he worked hard to keep the WPA orchestra together and performing. On November 19, 1935, the WPA moved the symphony's headquarters to Durham, although the orchestra remained in Asheville.[48]

The *New York Times* reported on December 15 that the orchestra would leave Asheville on January 1, 1936, for a winter season in Winston-Salem, and that "A number of concerts will be presented in the central part of the State."[49] By February 1, 1936, however, the orchestra was performing in Asheville instead, and it gave two concerts per week from February through April. From June 8 to 10 it played at the Asheville musical festival, which included performances by soloists, the Asheville Civic Ballet, and the Asheville Festival

Chorus. Then in the fall, Erle Stapleton, the new director of the WPA's Federal Music Project in North Carolina, moved the orchestra to a headquarters in Greensboro, where DeNardo anticipated twelve concerts and then a tour of the state in 1937. On May 25, 1937, the Junior League sponsored a concert in Greensboro. The program included selections from Beethoven, Schumann, Bizet, and Ravel, and Greensboro native Edward Cone, a concert pianist, appeared as a soloist. The guest conductor and another soloist was Dr. Benjamin Swalin, a new arrival to North Carolina. Swalin worked as a violinist and music instructor at UNC in Chapel Hill. He was destined to have a tremendous impact on the future success of the state orchestra and classical music in North Carolina.

But by the time of the Greensboro concert, that future seemed in jeopardy, amid controversy about the symphony's operations. Since the North Carolina Symphony Orchestra's inception in 1932, the North Carolina Symphony Society had played a large role in maintaining, scheduling, and promoting the orchestra. Its efforts had been bolstered significantly when the FERA provided money to pay musicians' salaries. But when the WPA took charge of the management of the orchestra in 1935, the Symphony Society lost its control and influence. The musicians went without pay for a time and threatened to pawn their instruments. Under the WPA, only those musicians who qualified for relief could receive federal salaries. A number of players left the orchestra. Arguments broke out among the society, the musicians, and Federal Music Project regional director Stringfield; and quarrels had developed about where the symphony's headquarters would be located and who would decide on schedules and performances. With no say in the orchestra's operations, the Symphony Society on January 3, 1936, withdrew its support for the orchestra in a letter from President Pratt to Bruce McClure, director for professional projects of the WPA. Without the continued support of the Symphony Society, and with the withdrawal of federal salaries for many of the musicians, the orchestra came near collapse. Some musicians still eligible for federal pay remained as a remnant of the orchestra at its headquarters in Greensboro, where they taught music in the public schools and in private studios and performed in a band. Although the North Carolina Symphony Orchestra had declined to only a shell of what it had once been, many of its advocates wanted to see it revived and back under local control.[50]

Even though a future for the state orchestra was uncertain, Lamar Stringfield had laid the groundwork for its survival. In his new position as regional head of the WPA's Federal Music Project, Stringfield took up the assignment to establish symphony orchestras in seven southern states, drawing upon the North Carolina program as a guide. He further sought to create a Southern Symphony Orchestra that would give classical concerts, encourage young musicians, and promote American compositions throughout the rural South.

He traveled to several southern cities to promote the idea, but his plans received no local support. His concept for a nationwide organization of symphony orchestras did result in the establishment of the Society of American Symphony Orchestras in the summer of 1940. But the society soon vanished with the onset of World War II. In the end, Stringfield's labors with the Federal Music Project proved disappointing for him. Marital problems also arose. In 1927 he had married Caroline Crawford. They had one child, a daughter named Meredith. Following a divorce in 1938, he accepted a one-year contract as associate conductor at New York's Radio City Music Hall. In New York, he was able to perform his own compositions, such as *On a Moonbeam*, for voice, flute, and piano (1938), and "Chipmunk" from his 1921 suite *Mountain Echoes*. In the meantime, he had composed music for Paul Green's symphonic dramas *The Lost Colony* and *Shroud My Body Down*.

The Second World War brought further frustration when the federal government declined to fund Stringfield's research project on using musical tones to treat shell-shocked soldiers and on the piping of music into service clubs and mess halls of the military. Stringfield taught music composition and advanced orchestration in a summer session at Claremont College in California and then, too old for service in the armed forces, found wartime work in the Vought-Sikorsky airplane factory. After the war, he returned to Asheville and a career in music, although the number of works he produced had declined. He composed the music for the sacred cantata *Peace*, for flute and string orchestra (or organ), first performed at the New York Avenue Presbyterian Church in Washington, D.C., in 1949. Other works included *Mountain Dawn*, for flute and orchestra (1945); *Georgia Buck*, for concert band (1949); *My Lonely Flute* and *About Dixie*, for chorus and orchestra (1950); and *Carolina Charcoal*, a musical comedy that he began in 1950 and continued to revise until 1955. Stringfield served for a time as conductor of the Knoxville, Tennessee, orchestra. He commuted from Asheville and declined to accept a three-year contract because it would require that he take up permanent residence in Knoxville. He then signed on for a time with the Charlotte Symphony Orchestra and served on the board of directors of the National Society of Music and Art and as regional consultant for the National Association for American Composers and Conductors.

Having a strong interest in actually manufacturing and selling a superior flute, Stringfield studied acoustics with a physics teacher at the Case Institute of Technology, learned to make castings and models, and set up a workshop in Asheville and then in his apartment in Charlotte. There he repaired woodwind instruments and worked to perfect the "Stringfield Design Flute."[51] A newspaper reporter who visited his workshop-apartment in May 1949 observed a living and work space in disarray, with "Ordinary plumbers tools, scissors, dental forceps, letter openers, crochet hooks and women's curling irons [that] make up part of his tools." The visitor also noted his erratic work, eating, and sleep habits. "I live like a dog," Stringfield declared. "I sleep when I'm sleepy, I eat when I'm hungry, I observe no hours nor schedules." A lathe stood next to the stove in the kitchen so that he could "turn a flute and whip up an omelet at once." He continued to practice the flute for six hours each day. "Even when talking," recalled the reporter, "he usually has the flute in his hands, running his fingers through the scales and touching it silently to his lips."[52]

The last years of Stringfield's life were marked by professional as well as financial decline. His last major composition, *Carolina Charcoal*, and some music for the short-lived Asheville play *Thunderland* proved unsuccessful. He received honoraria for performances as a flutist but failed to obtain teaching jobs at Mars Hill College and in the public schools. Stringfield made Asheville his final residence when his health began to deteriorate. His physical problems included hernia surgeries, a broken leg, sinusitis, and difficulties with alcohol. He died of lung congestion in January 1959 at the age of sixty-two and is buried in Asheville's Riverside Cemetery.

Stringfield's musical legacy in North Carolina quickly faded after his death, although he did receive some public recognition. For much of his life, he owned a flute crafted by the famous nineteenth-century flute maker Louis Lot of Paris. After he died, his daughter, Meredith Stringfield Oates of Knoxville, presented the instrument to the North Carolina Symphony. The Lamar Stringfield Society was formed to honor persons who include the symphony in their estate plans or endow musician chairs or special funds. In 1971, on Music Day of "Culture Week," established in the 1930s as an annual meeting of the state's historical and cultural organizations in Raleigh, the North Carolina Federation of Music Clubs presented a plaque honoring Stringfield to the Department (now Office) of Archives and History. His daughter, brother, and niece attended the presentation. The plaque, received by Archives and History director H. G. Jones, was intended to hang in the lobby of the agency's building and now resides in the collection of the North Carolina Museum of History. In 1988 the Office of Archives and History erected a North Carolina Highway Historical Marker on North Person Street in Raleigh commemorating Stringfield's nearby boyhood home. His papers are located in the Southern Historical Collection at UNC in Chapel Hill. Each summer the Lamar Stringfield Music Camp is held for young musicians at Raleigh's Meredith College.

Lamar Stringfield's career with the North Carolina Symphony Orchestra lasted only a few years. Nevertheless, he brought classical music to North Carolina on a scale that the state had never known before. He also earned a degree of national fame as a flutist, composer, conductor, and teacher of music. Although Stringfield's greatest passion was for composing and orchestral and instrumental performance, he worked extensively as a guest conductor for various orchestras, including the National Symphony Orchestra in Washington, D.C., the Baltimore Symphony, the New York Civic Orchestra, the New York Festival Orchestra, the Philadelphia City Symphony, the Virginia Symphony, and Radio City Music Hall.[53] That aspect of his career is ironic considering that in his early days as a young musician, he maintained that conducting was a form of "faking," inferior to performance with an instrument and an art attractive to its practitioners purely for its glamour. He still held to that point of view late in life, when he proclaimed that "it is far greater to be an artist on an instrument than merely to conduct an orchestra in its glamorous fashion," and he rated "the three phases of my professional qualifications: (1) as composer; (2) as an artist on the flute; (3) as a conductor ... in that order."[54]

Stringfield produced about four hundred compositions, of which 150 reached publication. Most of his large works were for symphony or chamber orchestras. However, he also composed some short operas; scores for plays, outdoor drama, and radio; and vocal and instrumental solos. He incorporated his love for North Carolina's folk traditions into the classical genre and is perhaps best remembered for such works as *From the Southern Mountains*, which earned him the Pulitzer fellowship and the most professional fame.[55]

The birth of the North Carolina Symphony Orchestra owed a great deal to Stringfield's devotion to folk music. It was, after all, through UNC's Institute of Folk Music—with him as director—that a way was found to establish a state symphony orchestra, an idea that some North Carolinians at the time thought was too highbrow to have much chance of success in a largely rural southern state. But the South had a strong folk music tradition from the earliest days of the nation's history. That tradition was particularly strong in the mountains of North Carolina, where it was given voice in the Mountain Dance and Folk Festival, established in 1928. The music was preserved, performed, and promoted by such musicians and collectors of songs and ballads as Bascom Lamar Lunsford, Artus Monroe Moser, Dellie Chandler Norton, "Song Catcher" Dorothy Scarborough, Cecil Sharp, and Olive Dame Campbell. Stringfield consistently incorporated the folk element into the orchestra's concerts by inviting such classical composers and artists as Grainger, Powell, and Vardell—with their emphasis on the folk genre—to perform and to have the symphony play their works. The largest audiences for and greatest interest in hearing the early North Carolina Symphony Orchestra occurred during the summer seasons in Stringfield's beloved mountains. Along with Powell and David Guion, a Texas pianist and composer, Stringfield was one of the three most prolific classical arrangers of southern folk music, and his emphasis on that motif did much to bring about the early success of the North Carolina Symphony Orchestra.[56]

Indeed, the folk tradition—particularly the ballad—has had a strong influence on classical music as both composed and performed throughout the United States and has traditionally helped foster the American public's appetite for the classical repertoire by native composers and artists as well as the European masters. "This is not to say," writes American music historian John Warthen Struble, "that all American classical music is based on the ballad or even that a preponderance of it is. But the most successful American composers (in terms of public recognition) have always been those whose music asserted a direct and uncomplicated melodic appeal, even when its other musical parameters have been rooted in more abstract, 'high-brow' concepts. This is amply demonstrated by the overwhelming popularity of such works as MacDowell's 'To a Wild Rose,' Gershwin's *Rhapsody in Blue*, Copland's *Appalachian Spring*, Barber's *Adagio for Strings* and many other such American classical 'hits.'"[57]

Time has obscured Stringfield's reputation and important role in establishing classical music and the first state symphony orchestra in North Carolina. But it was largely through his initiative and efforts that the Institute of Folk Music at UNC was created, and that set the state on course for founding a symphony orchestra supported by a society of enthusiasts and donors. With the backing of the FERA and the Symphony Society, Stringfield led the orchestra, which featured well-known guest conductors and artists, in bringing classical music to large audiences throughout North Carolina during a difficult time in the state and nation's history, when music helped lift the spirits of a demoralized population. The movement to bring an orchestra to the Old North State surged forward under his leadership and then declined as he saw his vision for classical music in North Carolina and the South fade. But the movement did not die, and revival loomed on the horizon.

3

The Swalins and the Orchestra's Renaissance

In the summer of 1935, a train pulled into the station of the North Carolina tobacco town of Durham. Aboard were musicians Benjamin and Maxine Swalin, a recently married couple who were destined to have a profound impact on the revival and future of the North Carolina Symphony Orchestra. Benjamin was on a six-week sabbatical from DePauw University in Greencastle, Indiana, where he taught violin and music theory. He had been invited by Glen Haydon, head of the Department of Music at UNC, to teach in the second session of summer school on the Chapel Hill campus. The two men once had been students together at the University of Vienna, from which they both graduated in 1932. Haydon and his wife, Helen, met the Swalins at the station and took them first to the Carolina Inn to meet guests and to play for them briefly, then on to the Haydons' house, where they were to live while the Haydons were on vacation.[1]

Benjamin Franklin Swalin was born March 30, 1901, in Minneapolis, Minnesota, to Swedish parents Benjamin and Augusta Swalin. His father arrived in the United States aboard a vessel in steerage at the age of eighteen. He found work in Minneapolis as a blacksmith, which included shoeing horses for the city's trolleys. As would his son later, the elder Swalin played the violin, often for Swedish dances. At one of the dances he met his wife, who had immigrated as a servant. With the encouragement of their parents, all the Swalin children played musical instruments. The young Benjamin's brother Arthur was a pianist, and Harry was a violinist. Both became leaders of jazz bands.[2] Benjamin showed talent with the violin at an early age. In addition to his parents' influence, he received guidance from his uncle N. B. Swalin, who taught music in the Minnesota town of Willmar, where Benjamin sometimes visited his two uncles and gave local recitals. "The young Benjamin is but 17 years of age," announced the *Willmar Tribune* on September 18, 1918, "but all who heard him predict a great future for him."[3] At another recital the following year, Benjamin and his pianist brother, Arthur, drew further local acclaim, as reported by the *Tribune*.

A musical recital was given at the beautiful new home of Mr. and Mrs. J. B. Swalin, 525 Fourth St., when about a score of invited guests were given an opportunity of hearing Benjamin Swalin, violinist, and Arthur Swalin, pianist, two most promising young musicians from Minneapolis, who are visiting their uncles at Willmar.

The young musicians gave some wonderful music. Everyone present was greatly and agreeably surprised at the high standard of their performance. There can be no doubt but that Benjamin Swalin is destined to become a great violin player. Tho but 18 years of age, he has besides his regular high school work, so applied himself to his musical studies that he now has promise fo[r] a membership to the first violin section of the Minneapolis Symphony orchestra.

Benjamin and Maxine Swalin in the 1930s (Benjamin F. Swalin and Maxine M. Swalin Papers, Southern Historical Collection, Wilson Library, University of North Carolina at Chapel Hill).

The musicale was in charge of Prof. N. B. Swalin, an uncle of the young musicians, who announced the numbers. It opened with Beethoven's "Romance in G Major," and at once it was evident that the young violinist had made great progress in his studies since he played for a Willmar audience some four years ago. Hardly less remarkable was the performance of his younger brother, 14 years of age, who handled the difficult piano accompaniments with such precision and understanding that it augurs a great musical future also for him.[4]

To develop and perfect his musical craft, Swalin studied with George Klass, second concertmaster of the Minneapolis Symphony Orchestra, who featured his pupils in recitals in Minneapolis.[5] Upon graduating from high school in 1919, Swalin auditioned for the Minneapolis orchestra (later the Minnesota Symphony Orchestra) and was accepted as its youngest member. "During my two years with the orchestra," he later recalled, "I learned a great deal from its experienced musicians; while on tour in Winnipeg, Canada, I bought a handsome Panormo violin, still one of my treasured possessions;

and I developed a desire for a university education, inspired by the numerous stops made by our touring orchestra at colleges and universities." But first he wanted further training from the violin master Franz Kneisel, with whom he studied for two years.[6] Although his parents wanted him to remain in Minnesota and teach music for a career, he gained admission to the Institute of Musical Art (later the Juilliard School of Music) in New York and continued under the tutelage of Kneisel at the institute and, in the summers of 1921–1923, at the master's house in Blue Hill, Maine. Around the time he entered the institute, Swalin received a scholarship from the Jenny Lind Memorial Foundation.[7] During his studies, he "learned not only from my lessons with the great master but also from hearing some of the eminent violinists who were his friends and colleagues, and from the summer chamber music sessions that were an important part of the Kneisel discipline." When Kneisel died suddenly in 1926, Swalin took further instruction from Leopold Auer, who had succeeded Kneisel at the institute.

While in New York, Swalin earned income in a number of jobs, including playing in the first violin section of the Capitol Theatre Orchestra, in three hundred performances of the show *Up She Goes*, and for the WOR Radio Orchestra. "To feed my mind," he enrolled in Columbia University, where he earned BS and MA degrees.[8] He also gave recitals at Columbia. "A violin recital by Benjamin Swalin will be given Wednesday afternoon at 5 o'clock at Philosophy Hall, Columbia University," announced the *New York Times* on August 10, 1930.[9] At about the same time, the literary scholar Carl Van Doren, one of his professors at Columbia, encouraged him to broaden his education and experience by accepting a fellowship to study music in Vienna.

In September 1930, Swalin began his studies in violin, composition, and conducting at the Vienna Musikhochschule. In addition he took courses at the University of Vienna, which led to his earning the PhD degree in two years. In January 1933, he began traveling throughout Europe, visiting Czechoslovakia, Berlin, Sweden, Copenhagen, and Cambridge in England. "I sought out the scholars and musicians whose work I had admired," he later noted, "and I was fortunate to meet them." Upon returning to New York, he found employment in music difficult to secure, and he accepted a position teaching violin and music theory at DePauw University in Indiana.[10]

Swalin had met his future bride, Maxine, while he was studying and working at Columbia. She was born Martha Maxine McMahon in Waukee, Iowa, on May 7, 1903. Her father, physician George McMahon, and mother, teacher Mary Wilson McMahon, early influenced her interest in music. "My parents had grown up in country churches," she remembered, "where singing was often unaccompanied. When they settled in Waukee, they formed a quartet. Father lent his rich bass to Mother's clear soprano, and their favorite alto and tenor from the church choir filled in the harmony." Maxine had two older sisters, Bea and Roxy.[11] While she was still an infant, her "father brought home a Victrola and some recordings," and before she started school, "my older sister [Bea] read to me from the Victrola Book all about Melba, Galli Curci, Madame Shumann-Heink, and Caruso. Then she taught me to read music and to play the piano."[12] When Maxine was in the fourth grade, her mother enrolled her in art and piano lessons in nearby Des Moines. On Saturday mornings she rode the train to the city. After her art lesson, she took the trolley to the Victoria Hotel, where she received piano lessons from Marie Van Aaken. Van Aaken was on the faculty of the Drake University Conservatory and gave private instruction at her apartment, where she lived with her sister, Kathrina, a violinist. "Miss Van Aaken taught me with particular care, sometimes guiding my hand inside hers," Maxine later recalled. "When she demonstrated a phrase her broad frame seemed to surround the keyboard."[13]

At school in Waukee, Maxine particularly delighted in Thursdays, when her class listened to radio broadcasts of Walter Damrosch and the New York Philharmonic, because "The music by Haydn and Mozart was so beautiful."[14] She also looked forward to the weekly visits by Harry True, a dentist who came from Des Moines to treat the teeth of her father's patients. He played the piano, and they performed duets from *Etude* magazine on the family's old Sterling upright. She once reflected that the "*Etude* melodies of opera and symphony excerpts tingled in my ears between each week's adventure in sight reading. Even in bed when I closed my eyes I heard them, and wondered, if I wished really hard, could I, would I ever get to see and hear anything as wonderful as an opera and an orchestra."[15]

Maxine's sister Bea contracted tuberculosis shortly after her marriage, and Dr. McMahon arranged treatment for her at a sanatorium in the Colorado mountains. Mrs. McMahon accompanied Bea and her husband, Floyd Straight, and they rented a house in Denver. Maxine soon joined them and enrolled for her first two years of high school in Denver. She also began piano lessons at the Blanche Dingly Mathews Piano School. "From my first lesson," she fondly remembered, "practice was happiness. Mrs. Mathews gave me ear-training and keyboard harmony, relating it to the compositions she taught me. Why had my eyes and ears never been opened before? Previous teachers simply gave me pieces and exercises to practice." Undeterred by the flu pandemic of 1918, "I pedaled across town to my lessons, wearing a mask." Dr. McMahon traveled periodically to Denver to check on Bea and visit with the family.[16]

When Bea's health improved, she, her mother, and Maxine returned to Waukee, where Dr. McMahon had modernized their residence. For Maxine's last two years of high school, she boarded at Frances Shimer School in Mount Carroll, Illinois. She was inspired by a number of her subjects but disappointed in her piano instruction, although "I never missed a lesson or neglected practice, but progressed mainly from accompanying the chorus and singers, and by practicing the way Mrs. Mathews of Denver had taught me."[17] Back home after graduating from Frances Shimer School, Maxine took summer classes at the Drake Conservatory. Her instructor, pianist Basil Dean Gauntlett, had trained in England. He convinced her to attend Stephens College in Missouri, where he would be teaching, but she left that small campus after a year. She then enrolled at Drake University, living with the dean of women at no charge in exchange for helping with the musical education of her children. At the end of a year, she had earned enough credits in education and music to receive a teaching certificate, and she took a job teaching in the public schools in Waukee.

Having lived at home and saved her money for two years, Maxine left Waukee bound for the Institute of Musical Art (Juilliard) in New York. Dissatisfied with her original instructor, whom she regarded as lazy, she considered leaving the institute to return to Drake University to continue her studies. But reassignment to taskmaster Elizabeth Strauss led her to endure two and a half years of study and graduate in 1926.[18]

It was at her graduation that Maxine first met Benjamin Swalin. She had seen him from time to time in the halls of the institute and the library at Columbia, and she became interested in meeting him. He finally approached her as she stood in her graduation line. "Congratulations, Maxine," he said. "Are you free tonight? I'd like to take you to a friend's restaurant to celebrate." She regrettably informed him that she had previously made plans for the evening with another suitor, a violinist, and must decline Benjamin's invitation. "I had missed what I wanted so much, having a date with Benjamin Swalin," she lamented.[19]

Upon leaving the institute, Maxine took a position teaching music theory at the Hartford School of Music in Connecticut. At first she was lonely, but in September, Swalin telephoned her and asked if he could visit on the weekend. She readily agreed. At the initial Saturday visit, they took walks, went to a museum, dined at her favorite restaurant, and discussed art and literature, including the beginnings of his master's thesis, "Rossetti and the Pre-Raphaelites." On subsequent Saturdays at Hartford, they played music together, with Swalin giving her additional guidance. She observed that "His six years of intensive training under Franz Kneisel had given him refinements of phrasing, nuance, touch contrasts and accents that no piano teacher had ever revealed to me. Gradually I set myself free from Mrs. Strauss' rigid training as my recital pieces improved." On occasions she visited Swalin in New York, where she accompanied him to his Saturday class with Van Doren, played with his violin students in New Jersey, and went with him to concerts, church, museums, fraternity dances, and on a boat trip up the Hudson River.[20]

As their relationship grew, they began to talk of marriage. Although

Swalin had mixed feelings about leaving New York after his commencement at Columbia, he considered his fellowship to Vienna to be the first priority. "Even an offer to join the music faculty at Oberlin College had not tempted him," Maxine recalled. "I was disappointed by that refusal. We could have been married, I reminded him, and I could study right there on campus. But he said that for both our sakes his Ph.D. came first.... Ben had seen Columbia scholars buffet the distractions and financial strains of family life before completing their dissertations, and wanted none of it." Prior to departing for Vienna, Ben toured with an orchestra in the White Mountains, and Maxine began applying to various colleges. She visited Wellesley, Smith, Vassar, and Radcliffe, and Smith offered her a scholarship. She ultimately decided, however, to attend Iowa University in Iowa City, where she completed a bachelor's degree in two and a half years, in time for Ben's return from Europe, when they planned to be married.

While studying in Vienna, Ben missed Maxine and invited her to join him, but she declined. Years later she would lament missing a youthful opportunity to live and study in the Austrian city of music and culture.

> Why hadn't I left Iowa City in 1931, when he had prepared the way for me to join him in Vienna? We could be together he underlined in his "walking on air" letter. Professor Steurmann of the Vienna Musikhoschule had promised to give me free piano lessons.
> But I had been too afraid to borrow money or give up my degree midway. A break with my family would have caused a crisis.... I am the result of the road not taken, ... and I'll always regret it.[21]

When Swalin arrived back in Depression New York in 1932 without a job, a dean at DePauw University offered him the teaching position. Maxine and her family "rejoiced that Ben now had a contract in hand." But their elation was short lived, for he wanted to delay accepting the position and their marriage. According to her, "our shock was genuine when he arrived at Minneapolis instead of coming to me, and worse, he was leaving again." Swalin now intended to enroll in summer school at the American-Russian Institute for International Relations in Moscow. Apparently, in Vienna he had developed an interest in socialism and wanted to explore it further. "I was puzzled, disappointed, and even humiliated," said Maxine. "Because of his Mother's [recent] death, I could understand why he went to Minneapolis before coming to me; but crossing the ocean again when our marriage was the next logical step upset and worried me." Her parents questioned his "common sense" and wondered if he was sincerely committed to the engagement. Swalin's father also expressed his concern and anger: "You've just arrived from Europe ready to settle down and now out of curiosity you want to go see the Bolsheviks. That's crazy!"[22]

Hurt and resentful of Swalin's behavior, Maxine nevertheless "still believed in our future marital happiness" and convinced herself that his trip to Russia was his "last student fling before settling down." In the meantime, she had taken a job teaching music and English at a high school near Des Moines and read with interest his letters from Russia.

When Swalin returned to the United States for the second time, he went directly to Waukee after landing in New York. From there he journeyed on to DePauw University to take up his duties teaching violin and theory, although he still wanted to postpone a wedding until he was established in his career. During the Thanksgiving holiday of 1934, Maxine visited the DePauw campus, and the couple window-shopped for furniture ideas for a possible house in the future. Swalin spent Christmas with his family in Minneapolis, and Maxine with her folks in Waukee. Shortly after Christmas Day, she visited a married friend and her church minister husband in the town of Mexico, Missouri. During a telephone call to Ben in which Maxine expressed her continued unhappiness at being apart, the two decided to get married right away. He immediately boarded a train and arrived in Missouri at midnight on December 31. They were married the next day at the friend's house, with the minister husband conducting the ceremony. The newlyweds then traveled to DePauw. Although they did not know it at the time, their stay there would not be a long one.

The Swalins' original plans called for Ben to teach the summer session at UNC and then return to DePauw, where Maxine intended to pursue graduate studies by commuting to Indiana University at Bloomington.[23] According to Ben, "My wife and I came to Chapel Hill in 1935 with no inkling that it was to be our permanent home." Within a short time, however, Glen Haydon proposed to Frank Porter Graham, president of UNC, that the university offer Swalin a teaching position on the Tar Heel campus. Graham invited him to join the faculty with a two-year contract. Swalin recalled that "Acceptance of the invitation was not automatic, however, because at that time I was employed at DePauw University and I had appreciated my work there, even though my teaching load was approximately thirty-three hours per week. But the DePauw contracts had been delayed due to the severity of the Depression, and members of the faculty had no absolute assurance of employment for the coming fall session (although a promise had been made by the administration that contracts would be available in September). My salary at DePauw had been $3,000, whereas at Chapel Hill I would start at only $2,750." Yet at UNC he would be able to direct an expanded university orchestra, do research in musicology, and make revisions to a book on the violin that he was writing, which UNC Press had expressed an interest in publishing. In 1941 the press did publish his *The Violin Concerto: A Study in German Romanticism*, with a subsidy from the American Council of Learned Societies. Swalin wrote to DePauw asking to be released from his contract. With that request granted, he accepted Graham's offer, and he and Maxine began a long musical career in North Carolina—a life's work that would leave an illustrious mark upon the cultural development of the state.[24]

As Ben settled in to teach his classes and direct the university orchestra, he and Maxine decided that she should pursue a graduate degree in music, even though it would mean a year's separation. She entered Radcliffe, where she earned an MA degree. At times during her year of study, she and Ben managed to meet in Washington or Philadelphia. He went to Cambridge for the awarding of her degree, and they vacationed in the Green Mountains before returning to UNC. "I was ecstatic to return with Ben to Chapel Hill," she remembered, "to practice, accompany his violin students, and copy musical examples for his book." For a time, they lived in an apartment; then they rented a small house on Columbia Street. Despite some disappointment and delay regarding Ben's salary and promotion, the Swalins enjoyed their early years in Chapel Hill. "Life was good," Maxine recollected. "We did all

Glen Haydon, head of the Department of Music, hired Benjamin Swalin to teach at UNC (North Carolina Collection, Wilson Library, University of North Carolina at Chapel Hill).

the normal things—went to parties, chaperoned Tin Can dances, listened to Charlie Jones's courageous sermons on civil rights and justice at the Presbyterian Church where I was choir director, and we cherished the friendships of faculty and townspeople." For a time, she taught at Chapel Hill High School.

One summer they purchased a secondhand Chevrolet and drove to Peterborough, New Hampshire, where Ben had a summer residency in music instruction and performance at the MacDowell Colony. Just before Germany invaded Poland and World War II erupted in Europe in 1939, they traveled to Vienna, where they visited some of Ben's former professors, and then on to Munich, where they toured museums and attended opera performances in the evenings. With hostilities threatening and German borders about to close, they narrowly escaped Europe through Hamburg and Oslo, arriving in the United States aboard the SS *Bergensford*. Back in North Carolina, Maxine suffered for months from a shoulder injury she had acquired aboard ship. But "How fortunate we felt to be in North Carolina and Chapel Hill instead of Germany!" she declared. They purchased the house they had been renting on Columbia Street; remodeled it to "open a place for our piano, for string quartets and madrigal singing"; and invited students to rehearse and perform there. They continued to own the home even after they subsequently moved out of Chapel Hill to a country site near Carrboro that they called Maxeben, a name formed from their first names. In later years, they moved back to the house in town.[25]

A degree of sadness intruded into the Swalins' marriage when, at age thirty-two, Maxine experienced a miscarriage. She had long wanted children and regretted delaying her marriage and pregnancy. She even felt that taking a year to attend Radcliffe had been a mistake, because it postponed having a baby. "It was a preposterous idea," she lamented, "and we suffered for it." After the miscarriage, "we thought and hoped that I would become pregnant again." But with the demanding schedule of a growing state orchestra that lay ahead for them, a child of their own was not to be. By the time they considered adoption, they "were ineligible."[26]

As their lives and careers unfolded at the university and in the surrounding community, Swalin began to think seriously about reviving the orchestra that had been launched by Lamar Stringfield, whom he had known slightly when the two studied at the Institute of Musical Art (Juilliard). He once described how his commitment to the project developed. "My responsibilities in the music department," he said, "included directing the University Orchestra, and I gradually developed the notion of strengthening that group by merging it with the remains of the WPA orchestra. I knew that such a project would require an adequate rehearsal hall and a source of funds, and I was not sure how these could be acquired. Nor was I sure how I could fit it into my teaching schedule. But it seemed a notion worth pursuing, and by early 1937 I had formulated a proposal to reestablish a permanent North Carolina Symphony Orchestra under the auspices of the North Carolina Symphony Society."[27]

He began by calling on society president Joseph Pratt, who, along with the society executive committee, supported the idea. Erle Stapleton, director of the WPA's Federal Music Project in North Carolina, agreed to move the agency's symphony from Greensboro to UNC if the university would agree to a merger of the two orchestras. Also, the North Carolina Federation of Music Clubs passed a resolution endorsing the plan to revive the orchestra. Swalin pointed out to the university that a number of WPA musicians might become students in UNC's music department and members of the university symphony. He planned a demonstration concert in Chapel Hill for May 24, hoping to obtain the university's cooperation in the renaissance of the North Carolina Symphony Orchestra. On the following day in Greensboro, he was guest conductor of the WPA orchestra at a concert sponsored by the Junior League. But UNC declined his proposal to consolidate the two symphonies. Music department head Glen Haydon flatly rejected the merger. He argued that the student musicians would simply be distracted performing with professional players from the Federal Music Project. At a campus meeting on May 29, Haydon read a short statement declaring that a North Carolina Symphony Orchestra "under the sponsorship of the university's Department of Music was not in line with the policy of the department." Despite the lack of support in the UNC music department, which wanted to emphasize musicology rather than conservatory training, Swalin enlisted a few musicians from the old orchestra and some of his students and continued to hold rehearsals.[28]

North Carolinians at large were also divided over the need, expense, and practicality of maintaining a symphony orchestra in their state. A UNC alumnus once remarked to Swalin that "The violin in my day was a fiddlin' instrument, and a fellow would be ashamed to carry a violin case across the campus or even talk about a symphony orchestra." At Winston-Salem in 1937, the Swalins attended a large meeting of leading citizens who convened to consider the feasibility of a plan to fund and expand the WPA orchestra and help keep classical music alive in the state. But at that gathering, a prominent corporate executive told Swalin that he was wasting his efforts, because "The people do not care for that kind of music." Swalin countered that classical music could enrich anyone's education and lifestyle and help ensure a well-rounded society. Despite his attempts at persuasion, the conference in Winston-Salem failed to produce any assistance for a state symphony orchestra.[29]

Without the university merger or private support that the Swalins and others sought, the WPA orchestra continued to limp along with limited outreach. It kept its headquarters at Greensboro and gave summer concerts in Asheville. The Little Symphony managed to present a few performances. On May 4, 1937, for example, the smaller orchestra played a mainly children's program at the Broad Street High School auditorium in Burlington. The Burlington Music Club sponsored the concert, and a small admission fee was charged. In the summer of 1938, the larger orchestra did not travel to Asheville but instead gave twelve concerts on Harbor Island at Wrightsville Beach, under the direction of Laird Waller from Chicago, while a smaller contingent remained in Greensboro and performed band concerts. By that fall, the band at Greensboro was the only part of the WPA orchestra still operating, and its concerts ended in 1940. The rest of the orchestra disbanded, with some musicians finding employment in North Carolina and others joining the Virginia orchestra directed by Waller.

The reality of a symphony orchestra for North Carolina seemed to be vanishing. But the Swalins and other loyal supporters were unwilling to accept defeat. After the May 1937 concert conducted by Swalin in Greensboro, Edward B. Benjamin, a prominent businessman and philanthropist of New Orleans and Greensboro, came away impressed. He approached the Swalins about reviving a state symphony that could sustain itself. He would remain a good friend of the Swalins and a proponent of a state orchestra.[30]

For the small number of musicians that he was rehearsing at UNC, Swalin hoped to find a way to provide at least "modest … compensation." But "Unhappily, there was virtually no money." Nevertheless, a number of sympathetic friends rallied to his cause of maintaining an orchestra. One was the playwright Paul Green, a product of UNC's Carolina Playmakers who had gained a national reputation for his dramas, including a 1927 Pulitzer Prize for his Broadway production *In Abraham's Bosom*. As noted previously, his symphonic dramas included *The Lost Colony*, for which Stringfield had composed music. Through his dramatic works and outspoken public opinions, Green had shown himself to be a liberal defender of the poor and a supporter of racial equality and other humanitarian causes, as well as of the arts. "I had been with him on only a few occasions," recalled Swalin, "before I began distinctly to sense that, in the parlance of the 1930s, we were on the same wavelength."[31]

Swalin found another active ally in Mrs. Athol C. ("Johnsie") Burnham, one of the earliest female violinists to perform with New York's Metropolitan Opera Orchestra. She had studied in Paris with Jacques Thibaud. A native North Carolinian, she returned to the state and settled in Chapel Hill after her husband's death. She had played with the state orchestra in its early days, then continued violin instruction with Swalin and believed strongly in reestablishing the North Carolina Symphony. Swalin's fledgling orchestra was sorely in need of funds for operating expenses and some percussion instruments and other necessities. So he, Green, and Burnham called at a bank and borrowed two hundred dollars in start-up money.[32]

More friends and supporters continued to help in the Swalins' crusade to revive the symphony, contributing time, effort, and moderate resources. Maxine remembered that "Our mutual best friends were Johnsie Burnham, violinist and raconteur, full of pungent stories about European mishaps during her travels with her husband, the Director of the International Red Cross after World War I; and Paul Green and wife Elizabeth who preferred North Carolina's native Harnett County and Chapel Hill to Hollywood. The [Fred B.] McCalls, Johnsie, and the Greens were founders, supporters, and trustees of the symphony from its dawn, and … encouraged Ben to revive it. This enduring link of friends became our Chapel Hill family."[33]

Although the initial efforts of friends and sympathetic devotees spurred its renaissance, the orchestra still faced serious obstacles, including "no rehearsal home, office, secretarial help, publicity chairman, personnel director, or business manager."[34] But the movement to launch a resurrected orchestra grew further when Pratt, on October 16, 1939, sent a letter to remaining and potential members of the North Carolina Symphony Society asking them to come

Playwright and Pulitzer Prize–winner Paul Green was a strong supporter of the Swalins' efforts to revive the North Carolina Symphony (photograph from 1939, courtesy State Archives of North Carolina).

together to discuss the orchestra's future and the society's finances and to elect officers. The society convened on October 20 at a dinner meeting in the Graham Memorial Building in Chapel Hill. The members pledged to support a plan for the reorganized orchestra to present an initial concert in Durham in late January or early February 1940. Rehearsals for musicians from various towns were to begin after Christmas. From the organization's 1932 roster, the society again elected Pratt as president, along with a slate of officers including vice president, secretary, and treasurer.

The original plan to hold the first concert in Durham soon changed. Instead, the event was scheduled for Jones Auditorium at Meredith College in Raleigh on March 16, 1940. Prior to that date, a demonstration concert took place in Chapel Hill, and Swalin held rehearsals for small groups at different sites. One group gathered in the WDNC studios in Durham, another at Woman's College of the University of North Carolina in Greensboro (now UNC Greensboro), and a third in Chapel Hill. On the day before the Meredith concert, the full orchestra of fifty musicians, largely from colleges and high schools, held a rehearsal in Pullen Hall at North Carolina State College (now University) in Raleigh. A final rehearsal occurred in the Meredith auditorium on the afternoon before the evening performance.[35]

At the concert, conducted by Swalin, the audience heard the Overture to *Prometheus* by Beethoven, the Concerto in B Minor for Violoncello and Orchestra, Op. 33, by Saint-Saëns, the *New World* Symphony by Dvořák, and the Overture to *Die Meistersinger* by Wagner. The guest soloist for the concerto was William Klenz, a graduate assistant at UNC who had graduated from Curtis Institute in Philadelphia. His appearance marked a tradition by Swalin "of introducing to North Carolina audiences exceptionally talented young soloists," which "provided many aspiring musicians unusual opportunities for musical development."[36] Tickets were sold at Meredith, and the orchestra raised about $90 in receipts. But finances remained a major problem. In February the society's assets from donations had totaled $424.64. After the Meredith event, the organization launched a membership drive, printing a leaflet explaining its mission and setting goals of a hundred members and $25,000 to sustain the orchestra. Categories of membership extended from $1 ("Active") to $1,000 ("Benefactor").[37]

The Meredith concert was followed by four others in 1940. The second one, part of the Student Entertainment Series at UNC, was performed on Sunday evening, May 5, before a mostly student audience in Hill Music Hall. Swalin retained the previous selections by Dvořák and Wagner but added Gershwin's *Rhapsody in Blue* and William Billings's *Chester*. The piano soloist for *Rhapsody in Blue* was another aspiring young musician, Thomas O'Kelly, who had studied with Severyn Eisenberger at the Cincinnati College Conservatory of Music. The forty-nine musicians derived from several communities and institutions, among them the Asheville Symphony Orchestra of 1927, the Musical Society of Asheville, the public schools, and the Institute of Folk Music at UNC.[38] The *Daily Tar Heel* of May 5 noted that—with the selections from Dvořák, Gershwin, and Billings—the concert was following the Symphony Society's policy of "encouraging the performance by North

Carolinians of American compositions." The newspaper billed the day of music as a "Double Feature."

> Local music lovers will be given two programs of classical, light classical and march music today. Under the direction of Professor Earl Slocum the University band will play light classics and march tunes in an open air concert this afternoon at 5 o'clock under Davie Poplar. Tonight at 8:30 the North Carolina Symphony, conducted by Professor Benjamin Swalin, will perform in Hill Music hall in a program of classics.
>
> These musical programs and others like them add much to what might otherwise be a dull weekend. Chapel Hill, located in a state and section in which "good music" often is not appreciated, is fortunate in being able to present two programs in the same day.[39]

The year's third concert took place on November 22 in the Fayetteville High School auditorium and was sponsored by the Southeastern Teachers Association. To selections from the first two symphony appearances Swalin added Weber's Overture to *Euryanthe* and Haydn's Symphony No. 104 in D Major. The fourth concert occurred at Mitchell College in Statesville on November 23. It was followed the next day by another performance in the Asheville auditorium, sponsored by the Asheville Civic Music Association. Local radio broadcast the concert from the auditorium.

In 1941 Swalin maintained his policy of rehearsing separate units of the orchestra at different locations prior to bringing all the musicians together for a final rehearsal just before a concert. To hold those individual practice sessions, he traveled to Asheville, Charlotte, Durham, Greensboro, and Raleigh, in addition to spending time with the musicians in Chapel Hill. For its first concert of the year, the symphony gave a performance in Elizabeth City's S. L. Sheep Auditorium on March 22. The Elizabeth City Music Club sponsored the event. Besides the aforementioned selections by Weber and Haydn, Swalin conducted an aria, "Vision Fugitive," from Massenet's *Hérodiade*, as well as Dett's *Juba Dance*, Brahms's Hungarian Dance No. 6, and Chabrier's *Espana Rhapsody*. The soloist who sang the aria was Paul Oncley, violist with the orchestra.

Three days after the Elizabeth City event, the orchestra gave the same program in the Aycock Auditorium in Greensboro. The concert was part of the Bundles for Britain campaign to provide aid for Britain, then under attack by Nazi Germany. Following the orchestra's presentation, the Kerenoff Ballet, accompanied by the symphony, performed *Dance of the Hours*, by Ponchielli, and dances from Bizet's *Carmen*.[40]

Early in the new season, the symphony followed the precedent set by Stringfield with the old orchestra and established a Little Symphony Orchestra in order to reach more audiences in the state. The Little Symphony gave its first concert in the far west at Western Carolina Teachers College (now Western Carolina University) in Cullowhee. Soon after the small symphony's debut, the Raleigh Civic Music Association sponsored a performance by the full orchestra in the capital city's Memorial Auditorium on May 11. Except for Mozart's Symphony Concertante for Violin, Viola, and Orchestra, K. 364, all the selections had been played in earlier concerts. The Mutual Network through WRAL Radio broadcast the first half of the concert, which featured conductor Swalin and violist Julia Mueller as soloists. Besides playing with and promoting the symphony, Mueller earned a reputation as a capable administrator with both the music department at Duke University and the North Carolina School of the Arts before her death in 1979. The orchestra gave the same concert on May 12 in Chapel Hill, sponsored by the Student Entertainment committee.[41]

Although the revived orchestra was off to a good start, it still faced "tough times." The musicians did not receive a regular salary but occasionally got an "honorarium." They paid their own expenses and traveled long distances from town to town for concerts. In his memoir, Swalin described the difficulties under which the orchestra had to operate.

> We were developing a rehearsal routine that in large measure was responsible for whatever success the orchestra was able to achieve. The members of the orchestra lived in Chapel Hill, Charlotte, Raleigh, Asheville, Durham, Kinston, Greenville, Wilmington—all over North Carolina. This made it very difficult to get together for rehearsals, and even for scheduled concerts. Our concerts almost invariably were scheduled for weekends. Prior to each concert we made detailed arrangements for lodging and rehearsal space, and we would see that each of the musicians received the necessary information. On the weekend of the concert we would all arrive at the designated place, perhaps a school auditorium or gymnasium, for rehearsal on Friday afternoon or evening and again on Saturday. This might be our only opportunity to go over the entire program together, and by itself it would not have been enough to ensure a polished performance. What made the crucial difference was that smaller groups of musicians would get together on the weekends between concerts whenever and wherever we could.[42]

Swalin himself was especially challenged by such a system as he struggled to fulfill his teaching duties at UNC and simultaneously maintain a demanding statewide rehearsal schedule. Maxine recalled that "After his last class on Friday afternoons Ben caught the bus from Hillsborough to a different rehearsal unit, generally standing because of crowded conditions. Musicians from each area, Charlotte, Asheville, Greensboro, Greenville, Durham, or Wilmington, rehearsed with him in borrowed places such as legion huts, school gymnasiums, cafeterias with chairs stacked on tables, and churches."[43]

By the time the United States entered the Second World War following the Japanese attack on Pearl Harbor on December 7, 1941, the Swalins and the Symphony Society had reestablished the symphony on a relatively sound footing. The war had an impact on the orchestra as well as the state and nation. It had to endure financial stringency, travel restrictions, and some public opposition to the luxury of having a symphony during wartime. The loss of forty-five musicians to the military draft over the course of the conflict posed a particular problem. Women players replaced most of the conscripted men. Before the war ended, two-fifths of the orchestra's fifty-five to sixty musicians were female.[44]

Swalin was forced to pursue a relentless recruiting effort, or "our symphony might soon be decimated." He also maintained an exhausting traveling schedule to rehearse individual units. "We were fortunate," he remembered about trips to rehearsals in Virginia,

> to find a group of experienced musicians in the Richmond, Virginia, area. That meant that I would have to go to Richmond to rehearse them, and this presented problems. On one occasion I had to sleep in the railroad station there because there was no hotel space! Generally, though, because it was possible to rehearse with the Richmond contingent only on Sundays, I would leave Chapel Hill early on a Sunday morning, park my car at the Seaboard railway station in Raleigh, and board a 7:30 train for Richmond. The coaches usually were crowded with military personnel, mothers with fretful babies, and piles of bulky baggage. On arrival at Richmond I would barely have time for lunch at the John Marshall Hotel before going up to the roof of the hotel for a rehearsal at two o'clock. Following the rehearsal, someone would drive me to the station to catch a 5:00 train for Raleigh, where I was due to arrive about 9:30 that night.[45]

Sometimes the musicians did not appear at a site for rehearsal. One observer of Swalin's harried schedule remarked: "Once Dr. Swalin traveled from Chapel Hill to Greensboro only to find an empty rehearsal hall. He then practiced alone on his violin."[46]

Despite the limitations of wartime, the orchestra managed to continue its mission of bringing classical music to the state's populace and even to expand that outreach with new financial support and the creation of a children's educational program. In 1942 the symphony presented six concerts, appearing first on February 27 in Kinston under the sponsorship of the local woman's club and then in Memorial Hall at UNC on March 20, supported and promoted by the Student Entertainment Series. The Symphony Society had recently implemented a plan for establishing local committees (later called chapters) to sell memberships to pay for concerts in their communities, which would include the bonus of a free children's matinee. So at the Chapel Hill performance, the symphony included a program for children in the afternoon. The evening concert featured a guest solo from Mendelssohn's Concerto in E Minor for Violin and Orchestra by the violinist Ruggiero Ricci, well known for his left-hand technique and his recording—especially of works by Paganini—and teaching careers. The orchestra next played at Memorial Auditorium in Raleigh on April 27 as part of the city's sesquicentennial celebration. A number of local musicians and singers participated in the concert. They included Edgar Alden from the Department of Music at Peace College in Raleigh, Paul Oncley of the Department of Music at Woman's College in

Greensboro, the Woman's College Glee Club, the North Carolina State College Glee Club, and the voice class from St. Mary's Junior College in Raleigh. The final two concerts of the year were a children's program in the afternoon and an evening performance in Durham on November 13. The Music Club of the Woman's College at Duke University and the Durham chapter of the Symphony Society sponsored the concerts.

Because much of the state's population was focused on winning the war, the orchestra performed only five concerts in 1943, three of which were for children. On January 30 in Asheville, the symphony played its first concert, a children's program sponsored by the Junior League. On March 21 and 22, it gave a children's matinee in Chapel Hill, an evening presentation at UNC's Memorial Hall, an afternoon performance for a large number of school-children at Memorial Auditorium in Raleigh, and an evening concert in the capital city's Needham Broughton High School auditorium. The Student Entertainment organization sponsored both Chapel Hill events.[47]

Amid the strains of war, Benjamin and Maxine Swalin continued to press for public support for the orchestra and classical music in North Carolina. They were joined by Mrs. Charles E. Johnson of Raleigh, who heard the sesquicentennial concert in 1942 and became a strong advocate of the orchestra. A Raleigh newspaper published a letter from her praising the symphony and criticizing the population for its lack of interest and support. She would later become president of the Symphony Society. In late 1942, Mrs. Johnson and the Swalins attended a meeting with Governor J. Melville Broughton that she had arranged. They asked for the governor's endorsement in obtaining funding through the state budget for the orchestra. They stressed the symphony's role as a valuable public education resource. The governor and his wife joined the Swalins, Mrs. Johnson, Johnsie Burnham, and other members of the society in urging the General Assembly to pass legislation to fund the orchestra.

The group's lobbying paid off when the General Assembly passed Senate Bill No. 248 in March 1943. Ten senators introduced the bill in February, and that same month, the Appropriations Committee held hearings on the proposed legislation before it was submitted to both houses for a vote. During the ensuing heated discussion, a number of legislators voiced their opposition to a spending bill they considered frivolous, often citing the demands of the war as a special reason for rejecting it.[48] One opposing member rose in the house of representatives to remark that on his way to Raleigh for the General Assembly session, he observed a woman at work in a field. He loudly proclaimed to his fellow lawmakers: "I thought to myself, that poor soul could have a son in World War II. What would *she* say if she heard that I voted for this horn-tootin' bill?" As a result of his label for the legislation, Senate Bill No. 248 was often referred to in the press and in conversations as the "horn-tootin' bill."[49]

Despite the objections to spending public money to support an orchestra in wartime, the bill passed. It placed the North Carolina Symphony Society "under the patronage and control of the State," and it authorized "the Governor and Council of State to make an allotment from the Contingency and Emergency Fund in aid" of the society's mission of "making fine music available to the people of the State and promoting interest and appreciation of fine music by the citizenship of the State." The appropriation was not to exceed $2,000 per year and was subject to state audit. The act emphasized the orchestra's "distinctly educational" role in "increasing the love and appreciation of music by the children of the State, by giving free concerts for the children." It specified that the North Carolina Symphony Society would have a board of directors with sixteen members, including the governor and the superintendent of public instruction. The governor would appoint four directors, and the society would select the remaining ten. The board of directors would make bylaws for the society.[50] The board appointed an executive committee for the society to guide it in its pressing obligations.

With passage of the "horn-tootin' bill," many North Carolinians considered their state government to be the first to provide a "recurring appropriation" for a symphony orchestra, although previously Indiana had allotted state funds for its orchestra to play a number of concerts. In the 1950s, Vermont's governor challenged North Carolina's claim in a letter of protest to Tar Heel governor Luther H. Hodges. He maintained that Vermont became the first state to subsidize an orchestra when it provided $1,000 for its symphony to perform at the World's Fair in New York in 1939. But according to Swalin, "That appropriation ... was quite different from the one given our symphony, which was a *recurring* subsidy. It was not until 1945 ... that the Vermont Symphony began receiving a regular appropriation from the Vermont state treasury."[51]

In 1944 the number of the symphony's public appearances exceeded that of the previous year, although several potential concerts were cancelled because of transportation limitations and a shortage of available musicians. Nevertheless, the orchestra gave twelve performances, four of which were for children. The first adult concert occurred on January 17 in Winston-Salem's Reynolds High School auditorium. It began with "The Star-Spangled Banner" and featured works by Bach, Borodin, Prokofiev, Tchaikovsky, and Liszt. Paul Stassevitch—violinist, pianist, conductor, and educator from Chicago Musical College and DePaul University—appeared as piano soloist. The orchestra followed the same basic program, with some variation, in its subsequent concerts that year. At the next adult performance, in Durham on February 5, Dutch pianist Egon Petri, an émigré from war-torn Europe noted for his renditions of Liszt, was the guest soloist. The first children's matinee of the year preceded that event. The second took place in Raleigh's Memorial Auditorium on

March 10. On the following day, the orchestra played at Needham Broughton High School, where Stassevitch again appeared as guest soloist. April proved a full month, when the symphony gave three adult and two children's concerts. The adult presentations took place in Greensboro, Chapel Hill, and Greenville, and the children's in Greenville and Chapel Hill.[52]

The orchestra gave its final performances of 1944—sponsored by the Student Entertainment Series committee and the Symphony Society—in UNC's Memorial Hall on December 9. On that Saturday morning at 11:30, the musicians played a children's concert featuring "The Star-Spangled Banner," Stringfield's "Cripple Creek," and selections from Mozart and Beethoven. Also on the program was "Miss Margaret Shaw, 13-year-old pianist of Macon, N.C., as guest soloist," who had received instruction at both Meredith College and Duke University. Foster Fitzsimons of the Carolina Playmakers served as commentator and interpreter for the orchestra's renditions. The audience at the evening concert heard Beethoven's Sixth Symphony, Goldmark's *Sakuntala* Overture, Stringham's Nocturne No. 1, and the Prelude to Act 3 from Wagner's *Lohengrin*.[53]

The state allocations specified for the Symphony Society in the first year under the "horn-tootin' bill" consisted of $500 for music, secretarial work, and supplies; $500 for travel expenses of the orchestra's musicians; $500 for travel expenses of a business manager or other promoter of the orchestra; and $500 for an assistant conductor, advertising, and concerts at "an army camp or factory or open-air stadium."[54] At a meeting of the society at UNC's Carolina Inn on June 27, 1944, members voted to provide a three-year contract beginning in September and to make Swalin the official musical director of the orchestra, with a salary of $100 per year. The agreement specified that when the society's financial circumstances allowed, Swalin's salary "should be increased until it reached a level of respectability in keeping with the dignity of the position and services rendered." The musicians still remained largely unpaid. At that same meeting, the society discussed expanding its operations by adding a business manager and a secretary, establishing fundraising districts in the state, hiring a consultant to help expand revenue, and creating a children's department for the orchestra.[55]

For its final meeting of 1944, the Symphony Society gathered in Chapel Hill on December 9 and endorsed an expansion program. As part of that plan, the society hoped to raise $150,000 in an Expansion Fund for the next two years of operation; to hire forty or fifty full-time paid musicians; to develop a Children's Division; to increase the number of concerts to cover twenty to thirty weeks; to employ a full-time music director, a business manager, and a secretary; and to engage the American City Bureau of Chicago as a consultant for fund-raising. To secure revenue for the Expansion Fund, the state would be divided into districts, each of which would be based in a city and headed by a local chairman. A local committee would assist each chairman in soliciting money for the orchestra. Before adjourning the society noted that revenue for the past year had been $13,178.97, with expenditures reaching $12,170.97, leaving a balance of $1,008.00 in the treasury. It also appointed a committee consisting of A. C. Hall (society treasurer), Mrs. Charles Johnson, and the Swalins to lobby state lawmakers to increase state funding for the orchestra. The committee's efforts were rewarded when, early in 1945, the legislature increased the state's contribution to $4,000 per year for the biennium.

In January 1945, with the war still hindering the orchestra's progress, the executive committee of the society met twice in Raleigh to discuss the expansion plan and get it underway. It terminated the contract with the American City Bureau, changed the name of the Expansion Fund to the Symphony Fund, and moved the fund's headquarters to Chapel Hill. To lead the fund drive, the committee appointed R. L. McMillan of Raleigh as chairman and J. O. Bailey from UNC as director. Bailey worked tirelessly to publicize the fund during a half-year leave of absence allowed him by the university. When that ended, Colonel Kermit Hunter, recently released from military service, became an efficient business manager, coordinating the symphony headquarters with the fund-raising districts.[56] UNC president Frank Porter Graham granted Swalin an indefinite leave of absence to work full time to make the drive and the orchestra a success.

Swalin remembered the fund's new home: "We set up headquarters in a small room on North Columbia Street in Chapel Hill at the rear of a grocery store. The office equipment consisted of a few inherited tables and chairs, a 'gel' machine, and a typewriter on which Dr. Bailey pecked out his letters with his index fingers. Water for our coffee and bathroom accommodations were supplied at the nearby Chapel Hill town hall. During the cold weather we were warmed by our own labors and by stoking a coal stove."[57]

The fund drive officially opened on July 26, 1945, with a statewide broadcast from Raleigh by WPTF Radio. The Swalins performed several musical selections, and Chairman McMillan and Governor R. Gregg Cherry spoke to the radio audience. They stressed the cultural importance of classical music and the public pride in having a first-class orchestra for the state. They described the ongoing efforts to expand the number of concerts to reach audiences throughout North Carolina, and the plans to make periodic broadcasts. In September the Symphony Fund drive reported that $10,643.75 had been received, along with projected contributions of $8,000 from Asheville, $5,000 from Greensboro, $4,000 from Raleigh, $1,200 from Kinston, $1,000 from an unnamed industry, $857 from Durham schools, $500 to $1,000 from Wilmington, and $500 from Washington, North Carolina.[58]

As the Symphony Fund got underway, Benjamin and Maxine Swalin threw themselves relentlessly into finding public support for the orchestra as they traveled throughout the state. They promoted the program to any audience that would listen to their appeals for financial backing. Maxine recalled that "Ben and I criss-crossed the state, and at each stop, wherever there was an adequate piano, played a few short pieces together. Ben then spoke to the towns people about the newly formed N.C. Symphony. He urged them to believe, as he did, that the orchestra should bring its music directly to the people and to their community."[59]

Benjamin Swalin conceived a plan to raise additional money for the orchestra by recording "pops" albums featuring American works for general audiences and renditions for children. He hoped for a reduced recording fee, and he appealed to the American Federation of Musicians for assistance. However, the president of the union refused, arguing that recordings aired on radio threatened the employment of musicians who played in radio orchestras. A nationwide strike by the union brought further complications, and negotiations for recordings at reduced costs ultimately failed.

The orchestra made significant progress during the difficult war years, gaining momentum for the postwar era with the implementation of the Symphony Fund. But, in addition to laboring under the distractions and limitations imposed on the state and nation by the war, the symphony had to face other obstacles and problems. A number of North Carolinians continued to consider a state-supported orchestra as an elitist waste of money and an unnecessary extravagance.

Ironically, major opposition to the orchestra also came from several officials at North Carolina's leading academic institutions. Led by Dean Hugh Altvater of the Woman's College in Greensboro, some administrators at UNC, Duke University, and Davidson College attacked the symphony in the fall of 1944. They maintained that their students who played with the orchestra were being taken away from their studies. They further claimed that the faculty who performed at the symphony's concerts suffered from fatigue that inhibited their teaching. They insisted that a state-funded orchestra was a threat to their musical programs and their funding and was not needed. At UNC the leading opponent of the symphony was Glen Haydon, who had originally hired Swalin to teach. Negotiations between the orchestra and the music departments produced some reconciliation and assurances that students and faculty would not be unduly burdened. Yet resentment and fears of losing funding continued among academic institutions with music departments.

Swalin took the criticism personally, expressing his hurt feelings about the resistance to his plans for bringing classical music to the state's population at large. "Although there were few opportunities for an open confrontation," he once lamented, there were occasions when the orchestra was denied the use of institutional facilities—such as a hall in which to rehearse, or even music stands or chairs. And there was a persistent effort to have me dismissed from the University's music department. Further, two University officials later told me that on three different occasions during my ten years of teaching there, I had been recommended for promotion to a full professorship—but because of my work with the Symphony and at the insistence of one individual on the faculty committee, my promotion had been denied.

Why is it that when a new idea develops and is being brought to fruition—I have pondered this through the years and the answer still eludes me—opposition crystallizes and seeks to make a project one of the seven deadly sins?

Nevertheless, he insisted, "The project grew in spite of harassment, and we were privileged to return year after year to the same communities and also to extend our tours. But it was an uphill road."[60]

A shortage of musicians, particularly string players, continued to present a worrisome problem. Volunteer members of the orchestra had other jobs and responsibilities and could not always show up for performances. No formal contracts required their presence at rehearsals or concerts, and the logistics of transportation, meals, and overnight lodging often proved difficult. But Swalin usually managed to make last-minute adjustments to ensure that a concert succeeded. He praised the commitment of the musicians, noting that "Had they been less willing to contribute their time, their energies, their expense monies, and, most importantly, their abiding and abounding faith in our project, the North Carolina Symphony would have died away quickly to silence." He persisted in advocating for paid full-time musicians.[61]

The orchestra began its 1945 season on April 7 with a concert, sponsored by Governor Gregg Cherry and his wife, at Hugh Morson High School in Raleigh. Two days later, the society's Durham chapter sponsored a concert in the city's Carolina Theatre. The performance was dedicated to Private Eric Schwarz, a double bassist with the symphony who had entered military service and was killed in battle in February. Conducted by Swalin, the program included "The Star-Spangled Banner," Beethoven's Symphony No. 6 in F Minor, Goldmark's *Sakuntala*, Richard Wagner's Prelude to Act 3 from *Lohengrin*, and Joseph Wagner's *Variations on an Old Form*. After that concert, the orchestra accompanied a choir of forty voices in recording "The Old North State," North Carolina's official song. The recording was intended for distribution to public schools and state agencies. On November 17–18, the symphony played four concerts at Camp Lejeune, the United States Marine Corps base near Jacksonville: one for adults, two for children, and a special program at the base hospital. The parents of Private Schwarz attended.[62]

One of the symphony's most significant achievements during the war years was the effective organization of the Children's Division. As part of its renaissance under the Swalins' leadership, the orchestra had added children's concerts to its itinerary, and the symphony's potential as a vital educational operation had been important in convincing the legislature to support it with state money. In fact, Swalin always maintained that "It was largely on the basis of our educational program for children that we had approached the General Assembly for funding in 1943."[63] That program received a large and lasting boost in 1945 when Adeline Denham McCall developed an extensive plan—creating the Children's Concert Division of the North Carolina Symphony—for bringing classical music to the schoolchildren of North Carolina.

McCall had an accomplished career as a classical musician, as well as a strong background in education, and she had helped arrange the earlier children's concerts. She had received training as a pianist in New York and Europe and at the Peabody Conservatory, as well as a degree from UNC in the 1930s. After arriving at Chapel Hill, she married Fred B. McCall, a professor at the university law school and also a timpanist. Before becoming educational director of the Children's Division, she taught and supervised music in the Chapel Hill public schools and played with various chamber groups. Through the UNC library's extension publication program in the 1930s, she published a number of study guides for use by local music clubs in the state. One of the most popular was *Adventures with Music and Musicians*.

McCall designed the Children's Concert Division to work closely with the public school system to introduce elementary students to classical music. She adopted a multimethod approach that included teaching pupils about the symphony orchestra and its instruments as well as musical themes and composers. McCall prepared a guide and other materials for teachers to help them instruct and prepare students prior to a visit by the orchestra. The children learned to accompany musical themes with rhythm instruments and singing. Rhythmic dancing and art projects were part of the division's plan, and McCall wrote a pamphlet titled *Symphony Stories* for distribution to the schools. Within two years, the orchestra performed for more than 100,000 schoolchildren throughout the state. In the coming decade, McCall added music workshops for teachers, which convened in Chapel Hill, as she expanded the outreach of the school program statewide. The Swalins assisted her in planning the orchestra's school appearances, with Maxine serving as coordinator and narrator at the concerts.[64] Although she and Adeline worked together tirelessly in making the children's program a success, they had differences of opinion, and their relationship was sometimes strained. "When we couldn't agree," Maxine once said, "Adeline's authority dominated and I gave in.... Though she had magnetism for children, with never the first disciplinary problem, I found her difficult; sometimes dictatorial and impatient."[65] Maxine did not, however, allow that personality conflict—or any other everyday strain—to affect her commitment to the school concerts or the orchestra's overall goals.

Adeline McCall of UNC established the North Carolina Symphony's Children's Concert Division to introduce elementary schoolchildren to classical music (North Carolina Collection, Wilson Library, University of North Carolina at Chapel Hill).

Maxine Swalin played an indispensable role in reviving and promoting the North Carolina Symphony Orchestra as she and her husband provided valuable leadership and devoted long hours to setting the organization on a new and enduring course. She remained consistently at Benjamin's side in the effort to expand and professionalize the symphony. An accomplished musician in her own right, she served as accompanist for rehearsals and performances. She functioned as an administrative assistant for the Symphony Society. She worked exhaustively with the Children's Division and gave lectures and pleas for support to music and women's clubs and civic groups.[66] "Without her," Swalin once remarked, "neither I nor the North Carolina Symphony could have accomplished what we did. As wife, she has been counselor, encourager, and supporter in many respects. As coworker, she has been the Symphony's pianist, harpsichordist, executive assistant, hostess, 'advance man,' children's concert coordinator and narrator, and whatever else was needed."[67] At the war's end in 1945, the orchestra had a budget for the coming year of more than $65,000—raised in largest measure by the Symphony Fund.[68]

Although World War II had presented difficulties, the Swalins, along with the Symphony Society and its fund drive and political allies, had proved persistent and effective in renewing and furthering the orchestra's mission of bringing classical music to the populace of North Carolina. They had secured financial support from private contributions, the Symphony Fund, and the budget of state government that would continue to grow in the com-

Students learned to accompany musical themes with rhythm instruments as part of Adeline McCall's education program (courtesy State Archives of North Carolina).

ing years. In cooperation with the public school system, they had launched a popular statewide program to introduce classical music to many young North Carolinians. Having undergone this renaissance, the North Carolina Symphony Orchestra was poised to take its show on the road from one end of the Tar Heel State to the other.

4

On the Road with the "Suitcase Symphony"

Supported with increased funding in 1946, the North Carolina Symphony Orchestra boarded chartered buses to take classical music to communities from the mountains to the coast. During that year's season—March 11 through May 17—the symphony performed 104 concerts in fifty communities. The Little Symphony, an ensemble of about twenty-five musicians, carried out the first phase of the tour, appearing mostly in small towns that could not provide any financial assistance or facilities to accommodate a full orchestra. From March 11 to April 8, it played in places from Cherokee County in the west to Pasquotank County in the east. It called at such towns as Andrews, Bryson City, Kings Mountain, Marion, Roxboro, and Jacksonville. The concerts varied to some extent from date to date, but they included selections by major composers.

After a full rehearsal on April 8, the main orchestra—which combined the Little Symphony with around thirty more musicians—began its tour with a concert in Shelby on April 12. It continued on the road with performances in a number of the state's largest towns, from Asheville in the west to Wilmington in the east. Its itinerary included such locations as Salisbury, Winston-Salem, Greensboro, Durham, Raleigh, Goldsboro, Rocky Mount, and New Bern. It played a more varied repertoire from town to town than did the Little Symphony. The composers whose works were performed included Brahms, Dvořák, Wagner, Haydn, Smetana, and Strauss. The orchestra also played Swalin's own composition *Maxeben*, an overture titled from his and Maxine's names combined. Some young musicians from North Carolina were invited to perform solos in a few of the concerts. Although the regular season ended in May, the orchestra performed two special concerts at the Camp Lejeune marine base in November.[1]

The plan of using both the small and large symphonies to reach out to as many North Carolinians as possible remained the system of operation

As the symphony traversed North Carolina, it drew large crowds, such as this one at the mountain community of Marshall in 1949 (courtesy State Archives of North Carolina).

for years. Swalin noted that "In this way we were able to utilize the services of musicians from larger professional orchestras, who could join us after their regular seasons were over." For him and the musicians, the tour "was a new and wonderful experience! For the first time, we were a professional 'Orchestra on Wheels,' traveling as a group in our own chartered buses for three months of concertizing."[2] At the conclusion of the regular season, the North Carolina Symphony Society met at UNC's Carolina Inn. Presiding was its new president, Spencer Murphy, a graduate of UNC, editor of the *Salisbury Post*, and a loyal supporter of the symphony and the arts. His father, Pete Murphy, served several terms in the state legislature, including as speaker of the house. The society expanded its operations by creating an endowment reserve fund to supplement the Symphony Fund. It designated Swalin as both director of the orchestra and director of the society in order to consolidate the musical mission with the administrative functions, including the membership campaign, of the society. Swalin would be assisted by the executive committee of the board of trustees. This system proved effective in coming seasons. In the fall of 1946, Swalin and some of the members approached the General Assembly for $15,000, which was appropriated. In seeking more funding, Swalin emphasized the orchestra's educational mission, pointing out that the past season had included fifty-three free children's concerts.[3]

That season also marked the beginning of the orchestra's Young Adults Auditions program. According to Swalin,

The purpose of these auditions was to give those with exceptional talent the opportunity to launch their careers by performing to professional standards—another aspect of our educational role.... Once each year we would bring together panels of from three to six eminent performers and teachers of music to judge the applicants in three categories:

instrumentalists aged seventeen or older; vocalists aged seventeen or older; and junior instrumentalists, aged sixteen or younger. Instrumentalists were judged by instrumentalists, and vocalists by vocalists. The panels were instructed to vote by ballot for a winner and a runner-up and to count the ballots *before* they consulted with each other. Our staff and I would listen to the auditions, but we never participated in the voting or discussions.

The music played by the applicants was to be selected from a list circulated well in advance of the auditions. Each performance was to be judged on both its technical and its aesthetic merits. The number of winners each year varied with the number and skill of the applicants, as did the number of concerts in which each winner performed. Adult winners performed in adult concerts and received honoraria for their performances. Junior soloists were featured in children's concerts without honorarium.[4]

In 1947 the North Carolina Symphony Orchestra—including the Little Symphony and the full orchestra—appeared in 115 concerts. Fifty-nine performances were for children. The orchestra opened the season on February 17 with a concert for state legislators at the State Capitol in appreciation for the lawmakers' recent allocation of $24,000 for the coming biennium. The Little Symphony began its east-to-west tour on February 21 and ended it on April 2. The full orchestra then performed from April 9 to May 16. The latter tour featured fifty different classical works, including four symphonies, nine concertos for various instruments, and three vocal arias. The orchestra also gave fifteen radio broadcasts. As its membership grew, the Symphony Society moved its headquarters to Swain Hall, which it shared with other organizations, on the UNC campus. (Previously used as a dining facility, the building had been dubbed Swine Hall by the students.) By the end of the year, forty-nine of North Carolina's hundred counties had formed chapters of the North Carolina Symphony Society, which then could boast 11,500 individual members, a large number of whom came from rural communities. The symphony adopted the motto "This Is Your Music."[5]

North Carolina's success with its symphony orchestra drew national attention. The *New York Times* noted that

> Symphony orchestras are expensive and finding the money and audience to support them has always been a problem. It has meant that, for the most part, smaller communities have gone without orchestras, for the wherewithal to support them has only been available in large cities. In North Carolina, however, various devices have been worked out whereby both the pleasures and the financial burdens of an orchestra have been distributed over the whole State. The North Carolina Symphony Orchestra is based at Chapel Hill, but it has a State appropriation and supporting subscribers from every part of the State. In return, the orchestra tours widely.... In towns where the cost of a full orchestra is prohibitive, Dr. Benjamin Swalin, the conductor, solves the problem by taking along a little symphony of twenty-three of the musicians.[6]

That success continued under the financial guidance of the Symphony Society's business manager, Albin Pikutis, and treasurer, A. C. Hall, as the

The orchestra performing for the General Assembly in the State Capitol in 1947 (courtesy State Archives of North Carolina).

orchestra strived to stretch every dollar in expenses. In July 1948, the society established Pikutis's salary at $3,600 and raised Swalin's salary to $6,000 and Maxine's to $1,500. For the four months that they were on the road, the musicians received $60 per week. Staff who drove their own autos on symphony business were allowed six cents per mile. Adeline McCall received honoraria

This symphony appearance took place in the auditorium of Hugh Morson High School in Raleigh in 1950 (courtesy State Archives of North Carolina).

of $100 for her annual student publications entitled *Symphony Stories*. Over the coming years, salaries continued to increase modestly.

From the time it was created in 1945, McCall's children's project made significant strides year after year as more and more teachers and school systems took advantage of the program and readied their students for visits by the orchestra on what were termed Symphony Days. Her leaflet *Getting Ready for the Children's Concerts* helped prepare the students for upcoming concerts by answering questions about the size and function of symphony orchestras and their conductors and instruments. Her *Symphony Stories* booklets, which were available for ten cents each or five cents if a hundred were purchased, provided more assistance. They included musical themes that the children could play on their recorder-like instruments and songs that they could sing. They also contained brief biographies of composers, information about compositions, and suggestions for further reading. The booklets were illustrated with cartoons by the national comic strip artist Les Forgrave, whose strip *Big Sister* was published by the King Syndicate. His cartoons for *Symphony Stories* depicted episodes involving a boy flutist and a horn player. Forgrave once lived in Chapel Hill, where his daughter had studied music.[7]

To train and update teachers and administrators, McCall maintained her summer workshops at UNC, supported by the university extension service and the state public school system. In 1958 McCall held three workshops for teachers in eastern and central North Carolina. At her workshop in Chapel Hill the following year, approximately one hundred teachers and supervisors attended.[8] Every participant in the summer sessions, she once asserted, "will have an opportunity to work with music materials, to exchange experiences, to solve specific problems related to the primary or upper grade curriculum." For years McCall's workshops and the children's programs remained popular in the public schools as the concerts drew large crowds of young North Carolinians, most of whom were instructed about and heard classical music for the first time.[9]

To make a Symphony Day especially appealing to young ears, McCall and the Swalins included among the classical selections shorter, popular, and lighter songs. Among them were such pieces as composer Leroy Anderson's "Sleigh Ride," "Typewriter," and "Waltzing Cat." Anderson toured with the orchestra and conducted his own works when he was stationed at Fort Bragg in the 1950s. From the folk music repertoire, the musicians played "Johnson's Old Gray Mule," "Old Joe Clark," and "Cripple Creek." From popular show

Adeline McCall's published guides included music that schoolchildren could play with recorder-like instruments (courtesy State Archives of North Carolina).

Top: These students are learning the roles of various instruments for an upcoming North Carolina Symphony performance of Prokofiev's *Peter and the Wolf* (courtesy State Archives of North Carolina). *Bottom:* In the era of racial segregation, the symphony played to separate audiences of schoolchildren of different races. Here a musician from the orchestra demonstrates the bassoon for a class of African American students before a concert (courtesy State Archives of North Carolina).

tunes, they rendered versions of songs like "Buttons and Bows." McCall and the Swalins also managed to secure some celebrities to appear at the children's events. When they heard that two sisters of the famed Trapp family were at Duke Hospital for a checkup, they persuaded them to appear in costume at UNC's Memorial Hall, where the student audience joined them in singing "Climb Every Mountain." A large crowd of children attended a concert in Memorial Hall when the famous ventriloquist Edgar Bergen and his puppets Charlie McCarthy, Mortimer Snerd, and Effie Klinker helped the orchestra entertain. About the success of the Children's Division, Swalin recalled:

> In cities throughout the state, and in consolidated school districts, children's concert audiences from one community sometimes numbered 5,000 or 6,000. At Elon College, for example, the gymnasium would accommodate 4,135 Alamance County children. The Greensboro Coliseum would seat 6,546 city children, followed by approximately the same number from the Guilford County schools. In the more rural areas each concert would attract children from many small schools and townships, and the program narrator at the matinees (generally, this was Maxine) made a point of reading off the names of the schools participating. For example, in western North Carolina when we performed in the Andrews high school gymnasium, children came to it in school buses from Hiwassee Dam, Hanging "Dawg," Martin's Creek, Peachtree, Tomatla, Marble, Hayesville, Mt. Pleasant, Walker, and Murphy. In the coastal section of the state, performances at Beaufort or Morehead City brought together school children from Sea Level, Atlantic, Harker's Island, Smyrna, and Newport.[10]

As the "Suitcase Symphony" traversed the highways and back roads of North Carolina, the miles and concerts piled up. In its 1948 season, it traveled 5,600 miles and appeared in 117 concerts, 59 for adults and 58 for children. Attendance at its adult performances totaled 55,000 and at the children's events 125,000. The Little Symphony's tour began on February 9 in Warrenton and ended on March 30 in Asheboro, covering more than thirty communities. The full orchestra went on the road on April 7 with a concert in Reidsville and ended its itinerary on May 20 in Salisbury. The next two seasons proved even more active. The symphony covered 6,200 miles in 1949 and 7,000 miles in 1950, playing in Tennessee and Georgia as well as North Carolina. In 1949 it performed 57 adult concerts and 73 free concerts attended by 150,000 schoolchildren. During that year's off-season, Swalin conducted the National University Symphony Orchestra in Mexico City on August 14.

The 1950s saw the Little Symphony and the full orchestra almost constantly on the road from February to May each year. In 1950 the North Carolina Symphony Orchestra gave 124 performances, 67 of them for children, and made 26 radio broadcasts, which included an hour-long program for the NBC network and a rebroadcast for Radio America.[11] The following three years witnessed the orchestra's covering even more territory each season. In 1951 it toured 8,000 miles and gave concerts in Florida, Georgia, and Tennessee as well as in North Carolina. Of the 134 performances, 60 were for adults and 74 for children. The attendance for adults was 40,000, which included 6,329 new "junior" members of the Symphony Society, and 103,000 students attended the children's concerts. The symphony also appeared at an Asheville orthopedic hospital, Central Prison in Raleigh, the State Hospital at Morganton, and the General Assembly in Raleigh. It performed 19 radio broadcasts, one of which was a full-hour network program.

The next season saw the musicians on the road for 9,000 miles, performing 140 concerts, 58 for adults (50,000 in attendance) and 82 for children (125,000 attending). The year's itinerary also featured 26 radio broadcasts, one of which on CBS celebrated the symphony's twentieth anniversary. The NBC network recorded the orchestra for its new broadcast series *The Culture of the New South*. In 1953 the symphony played at 123 concerts, 52 for adults and 71 for children. It traveled out of state to give performances in Alabama, South Carolina, Tennessee, and West Virginia. Two years later, the tour featured 112 concerts, 46 for adults and 66 for children, and in 1956 the symphony appeared on 107 occasions, at 44 events for adults and 63 for children. During that same season, its itinerary included a number of concerts at colleges and universities in North Carolina, Florida, and South Carolina; and it began a practice that resulted in at least one television performance per year.

Benjamin and Maxine Swalin talk with Governor Luther H. Hodges *(right)* in 1955 (courtesy State Archives of North Carolina).

The year 1957 brought 112 concerts, 41 for adults and 71 for children. One hundred and seven were given in 1958, of which 45 were for adults and 62 for children. The year 1959 concluded with 104 performances, 43 for adults and 61 for children. For the 1960 telecasts, the audience was estimated at 465,000.[12]

In 1962 the North Carolina Symphony commemorated its thirtieth anniversary, and Governor Terry Sanford designated February 4 through February 10 as Symphony Week. Sanford's predecessor, Governor Luther Hodges, had declared the first Symphony Week in 1956. During its tour in 1962, the orchestra traveled 9,171 miles and performed 116 concerts in 51 communities. A total of 137,550 children heard 67 of those concerts. The largest of the youth events occurred at the Greensboro Coliseum, where approximately 6,800 children were present. The number of adults who attended concerts totaled 48,463. The orchestra also played for 16 radio programs and made three television appearances before the year ended.

By that time, the orchestra since 1946 had traveled thousands of miles with its Little Symphony and full orchestra and played for hundreds of thousands of listeners. It had established a popular children's concert series embraced enthusiastically by the public school system. It had performed the music of most major European composers, as well as such Americans as Copland, Gould, Grainger, and Rodgers. It had auditioned a number of aspiring soloists between the ages of seventeen and thirty-five and given them a chance to appear in concert. And it had played on radio and television.[13]

As the orchestra's outreach grew in the 1950s, it began awarding prizes to selected composers of new works. At the beginning of the decade, the symphony launched its Composition Auditions Award to acknowledge local composers. Although the recipients did not receive cash prizes, their works were performed in concert by the orchestra. Before it was discontinued, the award was granted to several local composers. Perhaps the best known of these was Margaret Vardell, a teacher of organ at Salem College and the daughter of musician Charles Gildersleeve Vardell. She was a graduate of Salem and the Eastman Conservatory of Music at the University of Rochester in New York. She taught for a time at Oberlin College in Ohio before returning to her native North Carolina. She received the symphony's composition prize for her work *The Three Marys*. Throughout her career, she performed at numerous public recitals and concerts, winning several other awards. In December 1956, she married Clemens Sandresky, pianist and dean of the Department of Music at Salem College.[14]

In October 1952, benefactor Edward Benjamin of New Orleans and Greensboro offered a prize of $1,000 for a composition by a resident of the United States, Canada, or Mexico, which would be played at one of the symphony's concerts. At its annual meeting, the Symphony Society called for a committee to be established to judge the entries.[15] The *New York Times* took note of the competition.

> Edward B. Benjamin of Greensboro, N.C., is offering a $1,000 prize for an orchestral composition which he specifies must have a definite effect. It must be restful. Perhaps some idea of what Mr. Benjamin considers "reposeful" can be gained from the fact that he forbids the use of either a piano or a chorus.
>
> The piece is not to exceed 10 minutes in length. Besides the cash, the winning work is assured of at least one performance during the 1954 season of the North Carolina Symphony, which is directed by Dr. Benjamin F. Swalin.[16]

The first recipient of the Benjamin Award was Theron Kirk of Laredo, Texas, for his Adagietto. Kirk, whose composition was played and award presented in Greensboro in May 1955, held a bachelor of music degree from Baylor University. According to the *Waco News-Tribune*, "He has taught 15 years in Texas public schools, and this year composed all sight reading material for Interscholastic League choral contests in the state. He is director of vocal music at Laredo Junior College and a Laredo high school." Kirk also won a Federation of Music Clubs composition contest and a performance award at the Southwestern Symposium of Contemporary Music.[17] In the following year, the winner of the Benjamin Award was Gerhard J. Wuensch, on the faculty at Butler University in Indianapolis, for his Nocturne for Orchestra in F Minor. The orchestra performed his work in Durham on May 13, 1957. Wuensch was a native of Vienna, Austria, where he earned a doctoral degree. He came to the United States to study at the University of Texas on a Fulbright fellowship. He eventually became chairman of the Department of Music Theory and Composition at the University of Western Ontario in Canada.[18]

The next two recipients of the Benjamin prize were both organists as well as composers: John Cook and Jan Philip Schinhan. Cook was born in Essex, England. He became a scholar at Christ's College, Cambridge, before attending the Royal College of Music in London and then worked as a composer, conductor, and church organist. In 1954 he emigrated with his family to Canada, where he joined the faculty of the University of Western Ontario as professor of harmony and composition. He also undertook the duties of organist and choirmaster at St. Paul's Cathedral in London, Ontario, as well as conducting and composing for the Stratford Ontario Shakespearean Festival. In the 1960s he joined the music faculty at the Massachusetts Institute of Technology. His "Ecologue" received the 1957 Benjamin Award, and the symphony played the composition in Wilmington in April 1958.[19] Schinhan, professor emeritus of music at UNC, won the 1958 Benjamin for his Fantasy for Orchestra. A native of Vienna, Schinhan studied at the Academy of Music in Munich before coming to the United States as conductor of a German opera company. He earned BA and MA degrees at the University of California at Berkeley and served as an organist with the San Francisco Conservatory of Music, appearing at times with the San Francisco Symphony. He returned to Vienna to earn a doctoral degree before joining the UNC faculty. At the university, he headed the organ program and taught advanced piano, theory, composition, and musicology.[20]

The 1959 winner of the Benjamin prize was pianist Alan Hovhaness, who was born Alan Vaness Chakmakjian, of Armenian descent, in Boston in 1911. He studied composition at Boston's New England Conservatory of Music and attended Tufts College. In 1940 Hovhaness became organist at St. James Armenian Church in Watertown, Massachusetts, and two years later he won a scholarship for study at Tanglewood. He wrote numerous concertos and symphonies, which earned national recognition and many recording contracts. His rise to major fame came in the 1950s with his symphony *Mysterious Mountain*, which premiered under the baton of Leopold Stokowski conducting the Houston Symphony. Hovhaness won the Benjamin Award for his one-movement composition "The Celestial Gate."[21] In 1963 Benjamin Swalin himself received the Benjamin prize for "Sunday in Chapel Hill," played in concert for the first time that spring. The award was subsequently discontinued.[22]

Revenue for the orchestra continued to grow in the decades following World War II. From 1946 to 1953, for example, the Symphony Society consistently provided the orchestra with sizable funding from memberships: $58,125 in 1946; $53,068 in 1947; $49,685 in 1948; $56,726 in 1949; $54,601 in 1950; $60,515 in 1951; $62,048 in 1952; and $53,218 in 1953. Starting in 1948, the society's sustaining fund collected $2,515 in that year; $3,488 in 1949; $11,303 in 1950; $7,040 in 1951; $8,745 in 1952; and $9,837 in 1953. Much of the Symphony Society's success in raising money came from the persistent grassroots drives of the local chapters and their chairmen. In 1950 the Symphony Society had about 20,000 members, and in 1954 it had 26,000. By 1962 the number had grown to 34,000, located in 39 chapters.[23] Swalin gave much credit to the chapters.

> Crucial to our financial survival was the level of success we had with our various local Symphony chapters. The thermometer readings on those success charts ranged all the way from almost zero to normal, and occasionally to fever pitch.
> The initial impetus for the formation of a new chapter most often came from the hard work of our field representative, who would arrange to meet with local women's clubs and businessmen's associations in order to bring them the message of the Symphony.

Those local campaigns were not always successful. In many cases, however, persistence by Swalin, representatives of the society, and especially Maxine "on a trouble-shooting mission" brought results to an initially unproductive drive. Usually a local banquet, sometimes with musical entertainment, launched a fund-raising membership drive in a community.[24] Typical of those local drives was the one in Alamance County in November 1952. The Burlington *Daily Times-News* announced:

> The Alamance chapter of the North Carolina Symphony will this year attempt to raise $3,250 to sponsor free concerts for school children of this area.
>
> The chapter's membership drive will be launched at a banquet to be held for campaign workers Monday night at 7 o'clock at the Davis Street Methodist Church.
>
> If the fund drive is successful, a total of four concerts will be presented in this area. The memberships will entitle the holder to attend an evening concert and will aid in financing three other concerts to be of[f]ered free to Alamance County school children.
>
> Memberships ranging in price from $2 to $100 are already available at the Burlington Chamber of Commerce offices on West Andrews Street and may be purchased by calling 6-6311.[25]

Initially the largest share of financial support for the orchestra came from the Symphony Society. But the state legislature consistently increased its funding in the years following the Second World War. In the period 1947 to 1949, it budgeted $12,000 annually, and from 1949 to 1953, the amount was $15,000. Finances improved further when state lawmakers passed legislation in 1953 to allow towns and cities to subscribe for memberships paid for by tax-free funds. By 1957 the state's allotment to the orchestra had risen to $30,000 per annum. It increased to $61,000 in 1961. The General Assembly's appropriation reached $424,494 by the 1971–1973 biennium. In addition, corporations or businesses at times made direct contributions to support the orchestra. In 1949, for example, the textile manufactory Burlington Industries, led by its founder, president, and chairman of the board James Spencer Love, contributed $10,000.[26]

Even before the 1940s ended, the traveling symphony had garnered national attention. In a May 1949 article titled "On the Move," *Time* magazine reported:

> Honking merrily, the red & yellow buses bumped along the back roads of North Carolina. At Laurinburg (pop. 5,685) they pulled up in front of an old Air Force camp theater, and 60 musicians tumbled out with their instruments. An audience of kids, who had trekked in from all over corn- and cotton-raising Scotland County, was there already, waiting for one of the 117 concerts that Conductor Benjamin Swalin's peripatetic North Carolina Symphony Orchestra (and its 23-man task force) will play at more than 60 highway & byway spots in the state this spring.
>
> While the orchestra tuned up, kids swarmed over the stage, inspecting everything from tubas to tympani. But when husky Conductor Ben Swalin rapped his baton for attention, they scrambled to free seats [and] got set to listen. Swalin gave excerpts from Schumann's "Spring" Symphony (No. 1), a Mozart rondo, a serving of Vaughan Williams and Berlioz and a chicken reel. Before each number, the musicians held up the instruments to be featured so the kids could see them. And when the last chicken was reeled the youngsters hollered for more. So did the grownups at a second concert that night.[27]

John N. Popham, a Chapel Hill correspondent for the *New York Times*, sang the praises of the "Suitcase Symphony," riding throughout the state in its "red-and-yellow buses." By the end of the 1951 season, he wrote, "The nomadic tunesters will have brought fine music to the 'doorsteps' of North Carolina by playing in city auditoriums, ball parks, gymnasiums, high schools and, in one instance, under an evangelist's tent. They will also have given a special concert at the State Prison in Raleigh, and another for the inhabitants of lonely Ocracoke Island, in the state's 'outer banks' section, where the language spoken is 'olde Englishe' and the motion picture and television are virtually unknown."[28]

In February 1952, *Collier's* magazine reported:

> In most of the U.S. anybody interested in hearing "live," unrecorded concert music has either to live in a city with a symphony orchestra or travel a good number of miles to get to one. In North Carolina, though, the music does the traveling. Working out of the little university town of Chapel Hill, the North Carolina Symphony Society delivers music by the carload to tens of thousands who otherwise might never have more than a nodding acquaintance with the likes of Brahms. The symphony does it by packing itself into a couple of busses and spending its entire five-month season on the road....
>
> No ivory-tower society of amateurs, the North Carolina group is composed of young, accomplished, serious men and women who are willing to mix their sonatas with cat naps in jouncing busses.[29]

In the following June, *Newsweek* magazine remarked that the North Carolina Symphony was "that rare phenomenon: a symphony directly supported by state subsidy" and was "called the 'Suitcase Symphony' and the 'Symphony on Wheels' with good reason." Recounting the orchestra's rising success since 1943, when it first received state funds, the magazine noted especially how Maxine Swalin, as copartner in fulfilling the orchestra's mission, "has mothered the entire organization. And when asked once what would happen if she and her husband might be ill at the same time, she simply answered: 'We can't.'"[30]

Maxine carried much of the burden of the orchestra's day-to-day operations, serving as an administrative assistant to the executive director and as coordinator of the children's concerts under director Adeline McCall's school division. She handled a large amount of correspondence regarding engaging musicians for the upcoming season, booking concerts, renting musical scores, and even arranging for the appropriate dress for female players at matinee concerts. In September 1968, she wrote to the Don Loper clothing and costume design firm in Los Angeles asking about the acquisition of "black culottes or a black suit having the culotte fold-over skirt." Rehearsals would start soon, she noted, and the orchestra would need twenty-five of the culottes, which should be "one inch below the center of the knee because of the high stage problem."[31]

Some of the orchestra's proponents saw her efficiency as a good balance to her husband's often less regimented or attentive approach to administrative duties. Governor Terry Sanford once wrote that "But for Ben Swalin, the North Carolina Symphony would not be. But for Maxine, Ben would not have prevailed."[32] Maxine also developed a reputation among a number of the musicians as a driving force who spoke her mind and did not hesitate to critique and criticize their performances or personal habits. "She was pretty much the boss," remembered a tuba player whom she chastised after a concert for "playing a bass melody."[33] She once disapproved of the principal oboist's distinctive mustache, which she declared distracted from the orchestra's image and made him resemble "Lucifer."[34]

Maxine's contribution to the orchestra went far beyond handling logistics. She was a talented pianist in her own right and frequently played at rehearsals and concerts. She also played the celesta, a small keyboard instrument, and had unique skill with the harpsichord. Following an Asheville concert in April 1969, a local newspaper critic wrote:

> Tuesday in Asheville-Biltmore College's Lipinsky Student Center auditorium, Mrs. Swalin and the other members of the North Carolina Little Symphony West gave Asheville the final visit of the symphony's 24th season.
>
> Dr. Benjamin Swalin, the symphony's long-time director, conducted but both he and soloist Enrique Raudales had to share the spotlight with Swalin's wife.
>
> Mrs. Swalin's harpsichord added color to the baroque music of Telemann's "Overture in G Minor" as well as providing contrast to violinist Raudales' Vivaldi Nachez solo.[35]

Maxine was involved in virtually every aspect of promoting classical music in North Carolina. When in 1962 she was appointed the state symphonic chair of the North Carolina Federation of Music Clubs, its president, Mrs. Floyd D. Mehan of High Point, announced that "We could have combed the North Carolina map. Nowhere would we have found a musician better qualified than Maxine Swalin for symphony promotion in our organization." Maxine pledged that "We shall strive to make each N.C. child and adult conscious of good music as a source of cultural and spiritual strength—a useful medium for pleasure and community growth."[36]

Although the Swalins were steering the "Suitcase Symphony" along a route of growing outreach and financial backing, a number of roadblocks and difficulties still arose along the way. Despite increases in funding, sufficient finances remained a constant challenge. Swalin once said that "No matter how hard we worked, our treasury was never overflowing; our income was always uncertain."[37]

In May 1959, Swalin suffered public and legislative rejection when he and his supporters appealed to the General Assembly to designate a portion of North Carolina's tax on jukeboxes for the symphony. Taxing the estimated nine thousand jukeboxes in the state an additional five dollars would give the orchestra an extra $45,000 per year, they argued in a bill introduced by Representative Watts Hill. Jukebox operators opposed the higher tax, and some opponents proclaimed that jukebox patrons preferred popular music and objected to paying extra to promote classical music, which they considered limited to the interest of only a few elite listeners. "Should Elvis Presley be taxed to support Rimsky-Korsakoff?" asked the *Asheville Citizen-Times*.

> Rep. Watts Hill of Durham testified at a House Finance Committee hearing Thursday it would be "poetic justice."
> Pou Bailey, Raleigh attorney appearing on behalf of juke box operators, said it would be just as valid to tax billboards to support the State Art Museum.
> So went debate on Hill's bill to levy an addition[al] $5 tax on juke boxes for the benefit of the North Carolina Symphony.
> The committee made no decision on the measure, but it listened raptly as Dr. Benjamin Swalin, symphony director, invoked Goethe, Henry Adams, Emerson and George Washington in support.
> "We are seeking to elevate the public's taste," the conductor said, in the face of an avalanche of trash.[38]

To support his position, Swalin quoted a popular rock-and-roll song titled "Ape Man," with its lowbrow lyrics. The *Charlotte Observer* saw Swalin's point and declared that "Music like that oughta be taxed."[39] The *Greensboro Daily News* also took note of the "Proposed Juke Box Tax Bill" and lampooned the symphony and "Dr. 'Scat' Swalin" in a cartoon portraying musicians playing and singing "Put A-nother Nickel in ... in the Nic-kel-o-deon."[40] Ultimately the juke box tax bill failed to pass the legislature.

But financing improved to some extent when Swalin appealed successfully to the federal Department of Internal Revenue to exempt the symphony from paying taxes on income from memberships. New expenses were also avoided when he convinced the state's Division of Purchase and Contract to rent the buses transporting musicians to appearances, thus avoiding having to pay a proposed tax on miles traveled by buses rented directly by the symphony.[41] In 1957 Swalin testified before Congress in hearings about establishing a Federal Advisory Commission on the Arts. When asked, "Are you not afraid that the government will tell you *what* to play?" he responded, "We shall be glad to perform the *Blue Danube Waltz* on many occasions if the federal government will honor us with an appropriation!" Federal support for the arts—including music—gave a boost to the cultural life of the nation when Congress passed an act creating the National Foundation on the Arts and Humanities in 1965. That organization began providing direct grants to organizations that met specific criteria. In 1970 the North Carolina Symphony Orchestra received a grant of $25,000 from the foundation's National Endowment for the Arts that helped extend its 1970–1971 season and end it with a surplus of $16,000.[42]

Emergency contributions by generous individuals helped the orchestra when it suddenly found itself short of money, as in 1960, when it fell seriously behind schedule because bad weather stranded the musicians in the mountains for several days. Gifts to the symphony's endowment fund also bolstered the orchestra's coffers. In 1960, for example, Mrs. Eli T. Watson of Hickory and New York wrote a check for $5,000. In the following year, Elsie F. Holder of New Jersey bequeathed almost $35,000 to the endowment in her will. Making the most of its resources, the orchestra in 1967 managed to extend its season by two months each year, to add another Little Symphony, and to hire its musicians for the entire season. Under the new arrangement, the full orchestra toured from November to February and then split into two Little Symphonies—one for eastern North Carolina and the other for the west—

Symphony musicians after disembarking from their bus during a tour ca. 1960 (courtesy State Archives of North Carolina).

and performed again from March through April. For the first time, the orchestra collaborated with the North Carolina School of the Arts in a production of Tchaikovsky's *Nutcracker* ballet during the 1968–1969 season.[43]

Some members of the Symphony Society advanced the idea of holding a symphony ball as a fund-raiser for the orchestra. Maxine Swalin had reservations about the plan, fearing that the ball—with guests formally attired and paying $100 per ticket—might suggest an elitist atmosphere and become a social distraction from the orchestra's mission of bringing music to the people. Nevertheless, with the support of Governor and Mrs. Terry Sanford, the first Symphony Ball was held at the Governor's Mansion in Raleigh in 1961 and secured more than $11,000 for the symphony's endowment. When the ball took place again at the Governor's Mansion two years later in May, Eleanor Steber of the Metropolitan Opera appeared in costume as a soloist. A few days after the ball, she made a guest appearance with the orchestra in Page Auditorium at Duke University. Subsequently, the Symphony Society moved the ball to such sites as Morehead Planetarium at UNC, Minges Coliseum at East Carolina University in Greenville, and a country club in Pinehurst. A part of the orchestra provided the music for the dances. The ball of 1968–1969 raised more than $15,000. To accommodate eastern and western North Carolina, two events were held in 1970: the Azalea Ball in Wilmington and the Western Ball in Asheville. When the ball took place in Raleigh's Memorial Auditorium in April 1977, a sit-down dinner was added to the festivities, preceded by a reception hosted by the governor and his wife at the Executive Mansion. In later years, fund-raising "galas" replaced the ball.[44]

The old "horn-tootin'" attitude and objections by some citizens and legislators about "wasting" government funds on the arts continued to hang over the orchestra. Nevertheless, North Carolina's lawmakers generally supported the orchestra with consistent, if limited, increases of funds, and the state's governors lent their endorsement. In 1964 Governor Sanford delivered a speech at a Detroit convention of the American Symphony Orchestra League in which he "said his state furnished a prime example of successful involvement in the arts by a state government." He pointed specifically to the "North Carolina Symphony ... and the North Carolina School for the Performing Arts, which will open next year" and declared that "North Carolina, I believe, is building an audience for the arts," which included supporting its symphony orchestra and the promotion of classical music. But as consummate politicians, lawmakers and governors—always conscious of taxpayers' concerns regarding government spending—qualified their remarks of support and took care to reassure the public that state monies were not being spent frivolously on non-essential services. When he spoke in Detroit, Sanford made the special point that "Our policy is not direct support of the artists themselves, but we are creating a climate for the artist in North Carolina."

The *New York Times* noted that "Governor Sanford termed the attitude of the state toward the arts just as important, in many cases, as financial support."[45]

In late 1965, Swalin learned that the Ford Foundation of New York had projected grants totaling $81 million to sixty orchestras in the United States, and North Carolina was not to be one of the recipients. Early in the new year, however, a representative from the foundation invited him to come to New York to appear before a board and answer questions about North Carolina's orchestra. The meeting lasted two and a half hours, and Swalin remembered it as "the most austere confrontation I had ever endured." At the session, the board made a number of comments and suggestions about the North Carolina program.

> [A] season of four months is inadequate; the ratio of rehearsals to performances is inequitable; the salaries of the musicians must be upgraded; a thinner distribution of concerts is essential; the working conditions of the players could be subject to examination; a home base for the orchestra is imperative; the racial policy should be defined; a plan for increasing employment for musicians is needed; the program should be a realistic one, even though the present plan is "interesting"; and the orchestra should not become a "traveling show."[46]

After the New York meeting, correspondence ensued as the foundation considered North Carolina for a grant. It requested numerous completed forms and reports about facets of the symphony's operations such as budgets, gifts, salaries, schedules, and recordings of actual concerts. The foundation also called for the creation of a ten-year plan and an expansion of the orchestra's sustaining fund.

Then in June 1966, word came that the Ford Foundation had awarded a challenge grant of $1 million to the North Carolina Symphony Society. The grant would provide an "outright gift" of $250,000 to be paid in annual payments of $50,000 in "expendable funds" and stipulated that the society raise $750,000 from other sources within a five-year period to match the balance. The Symphony Society was also mandated to come up with a yearly sustaining fund of $42,500, based on reports to the foundation of its "non-earned non-state income." That amount would not be "counted as part of the grant-matching total."[47] The exact provisions of the challenge grant were

1. That the Endowment Funds, which shall be held in a Trust established by the Ford Foundation for a period of ten years, should be matched by the Orchestra within the five-year period July 1, 1966, through June 30, 1971, through contributions from sources other than the Foundation amounting to one dollar for each Endowment dollar granted by the Foundation.

2. That the Orchestra shall continue its regular operations and shall not suspend its activities for a significant period of time during the ten-year period of the program, July 1, 1966, through June 30, 1976.

3. That funds raised by the Orchestra in its annual maintenance or sustaining drives during the first five years of the program will not be less than $42,500 per year.

4. That non-restrictive practices with regard to audiences at public concerts and non-discriminatory personnel practices inclusive of open auditions are observed by the Orchestra.

5. That the Orchestra is exempt from Federal income taxes under the provision of Section 501 ... of the Internal Revenue Code.[48]

By the deadline of June 30, 1971, the Symphony Society had not only met its five-year mandate for $750,000 but had exceeded it, with a total amount of $843,171. The Ford Foundation announced that "fifty-five of the sixty orchestras that received endowment shares subsequently met or surpassed the matching requirement.... The principal of the trust will be distributed at the conclusion of the program in 1976. In the meantime, the orchestras will continue to receive dividends from the trust." The monies that would have gone to the five orchestras that did not achieve their matching goals would be distributed among the fifty-five that did, including North Carolina's symphony. Ultimately, in 1977, the foundation granted $882,153 to the North Carolina Symphony Society, which sum was then added to the society's matching $843,171 for a total of $1,725,324.[49]

Although successful in the end, the Symphony Society's efforts to secure the Ford grant did not proceed without trials and setbacks. The hiring of a New York fund-raiser in 1966 proved a failure and had to be abandoned. By that time, Swalin had turned over responsibility for the Ford grant drive to a committee from the Symphony Society's board. But problems ensued, including maintaining an effective chairman for the committee and the disappointing performance of another employed fund-raiser, a North Carolinian, who resigned. In 1970 the society placed Swalin in overall charge of the Ford Foundation Challenge Campaign. Contributions came from local chapters and various businesses, institutions, communities, and individual donors. Governor and Mrs. Robert W. Scott added their influence to the drive and held dinners at the Executive Mansion at which they called on guests to contribute. Maxine Swalin instigated a series of luncheons held by sympathetic hostesses that raised almost $26,000. Even public school students—authorized by the governor, the superintendent of public instruction, and local school districts—donated $7,193 in nickels and dimes.[50]

One disadvantage that had plagued the orchestra for years was not having a permanent facility for practice. Swalin and his musicians rehearsed in whatever barely adequate vacant buildings they could find in various locales. UNC had been providing free office space in Swain Hall and then at other sites on campus, including trailers. But rehearsal and office space remained a problem. Chancellor Carlyle Sitterson appealed to the General Assembly for an appropriation to enlarge UNC's Memorial Hall; however, the legislature denied the request. Several communities considered providing a home for the orchestra but did not follow through. Although the symphony offices remained in Chapel Hill, for several years the musicians practiced in Durham at the city's Erwin Auditorium Arts and Crafts Center on the site of the former Erwin Cotton Mills and then at Page Auditorium on the campus of Duke University.[51]

In 1968 orchestra business manager Hiram B. Black attempted to secure a rehearsal facility in Raleigh but failed. On September 20, he wrote to Mayor Travis H. Tomlinson: "Of course, our first choice for a rehearsal hall for the North Carolina Symphony is Raleigh's fine Memorial Auditorium. Unfortunately, we do not have the $4,000 to $5,000 which we estimate would be required for such rehearsals at the Auditorium this season." The armory at Pullen Park would not suffice because of its inadequate and noisy heating system. "Therefore, due to this critical factor and the brief time left to us before the opening of rehearsals on October 21, we have decided to accept the facilities offered by the city of Durham for the current season."[52] Not until 1975 did the orchestra find a permanent home with sufficient office and rehearsal space in Raleigh's Memorial Auditorium, recently renovated as part of the city's urban revitalization plan.[53]

The rigors of a full schedule and many miles of travel by bus took their toll on the Swalins and their musicians. Living out of suitcases and enduring long hours on the road sometimes strained the tempers and personalities of the troupe. Overnight lodgings in cheap rooms were far-less-than-luxurious accommodations. One musician described a night spent in such miserable surroundings.

> Once the orchestra stayed at a motel somewhere along I-95 that was listed as H. Johnson on the schedule. All of us were excited by the prospect of staying in a nice place, instead of the usual roach motel. We were crestfallen when we arrived and found ourselves consigned to yet another flea-bag. We all noticed, on closer inspection, that the owner, presumably someone named H. Johnson, had parked ten derelict cars in the parking lot to create the impression that people were actually staying at the motel. The conditions were abysmal, and after a fitful night spent listening to trucks barrel down I-95, we awoke to find that there was no hot water.[54]

Another musician referred to such motels and hotels, with lumpy mattresses and poor plumbing, as "homey monsters." Swalin recalled that "Living in these hostelries and in such proximity to one another during almost continuous travel in the winter months, the Little Symphony musicians sometimes showed increasing irritation. For reasons of economy, and also because hotels and motels infrequently had enough single rooms, our musicians generally were assigned to double rooms. Privacy became a rare privilege. Nerves were frayed."

Another challenge was that playing the same program selections repeatedly could prove monotonous for the musicians. A flutist once remarked, "There must be something wrong with me. I'm beginning to *like* the *Blue Danube Waltz*." Concert halls did not always have the best acoustics or dressing facilities. Bad weather could delay the arrival of the symphony buses or cancel concerts entirely. Once, for example, a tremendous rainstorm denied the orchestra the opportunity to be filmed by the National Broadcasting Network's television cameras at a ballpark in Rocky Mount. On another occasion, a bitter winter storm prevented the musicians' crossing from the mainland to Ocracoke Island for a concert and photographic coverage by *Life* magazine.[55]

A persistent problem for Swalin was enlisting and keeping first-rate musicians, many of whom played with other orchestras when not performing during the North Carolina season. Each year during the off-season, he visited New York, Chicago, Cleveland, or other cities to audition and recruit musicians. He particularly had difficulty finding string players, apparently a dilemma for orchestras nationwide. "Two recent developments indicate how stringent is the shortage of string players," announced the *New York Times* in January 1959. "Dr. Benjamin Swalin came to New York hoping to recruit some for the North Carolina Symphony's fourteenth season. He did not succeed in snaffling one. And the National Orchestral Association has found it so hard to get string players to round out its training ensemble that it is offering fellowship grants to worthy string players, who will play with the other trainees."[56]

The situation improved somewhat in 1967, when the season—with full pay for the duration—was extended, but the challenge continued. In September 1968, Swalin wrote to Warren Benfield of the Chicago Symphony Orchestra asking about the availability of string players. He would be in Chicago recruiting on October 10 and declared that the North Carolina Symphony had "openings for strings" and was "especially in need of capable double bass applications." He asked Benfield if he "would be good enough to direct this information to any of your excellent students, or other friends, who would be available for our season starting October 21st and concluding on April 26th. The salary is approximately $130 weekly in addition to room accommodations when the Orchestra is away overnight from the home area." He also wrote to friends Mr. and Mrs. Josef Schoenbrun in Hollywood, California, that "We are in need of good violinists and a few other string players and I wonder if there is a chance that either or both of you might be able to join us this season." He asked Joseph Silverstein of the Boston Symphony Orchestra if, "perhaps, you might have some students both musically and personally—special students or graduate students."[57]

The orchestra did enjoy the advantage of having a number of talented guest musicians, soloists, and conductors appear at its performances. Swalin launched a project of inviting foreign musicians to play with the orchestra each season as a mutual learning experience. Over the years, performers from Japan, Australia, Canada, Germany, South Korea, and Columbia participated. One such visiting artist, young violinist Kenji Kobayashi, was a particular favorite with audiences. He came to the United States to study at Juilliard. In addition to performing as a soloist with the symphony, he served as concertmaster in 1966. Kobayashi subsequently became concertmaster of the Metropolitan Orchestra of Tokyo. When the Swalins traveled to that city in 1974, he visited with them at their hotel. After Benjamin conducted and the Swalins vacationed in Guatemala in the summer of 1968, business manager Hiram B. Black sent a contract to musician Enrique Raudales of that country to play with the orchestra in the upcoming season, contingent upon his securing a visa through the labor and immigration authorities and permission from the national musicians' union. When principal oboe Ronald Weddle arrived to play with the orchestra in 1968, he observed that it included a number of Guatemalans. Black also offered a contract to Katsuko Esaki for that upcoming season.[58] The international program was terminated when the Swalins left the orchestra in 1972.

During his years with the symphony, Benjamin Swalin invited numerous musicians to appear as soloists, and he and Maxine developed lasting friendships with several of their favorite players, who returned season after season. Typical among these was oboist Beth Sears, who performed with the orchestra for thirteen years, and Swedish violinist Beatrice Griffin, whose instrumental artistry was "impressive, for her violin tone was succulent, the execution extremely facile, and her artistic taste was impeccable." Another among their musician friends was Christian Kutschinski, a violinist who served as chairman of the music department at North Carolina State University before retiring and touring with the symphony. "Such a human spirit," Swalin once said of him, "is unusual in the competitive musical marketplace—he was a fine gentleman, a versatile musician, a teacher, and a friend."[59]

Two guest conductors were John Frederick Shenaut, in 1967, and Valter Poole, in 1970–1971. Shenaut was an Illinois native and violinist who held teaching positions, among them an appointment at Louisiana State Normal College (present Northwestern State University) to create an orchestra program offering scholarships for string players. In 1948 he established the Shreveport Symphony Orchestra, which he conducted for thirty-three years and built into a well-respected musical organization. Known locally as the Maestro, he conducted hundreds of concerts each year and shared Swalin's devotion to the educational mission of bringing classical music to public schools.[60] Poole, who conducted the North Carolina Symphony on several occasions while Swalin was busy on the road raising funds, was a native of Oklahoma who served the Detroit Symphony Orchestra as violist and also acted as district supervisor of music for the Detroit public schools. In the 1937–1938 season, he joined the new Detroit Civic Orchestra and quickly rose to become its conductor. When that orchestra dissolved a few years later, he returned to the Detroit Symphony and became assistant conductor and then associate conductor and educational director. He was also professor of music at Wayne State University.[61] Backing up Swalin as assistant conductors in the last decade of his tenure were Marion Rogers (1962–1966), William Kirsche (1967–1969), Jackson Parkhurst (1970–1971), Thomas Conlin (1971–1972), and Alfred Heller (1971–1972).[62]

From the end of World War II until the Swalins "resigned" their leadership in 1972, the North Carolina Symphony Orchestra maintained a constant and demanding pace in bringing classical music to North Carolinians. At its appearances, audiences heard the works of the master composers such as Bach, Beethoven, Brahms, Debussy, Dvořák, Haydn, Mozart, Rossini, Tchaikovsky, and Wagner. Among the twentieth-century European composers featured were Bartók, Prokofiev, and Vaughan Williams. From the beginning, the Symphony Society had called for works by American composers, and compositions by United States residents such as Copland, Ives, and Stravinsky featured in the programs.

Besides in concerts sponsored by the Symphony Society's chapters, the "Suitcase Symphony" appeared regularly at performances hosted by other institutions. Among these were the state's colleges and universities, including Appalachian State Teachers College (later Appalachian State University), Atlantic Christian College (later Barton College), Elizabeth City State College (later University), Fayetteville State Teachers College (later Fayetteville State University), Lees-McRae College, Mars Hill College, and UNC. It regularly gave public-service performances at places such as the mental hospitals in Morganton and Goldsboro, the veterans' hospital in Salisbury, the state prison in Raleigh, the Caswell Training School in Kinston, the polio hospital in Greensboro, the orphanage in Oxford, and an orthopedic hospital in Asheville.[63]

Large audiences invariably attended the concerts, which were covered by critics from the local press and often featured local composers and players, including selected promising young musicians. Correspondent Gertrude Ramsey of the *Asheville Citizen-Times* reported on the program of and public response to a typical concert held in that city on May 13, 1954.

> An appreciative audience of some 2,000 persons last night attended the annual adult concert of the North Carolina Symphony Orchestra in the City Auditorium.
> Under the inspired leadership of Dr. Benjamin Swalin the orchestra presented a program which ranged from a delicate interpretation of Bach's Prelude from the Suite No. III for Violin (arranged for orchestra) to the magnificent Firebird Suite of Stravinsky....
> Miss Jayne Winfield of little Washington and Greensboro completely won the audi-

ence with her playing of Beethoven's Emperor Concerto. Beautiful, charming and remarkably gifted in her talent, Miss Winfield displayed a mastery of the piano almost unbelievable in one 18 years of age, and her interpretation of the great concerto of one of the masters of the ages could not but have won the most exacting of critics.

Miss Winfield has grown up in the Symphony, having appeared with it almost every year since she was 10.

Edwin Stringham's symphonic poem, "The Ancient Mariner" was a highlight of the unusual program presented by the symphony. This work, which is truly a literal translation of Coleridge's "Rime of the Ancient Mariner," is pictorial in its imagery, as it evokes the scenes which tell the story of the man who shot the albatross.

The audience expressed great approval of this work which, although composed in 1926, was given its first Asheville performance last night, and greeted Stringham with an ovation.

Miss Marian Perley of Black Mountain, harpist, was heard in "Caprice," an unprogrammed answer to numerous requests. This delightful and melodic selection gave the gifted young musician an opportunity to display her considerable talent.

Paying a brief tribute to Sen. Clyde R. Hoey, who died Wednesday in Washington, Dr. Swalin led the symphony in the last movement of Tschaikovsky's [sic] Sixth Symphony, the Pathetique, as an elegy. Played with particular measured timing an[d] sonorous interpretation, it was greeted with a few moments of impressed and respectful silence before the audience expressed its appreciation of the tribute.[64]

A reporter for the *Greensboro Daily News* at a performance in May 1957 marveled at how an "enthusiastic audience" gave the orchestra a "warm reception" and persistently called for an encore.[65] "Last night," reported a staff writer of the *Asheville Citizen-Times* on April 26, 1967,

the North Carolina Symphony Orchestra played its annual spring membership concert in City Auditorium, to an audience of some 2,500 persons. (Some 12,000 students of city and county schools attended four free daytime concerts.)

The evening was charged with electricity; it was one of those times, rare times, when the audience, the orchestra and the conductor are as one three-part whole. The stillness with which the audience remained rapt during each number, and the thunderous applause which cut across the closing of each selection, evidenced this rapport.

A standing, applauding and in some instances, yelling, audience greeted Eudoxia de Campos Barros, Brazilian pianist, when she drew back from the keyboard after playing the Rachmaninov "Rhapsody on a Theme of Paganini." No one who heard it last night will ever forget, nor ever hear it better done.

The concert opened with the Overture to La Forza del Destino, a showpiece for every instrument. Early in this, it was evident that this would be a night to remember. The North Carolina orchestra is particularly rich in the strings section, soaring, rich, exciting. Major orchestral number of the program was Beethoven's Second Symphony, and the programmed numbers ended with a Suite from Stravinsky's ballet music "The Firebird."

The audience stood, not to leave, but to pay tribute to the orchestra and to demand "More." Prelude to the third act of Lohengrin and music from Smetana's "The Bartered Bride" sent the audience on its way.[66]

Such were the customary responses that audiences gave the orchestra in its appearances throughout the state. But there were occasions when some listeners were not responsive, appreciative, or even respectful. "Our most difficult audiences," recalled Maxine, "were the unwell and erratic listeners at institutions; at the hospital in Salisbury, the veterans surprised us with their sporadic hissing during the Star Spangled Banner, and they were more restless than the mental patients at Morganton. We wondered if our playing really helped the disturbed youths at Kinston, but the problem patients who sat on the front rows at Camp Butner were deeply absorbed, perhaps enjoying some happiness." At a morning concert at the state prison in Raleigh, the inmates "gave rapt attention and applauded roundly." In the evening, the orchestra performed for the state legislature in the Capitol, and "we thought it a special day; playing for the law-breakers in the morning, and the law-makers in the evening."[67]

The orchestra had no greater success than its children's concerts, which reached many thousands of elementary students. Though some were inattentive or restless during a performance, most young listeners responded with interest and active participation, for which they had been prepared by their teachers prior to the symphony's arrival. A number of teachers had them write about their experiences. In 1963 a third-grade pupil at Rocky Mount's Bassett School wrote in her essay "My Trip to the Symphony" that "I heard Swan Lake and many other songs too. I saw a trombone. We all played like we were playing bells because they did not arrive on time. I saw the Violins, and the drums too. The music was beautiful and sweet." Another wrote that "Yesterday I went to the Symphony. It was a very good symphony. The music was great. I am glad we get to go to the symphony free. The leader was a good one. He had a lot of dignity. He stood very straight and that meant he was polite. The players can play good. They sit very still too."[68] Many of the musicians took special pleasure and satisfaction in bringing classical music to young ears. "We did something for those kids," one former player recalled, concerned that now, in the twenty-first century, "we are not educating young people to appreciate classical music."[69]

Having a special affection for the children's concerts, Maxine once declared:

> My favorite children's audiences were at Cherokee and Pembroke, Valdese, Sparta, and Elon College. Not only did the teachers endear themselves to us, so did their wide-eyed expectant pupils. I wondered if the quiet Indian children knew about such rivers as the Watauga and Catawba, the Pasquotank, Hiawassee, and Chowan. But Valdese children knew about their Waldesian heritage, and could tell us stories about why and how Sunbeam bread produced in their town, reached tables across the South. Arriving in Sparta was like a Greek festival, with everyone participating. Children's paintings covered the auditorium walls, and upon arrival I was privileged to judge them. Prize money came from a local art enthusiast. As for Elon College, we were always convinced that the wheels of music were lubricated when Alamance County school buses deposited

more than four thousand children at the barn-like college gym with its risky sound system. High in the bleachers we saw mothers nursing their babies.[70]

Southern segregation laws enforced separation of the races at the children's concerts, a practice that troubled the Swalins. Maxine lamented that "we were saddened by the shoeless, unwashed misery of black children in some neglected schools. They crowded together on benches in front of a stage, the walls generally flaked with blue paint. Worried about the lethargy against change, Ben took his concerns to legislators." He was told to "Be patient" regarding school integration and racial equality.[71]

But for African Americans throughout the South, patience for equal civil rights was running out, as members of the North Carolina Symphony witnessed in May 1963. The musicians had gone to the Governor's Mansion in Raleigh to play waltzes and other selections for the Symphony Ball, where opera singer Eleanor Steber was performing. Suddenly a loud disruption "drowned out" the music. A large crowd of black civil rights protestors, many of whom had been demonstrating in Raleigh during the day, had gathered on the mansion lawn and demanded to be heard by Governor Terry Sanford. In an article titled "Negroes Boo Gov. at Mansion," the *News and Observer* described the incident.

> The anti-segregation demonstrators, most of them college students, marched to the Mansion about 10:15 p.m., while a North Carolina Symphony ball was in progress there.
> Boos and shouted remarks from the crowd interrupted the Governor, who finally came out onto the Mansion's south porch after the Negroes had sung hymns and chanted, "We want the Governor," for nearly 20 minutes.
> "I have enjoyed the singing," Sanford told the crowd.
> He was interrupted by boos. An unidentified leader of the Negroes called for quiet.
> "I'll be glad to talk to you about any of your problems, any of your grievances, any of your hopes," Sanford said. "This is not the time or the place.... You are not bothering me at all. You can stay here another hour or so if you like. I've enjoyed the singing."
> From the crowd someone shouted, "We are not here to entertain you, Governor."
> Sanford shot back: "You are not here at my request, either, friend.... If you want to talk to me at anytime about your plans and your problems, let my office know. You have not come to me with any requests."

More boos and shouts ensued, but the crowd dispersed as urged by some of its leaders. In the meantime, some dozen highway patrol troopers had arrived at the mansion.[72] During the altercation, the guests and the musicians grew increasingly apprehensive. The Symphony Ball ceased to be held at the mansion thereafter.[73] Of course, the civil rights movement, of which the mansion incident was a manifestation, continued to grow in the South, ultimately leading to the Civil Rights Act of 1964, the Voting Rights Act of 1965, and an end to racial segregation and black disfranchisement.

The first major African American guest artist to perform with the North Carolina Symphony Orchestra was soprano Wilma Shakesnider, who appeared in November 1970, first in UNC's Memorial Hall and then in the Statesville High School auditorium. According to an announcement by the Statesville newspaper, "The 28-year-old soprano will sing works by Marx, Mozart, Duparc and Verdi." Shakesnider was a graduate of Howard University and Juilliard. Her honors included an award by the Washington Friday Morning Music Club, a William Mathius Sullivan Foundation scholarship, the Liederkranz award, a Zeta Phi Beta sorority scholarship, and the Minnie-Kaufman award for a promising artist. After her concerts in North Carolina, Shakesnider was scheduled for performances with the New World Symphony at Philharmonic Hall in New York, and in Europe.[74] She became best known for her role as Serena in *Porgy and Bess*, traveling with the Houston Grand Opera Company to concerts in cities such as Washington, Philadelphia, New York, and Los Angeles.[75] New York critic William Glover, apparently not overly impressed with "George Gershwin's pseudo-folk opera," nevertheless praised Shakesnider's performance: "Clamma Dale as Bess and Wilma Shakesnider as Serena were absolutely magnificent sopranos both of transcendent range and melodic coloration."[76]

In between grueling seasons with the symphony, the Swalins managed to find time for one of their other passions, European travel. Periodically in the summers of the 1950s, they traveled to Europe, booking free passage on the Holland-America Line in exchange for Swalin's lecturing to traveling students onboard ship about European music and festivals. Landing in Rotterdam on one trip, they journeyed on to visit museums and friends and attend concerts in such cities as Amsterdam and Innsbruck.[77] In the summer of 1962, the North Carolina press announced that

> Dr. and Mrs. Benjamin Swalin ... flew from New York's Idlewild Airport on Sunday, for a seven weeks' jaunt through their favorite European cities....
>
> The Swalins will travel by Pan American Airlines on one of the six special planes reserved by the University of North Carolina for educational personnel. After arriving in London for their first European jaunt since 1958, the Swalins will follow a flexible itinerary together, traveling independently of tourist groups.
>
> With eight symphony orchestras performing in London all summer, the Swalins expect to be shuttling in and out of town to hear as much music as they choose. Their mutual interest in foreign languages will carry them to Paris where they may enroll for a brief refresher course at the Alliance Francais, famous school of languages. Close-by they expect to renew acquaintance with the American School of Music at Fountainbleau [*sic*], and hear some French music too.
>
> Traveling by train through the Italian provinces, the musicians look forward to a return to Florence, their favorite Italian city. Rome, of course, will be included. However Innsbruck and the summer opera season at Munich, Germany, are their preferences. "In Munich we can get away from the rush of tourists," they say.[78]

While Ben was attempting to compose his overture *Maxeben*, he and Maxine again traveled to France in the summer of 1966 so he could study composition with Nadia Boulanger at the music school at Fontainebleau. The experience led Ben to conclude that he had his limitations as a composer. Perhaps Maxine derived the most pleasure and benefit from the trip. She reflected that "While Ben labored on his manuscript I audited classes in painting and architecture on the top floor of the palace, and visited and revisited Napoleon's lavishly furnished chateau for Empress Josephine.... Invisibly etched into my life and memory was the inspiration of Mlle. Boulanger. As Ben's wife I had been privileged to observe her 'genius-teaching' and I returned home determined to study, learn, relearn, read, read, and to practice with more understanding."[79] The Swalins also traveled to other parts of the world, as when, for example, the summer of 1968 saw them vacationing in Guatemala.[80]

By 1971 the Swalins had brought the North Carolina Symphony a long way since they first arrived in North Carolina. With the resurrection of the Symphony Society and its local chapters, they had led the renaissance of the orchestra in 1940. Since the end of World War II, the "Suitcase Symphony" had traveled thousands of miles with its little and full orchestras and played for thousands of listeners. It had established a popular concert series for schoolchildren, which was embraced enthusiastically by the public school system and introduced vast numbers of students to classical music for the first time, an ongoing mission that has impacted generations of North Carolinians. One resident of eastern North Carolina recently recalled that "a memory forever etched in between my ears is my second grade trip to hear Dr. Benjamin Swalin conduct the North Carolina Symphony."[81] With Swalin as director, the orchestra had awarded prizes to composers of new works and also held auditions for the compositions of local musicians and given them the opportunity to play their works at its concerts. The Swalins, along with the Symphony Society, had been relentless in raising funds for the orchestra, securing the first state support in the "horn-tootin' bill," as well as monies raised by the society's local chapters and from donors. In the final season, 1970–1971, before their departure, the symphony scheduled 150 concerts in 64 communities.[82]

Although an excellent musician and an effective organizer and administrator, especially in fund-raising, Swalin was not known as an accomplished conductor. "He was not particularly good with a stick," a musician remarked.[83] But he recognized that deficiency and in April 1940 wrote to Dimitri Mitropoulos, conductor of the Minneapolis Orchestra, asking him to teach him how to conduct. Mitropoulos replied:

> I appreciate your confidence in my ability to teach you the art of conducting; but it is a principal [sic] of mine never to give lessons. It does not seem that such a thing can truly be taught.
>
> The only way is through intelligent application: following the rehearsals of some experienced conductor, the thorough study of composition and orchestration.
>
> If one seriously applies himself in this way and is gifted, in the beginning, with a musical talent; he may arrive.[84]

One of Benjamin Swalin's greatest achievements was his success in obtaining the Ford Foundation grant, as he traveled hundreds of miles throughout the state in a seemingly never-ending effort to reach the goal of matching funds. During his years with the symphony, Swalin had oversight of virtually all its activities: concerts, auditioning and hiring of musicians, publicity, and fund-raising. He served simultaneously as music director and executive director, controlling both the symphony's administrative and its artistic operations.

Contracts between the Symphony Society and musicians—with final approval by Swalin, who signed as music director—spelled out in detail what was expected of the musicians hired. A contract for the 1962–1963 season, for example, specified that employment would begin with rehearsals in October, and that the concert tour would last from April 6 to May 24. It stated that a musician would be paid ninety dollars per week, a salary raised in later years, "for his/her services during the said period including all services at rehearsals, concerts, radio and television broadcasts, and other performances." The salary satisfied "the requirements of Local No. 500, A.F. of M. [American Federation of Musicians], and the Musicians' Unions in North Carolina." A player was hired "with the understanding that he/she is a member in good standing of the American Federation of Musicians," although North Carolina's right-to-work law of 1947 prohibited union membership as a requirement for employment. Musicians had to travel together on tour, with transportation supplied by the Symphony Society, and could not use private vehicles. They had paid room accommodations ("twin bedrooms with bath"). However, the contract stipulated "That since the North Carolina Symphony is a State Symphony, it is 'at home' all over the State of North Carolina; therefore, according to regulations of the Musicians' Unions, it does not compensate the musicians for meal expenses incurred in North Carolina. For out-of-state engagements, the Society will pay the Musician for meal expenses on the basis of $.75 for breakfast, $1.25 for lunch, and $1.50 for dinner." Musicians were not allowed a leave of absence during the season, but they received one day of sick leave for each month of service. They had to furnish their own instruments and "to observe high principles of moral conduct and to refrain from excessive drinking of intoxicating liquors."[85]

While serving as music director and executive director of the symphony, Swalin kept his connections to UNC. In June 1967, Chancellor J. Carlyle Sitterson wrote to him: "It gives me pleasure to inform you that the Board of Trustees of the Teachers and State Employees Retirement System has approved your continuation in service for the University to July 1, 1968."[86] By the 1970s, however, new changes were taking place in the orchestra, and the Swalins' tenure would soon come to an end, though not without considerable controversy and animosity.

5

A New Image

The North Carolina Symphony began making changes to its mission and organization as it embarked on a new course beginning in the 1960s. The orchestra's composition of musicians underwent major change in that decade. Recruiting professional players every year grew more difficult as other orchestras lengthened their seasons. Swalin increasingly had to rely on retirees and recent conservatory graduates seeking their first jobs. "When I came to the North Carolina Symphony in 1969," recalled former principal clarinetist Jimmy J. Gilmore, "the demographic of the orchestra was strangely split between those over sixty and those under thirty." The older musicians supported the status quo and Swalin's leadership, but the young instrumentalists wanted change. According to Gilmore, "With an age gap in the middle of the orchestra population, there was no group to act as a buffer between the extremes. The oldsters, including Dr. Swalin, watched warily as the younger members began to agitate for better working conditions and direct representation in contract negotiations." Amid the growing disagreement, Gilmore and then–principal oboist Ronald Weddle led "the formation of the first Orchestra Committee in North Carolina Symphony history. The fledgling committee began to lay the groundwork for more orchestra involvement in contract negotiations between the musician's union [American Federation of Musicians] and management."[1] Swalin, who theretofore had held the final say over contracts, saw this movement—which he considered a "threatened strike"—as an attack on his authority and leadership.[2]

Around the same time, a climate for change was also growing among some members of the Symphony Society who wanted to see the orchestra expand its reputation and modernize and professionalize its administration. Those calling for innovation wanted the orchestra to shake loose its "Suitcase Symphony" image and establish itself as an organization of national renown. They, along with some of the young musicians, believed that in order for the orchestra to move forward in a new direction, Swalin should be asked to step down as music director. A number of them noted that his recent and frequent lapses in memory (he eventually was diagnosed with Alzheimer's disease), limitations as a conductor, and old ideas were inhibiting his ability to lead the orchestra. Supporters of Swalin rallied to him, and quarreling within and outside the symphony ensued. In general the older musicians supported retaining Swalin, and the younger ones called for his ouster. In March 1972, a number of the musicians sent a letter to the Symphony Society's board of trustees asking that Swalin be replaced.

The movement to bring new administrative organization and modernization to the orchestra was led by C. C. Hope, Jr., who had become president of the Symphony Society in 1970. Hope was a prominent banking executive from Charlotte who brought considerable financial and managerial experience to the task. He launched a plan of reorganization that would set the orchestra on a path toward gaining a larger national reputation. He maintained that such progress required the removal of Swalin, whose old system of dual control as executive and music director was holding back the orchestra.[3]

Hope and the Symphony Society's executive committee took specific steps to remove Swalin at a Saturday afternoon meeting at the Sheraton Motor Inn in Southern Pines on April 22, 1972. The Symphony Ball was scheduled to take place that evening in the town. Hearing of the meeting, Swalin requested to appear before the committee to express his views about the state of the orchestra and his continuing role as music director and conductor. Hope also invited two musicians who were members of the Orchestra Committee and wanted to speak on behalf of the orchestra in opposition to Swalin: committee chairman Gordon Stenger and Lorentz Ottzen. Speaking first on the agenda, "Stenger, chairman of the Orchestra Committee, ... stated that the Orchestra felt very strongly about the resolution that they had passed in March and mailed to the Executive Committee that Dr. Swalin be replaced by September 1, 1972. He stated that the incidents concerning defacing the bus in Fayetteville [by musicians dissatisfied with Swalin] were deplorable and that they had written a letter of apology to all the trustees." The executive committee than asked Stenger a number of questions regarding his position against Swalin. "He emphasized again that the Orchestra felt a new conductor should be selected as soon as possible."

After Stenger and Ottzen departed the meeting, Maxine Swalin appeared before the committee to speak on behalf of her husband. He had planned to speak to the executive committee in his own defense, but the night before, the Swalins decided that she would attend instead to argue his case. She insisted that "the Board needed to make the decision as to whether the Board and Symphony would be run by a small group of players within the Orchestra." She downplayed the musicians' complaints, telling the committee that

"Players always get restless in the Spring realizing that the season is about over and they have no jobs," and that "the restlessness could last another ten years if the trustees did not stand firm" against the musicians' grievances leveled at Swalin—who, she claimed, had not received his fair share of publicity recently. The board of trustees "must be firm and tighten up," she strongly advised. She concluded her remarks by calling for "a different make-up of the Orchestra Committee—2 orchestra union members; 2 trustees; 2 management and 2 outside the union." George Norman of the executive committee responded to her suggestion by saying that "we cannot tell the Orchestra that they cannot have a committee or how it will be composed or what they can discuss." Hope thanked Maxine for her appearance and reminded her that her husband had "a five-year contract but only one year (1971–72) as conductor before a new conductor was elected but that the salary was a five-year contract." Maxine then left the meeting, and the executive committee voted to accept her comments "as information."[4]

At the same meeting, the executive committee discussed the concept of making the orchestra a state agency. Sam Ragan, secretary of the North Carolina Department of Art, Culture, and History (later the Department of Cultural Resources and most recently the Department of Natural and Cultural Resources), attended to participate in the discussion. According to the minutes, "Mr. Ragan stated that he would like to see the North Carolina Symphony become a full State Agency but that all internal problems must be settled before it could be presented to the General Assembly. He stated further that he feels the 'time is ripe' to make the North Carolina Symphony a full State Agency."[5]

The society set about solving its "internal problems" by appointing a committee to find a new music director/conductor for the orchestra. The members were chairman James Cobb, Sara W. Hodgkins (subsequently president of the society and later secretary of the Department of Cultural Resources), Laurence Stith, Mary Duke Biddle Trent Semans, and Sam Ragan. When the executive committee met at the Airport Hotel conference room at the Raleigh-Durham Airport on October 3, 1972, "Dr. Cobb went into great detail on how the [selection] committee went about its work beginning on July 5, 1972." He "stated that they had received over 125 applications for the job of Artistic Director/Conductor of the North Carolina Symphony and that they interviewed some in person, some by telephone, several by members of the committee while they were in New York, and that the committee contacted numerous experts in the field of Symphony conductors and music." In reaching its recommendation, the selection committee considered:

1. Availability—could [the candidate] come in immediately and spend most of his time with us this year and full time after 1972–73 season.

2. A person with the ability to help us develop a major Symphony Orchestra.

3. Connections that he had in the field.

4. Educational background.

5. Professional background.

6. Recommendations of professional authorities.

Cobb then declared that the selection committee was unanimous in recommending John Gosling, who had been conductor of the Erie (Pennsylvania) Philharmonic Orchestra for five years, to be the new artistic director/conductor of the North Carolina Symphony. He proposed that the executive committee offer a three-year contract to Gosling, effective as of October 3, 1972. His motion was seconded and approved unanimously.[6]

Convinced that it had met all the requirements of Swalin's contract, the executive committee then determined how news of the change in conductor would be released to the public. First a committee would "go to see Dr. and Mrs. Swalin on Wednesday morning, October 4, as early as possible to tell them of the action of the Executive Committee." Appointed to carry out that task were William N. Westphal, Sara Hodgkins, Paul Green, and Sam Ragan. Next "All trustees would be notified of the Executive Committee action by telegram immediately after Dr. Swalin had been informed." That action would be followed by a press release to "the papers, radio and T.V." for Friday, October 6. Finally the members unanimously approved the election of Swalin as conductor emeritus of the symphony. Guilford Daugherty, general manager of the orchestra, was instructed to inform the other applicants of the decision to hire Gosling and to notify the society chapters.

That business completed, Gosling and his wife were then invited into the meeting and introduced and welcomed. Mr. Gosling stated that he was happy to have been selected and that he admired Dr. Swalin and what he has done for the North Carolina Symphony and that even though he had not met him he had known of his great work. He stated that we owe Dr. Swalin a great deal of gratitude and appreciation. He stated he wanted to work with Dr. Swalin and would ask him to con-

John Gosling served as artistic director/conductor of the symphony from 1972 to 1980 (courtesy State Archives of North Carolina and Raleigh *News and Observer*).

duct some during the year. He said he wanted to have the opportunity to meet with Dr. Swalin as soon as possible and receive suggestions from him as he had great respect for him and would appreciate his friendship and suggestions.

Mr. Gosling then stated he wanted only the best for the North Carolina Symphony and that he was ready to go to work immediately. He mentioned that it would be necessary for him to be away about five weeks during the year to complete his contractual duties with the Erie Pa. Symphony.[7]

Benjamin and Maxine Swalin did not accept the news of his dismissal without hurt feelings and resentment. They considered the decision to be a premature and unfair judgment of his capacity to conduct the orchestra, as well as a result of vindictiveness on the part of the newly unionized musicians and an illegal and misguided policy by the society's new business-minded executive committee and board of trustees. The Swalins were not mollified by the society's overtures to salve their injured pride.

John Gosling came to North Carolina with respectable credentials. He was born to a musical family in Trenton, New Jersey, in 1928. He graduated from Juilliard, where he studied the trumpet (which he had played since youth) under William Vacchiano, as well as conducting. For a number of summers, he taught trumpet and conducted some concerts at the Transylvania Music Camp (now Brevard Music Center) in Brevard, North Carolina. In 1950 he joined the Marine Corps Band (the president's band) in Washington, D.C., as assistant principal trumpet and as a member of the conducting staff. The band played for official government functions and at the White House. During his ten years in Washington, Gosling earned a doctoral degree at the Catholic University of America, where he served on the faculty and as artistic director/conductor of the orchestra and chorus. He joined the American Symphony Orchestra League and was selected to participate in conducting workshops led by Richard Lert, who prior to coming to the United States had been director of the Berlin Conservatory of Music and a protégé of the well-known conductor Bruno Walter. In 1960 Gosling was hired as conductor and music director of the Monterey Symphony Orchestra in California. During his tenure, the orchestra grew in size and scope and was selected by Community Concerts of Columbia Artists to tour in central California. He also began the Monterey Peninsula Youth Orchestra, which trained young musicians and gave school concerts throughout the state.

Gosling's career in music included selection as one of several American conductors for the International Conductors Competition and performing with England's Royal Liverpool Philharmonic Orchestra, for which he received a grant from the American National Theater Academy. He made a number of guest appearances in the United States, Canada, Mexico, Puerto Rico, England, Scandinavia, and Europe. He was a guest lecturer at the Vienna Conservatory and conducted the world premiere of the television opera *The*

Decorator, by Russell Woollen, for NBC. He was the founder of the Bear Valley Music Festival, held each year in California's High Sierra. The festival featured orchestral and chamber music, opera, classes, lectures, and guest artists from the United States and abroad. It was televised on NBC's *Today Show*.

When Gosling accepted the position with the North Carolina Symphony, he had since 1967 been conductor/music director of the Erie Philharmonic Orchestra, a major metropolitan orchestra that had performed in northwestern Pennsylvania, northeastern Ohio, and northwestern New York. While at Erie, he led the establishment of a youth program that featured concerts for children, young artist competitions and clinics, and a summer camp. The Erie orchestra received grants from the Pennsylvania Council on the Arts and the National Endowment for the Arts. With its school and industrial concerts and radio and television broadcasts, the symphony in Pennsylvania reflected closely the educational mission that characterized North Carolina's program under Swalin.[8] Gosling said that he wanted "to expand the ranks of the North Carolina orchestra and broaden its offerings to include more contemporary music." He also intended "to work with the North Carolina School of the Arts in Winston-Salem to bring ballet and fully-staged operas to North Carolinians."[9]

Gosling went to work as conductor almost immediately, and his initial efforts met with general approval. After he and sixty-five members of the orchestra performed on the campus of UNC Asheville on Tuesday, November 28, 1972, Bill Mebane in the Sunday edition of the *Asheville Citizen-Times* praised Swalin's past leadership and reported that "Gosling has plenty of Dr. Swalin's missionary zeal." Prior to the evening concert, Gosling spoke to several members of the local Symphony Society chapter at a dinner, reminding them of the orchestra's past success in "making symphonic music a feature of state supported education." He asserted that "We're not afraid of our product. There is something here for an awful lot of people, and if they can't come to us, we'll take it to them." One of his major concerns was that as Americans turned to "canned," or recorded, music, live performances might become phenomena of the past within fifty years. Without the personal experience of physical contact with a symphonic orchestra, he said, "our lives ... become little square boxes." Mebane approved of Gosling's message about public performances and declared that "As he and his musicians demonstrated later in the evening, there is no substitute for the experience of sitting in the same hall with a good orchestra while it gives life to art for each audience alone." The shared experience of "one of the highest forms of communication" began with "Dr. Swalin's orchestra," and "It is going to get even better under Gosling's direction."[10]

Shortly after taking up his duties in North Carolina, Gosling invited

Swalin to conduct concerts with the Little Symphony, but apparently Swalin never accepted his offer.[11] He and Maxine resented Gosling's replacing Ben, and at times they denounced him and his reputation as a conductor. She once told a close friend that he was a "fake" and "without credentials."[12] His disappointment at being displaced by Gosling led Swalin to try to discredit the new conductor with accusations that he had misrepresented his past career. Swalin wrote to several orchestras in an attempt to prove that reports of Gosling's having made appearances with them in the past were false. At a meeting of the Symphony Society's executive committee in December 1974, "Dr. Swalin asked to speak and stated that he was concerned with the publicity the Symphony was putting out on John Gosling. He stated that he had written to places where Mr. Gosling is supposed to have conducted and has letters to prove that he has not conducted at all the places he claimed he has. Dr. Swalin stated on this basis, and on other information that he has, he feels John Gosling should not be given another contract and ... this was deliberate lying on the part of John Gosling." The executive committee appointed a committee to "ask Mr. Gosling to verify his credentials as we now have them." His contract was subsequently renewed.[13] The Swalins, however, never relinquished their resentment of Gosling and their efforts to diminish his qualifications and success. Once when Ben heard rumors that Gosling was having some conflict with the orchestra, he wrote that such news "is not surprising—in fact, what is surprising appears to be the fact that he has lasted this long."[14] Despite the disparagement and accusations by the Swalins and their supporters, Gosling remained artistic director/conductor of the North Carolina Symphony until June 1980.

With a new conductor and sense of direction in place, the North Carolina Symphony Society set some goals for the future. At its annual meeting at the Velvet Cloak Inn in Raleigh during Culture Week on November 30, 1972, President Hope told the members "he believed that the North Carolina Symphony was without question on the threshold of its greatest period of growth." Three future projects of the board of trustees were to raise the pay of the musicians, to extend the orchestra's season, and to increase the size of the orchestra. Two other important objectives were finding a permanent home for the symphony and obtaining full state agency status for the organization.

Sam Ragan, secretary of the Department of Art, Culture, and History, proclaimed that "he felt the North Carolina Symphony is on the threshold of greatness," and that his plan for the coming year was to have the General Assembly "make the Symphony a full State Agency," which was getting a "good reception.... The bill is being drafted now." He expressed his thanks to Duke University for providing a temporary rehearsal hall and stressed the serious need for a permanent site for the orchestra's rehearsals and office space. He then explained a plan for the symphony to make its permanent headquarters in the Museum of Art building in downtown Raleigh. "He proposed this plan to the Museum of Art Committee and the committee accepted the plan. He stated that $4,000,000 had already been appropriated by the last General Assembly and that this year the General Assembly would be asked for $7,000,000 more for the building." The symphony, however, never moved into the space. The building was occupied by the art museum until it moved to a site away from downtown in 1983.

At the Culture Week session, the society members thanked Hope for his service. "It was then announced that the Nominating Committee would at the Board of Trustees meeting nominate Mrs. Norris L. Hodgkins Jr. [Sara W. Hodgkins] of Durham as President of the North Carolina Symphony Board of Trustees." Before the meeting concluded, Gosling was introduced to the members. He expressed his pleasure at being selected as artistic director/conductor and "stated that the challenge was tremendous and that it would take 3 to 5 years to build a great major orchestra." That evening he conducted a concert at Meredith College, followed by a reception in the college's Johnson Hall Rotunda.[15]

Benjamin Swalin, however, was not going to retire to an office in Chapel Hill as conductor emeritus without expressing his anger to the society about his ouster. After he and Maxine returned from a trip to Norway, where he acted as a guest conductor, he requested an opportunity to air his grievances before the board of trustees of the Symphony Society. When the executive committee of the society met in the symphony offices in Chapel Hill on February 7, 1973, Sara W. Hodgkins had succeeded C. C. Hope as president. At that meeting, "J. Sibley Dorton, Jr., made a motion that a meeting be held to allow Dr. Swalin to present his grievances. After much discussion, the Executive Committee decided to leave the matter in the hands of the President and a motion was passed to allow the President to use her discretion on dealing with the situation."[16]

Before the executive committee held its next meeting, Swalin attempted to find support for his position and reinstatement as artistic director/conductor among members of the newly elected state government. In 1972 the Republican Party had gained seats in the legislature, and the state had elected its first Republican governor since the 1890s, James B. Holshouser, Jr. Swalin wrote to Republican senator Hamilton Horton congratulating the party on its success and remarking that an "opposition party, as in Great Britain, is a healthy one in a democratic government." He called on Horton to initiate an investigation of improprieties in the North Carolina Symphony.[17] He also wrote to Holshouser about the orchestra's unscrupulous activities and informed the governor that he and Maxine would not be attending the next Symphony Ball in protest.[18] When society president Sara Hodgkins extended a special invitation to the Swalins to attend the upcoming ball, Swalin declined, "unless such an invitation is preceded by other developments which could ... rectify inequities."[19]

When the executive committee next met, on April 28, 1973, "The President took note of the fact that Dr. Swalin had sent a letter to trustees and others seeking their request to call a meeting of the Board of Trustees for June 1st. Inasmuch as the President had other matters to be discussed by the Board of Trustees, she told the Executive Committee of her plans to call a meeting of the Board of Trustees and invite Dr. Swalin to attend the meeting and that he be given ample time to present matters he would like to have discussed." The executive committee voted to hold the board meeting on May 29. The last item on the agenda would be Swalin's presentation of his grievances, and notice of the meeting would be sent to him.[20]

At the May 29 trustees' meeting in Southern Pines, the main item on the agenda was the establishment of the North Carolina Symphony as a full state agency, which had been proposed in a bill introduced by legislator Robert Wynne.

> Mrs. Grace Rohrer, Secretary of Culture Resources of the State [who had succeeded Sam Ragan], spoke on the status of the State Agency Bill that was presented to the last General Assembly. She stated that there was some opposition to the bill and some legislators did not want the State to become involved in making decisions on the arts and some felt the State should not take on another agency at this time. She stated that she and others felt it was best not to try to push the Bill through this year but leave it in the Sub-Committee. She stated that the first step was taken toward the Symphony becoming a State Agency by having the budget divided into Administrative Expenditures and Musical Expenditures. The Department of Cultural Resources will administer the administrative part of the budget and the Musical Expenditures will be carried out by the Society as usual. She stated that she hoped to keep the issue of State Agency alive in this way and felt this was better than having the Bill defeated on the floor.

Also present, former secretary Sam Ragan said that Rohrer's "was the best solution" for the time being, but "we should still work for the State Agency status because there are some legislators who feel that Grants-in-Aid should be wiped out completely so we need to have the security of the State Agency status."[21]

When given his opportunity to speak at the meeting, Swalin "stated that he came to speak as a life-time trustee and that in a democratic society he should have the right to speak freely." He then launched into a long list of issues and complaints against the trustees and his treatment, which were recorded in the minutes as follows:

1. Multiple resignations from the Board of Trustees.
2. Multiple dismissals from the Orchestra.

3. Current financial problems of the Orchestra.
4. Illegal assumption of authority on the part of the Executive Committee.
5. Secret meeting of the Executive Committee.
6. Discussion of his personal contract with Orchestra and others.
7. The validity of his retirement account.
8. President meeting with Orchestra.
9. Meetings of staff with President and Executive Committee.
10. Actions of the Orchestra Committee with Orchestra toward him.
11. International programs and guest conducting opportunities.
12. His being dropped as a member of the Executive Committee.
13. Censorship in the Symphony Public Information office.
14. His authority and responsibility as Conductor Emeritus and his freedom to accept guest conducting offers.
15. The number of concerts he would conduct a year.
16. His office and secretary.

He urged the society to make the following adjustments to the orchestra's operations.

1. That his contract be amended.
2. That all meetings of the Board and the Executive Committee be open meetings. That the press should be invited to all meetings of the Society, Board and Executive Committee.
3. That the duties of General Manager and Conductor be spelled out.
4. That the 10-year plan presented to the Ford Foundation be examined.
5. That we discontinue efforts to achieve major symphony orchestra status.
6. That he would be told which concerts he could conduct and that he be able to plan his own programs.
7. That all terms of officers be limited—Board members, Executive Committee, officers, etc.
8. That a retirement plan for the orchestra be started.
9. That "Honorary Trustees'" duties and responsibilities be defined.
10. That politics be eliminated from the Symphony.
11. That the term and duties of Conductor Emeritus be defined.
12. That the investigation of all these recommendations be made and reported to the Trustees.

On the recommendation of the members of the board, President Hodgkins informed Swalin that a committee would be formed to study his grievances and suggestions.[22]

Feeling abandoned and ignored by the Symphony Society, Swalin continued to solicit political help for redress of his removal from the orchestra.

He visited Lieutenant Governor James B. Hunt, Jr., a Democrat, to express his dissatisfaction with the orchestra and the illegality of the injustice done him by the society's executive committee. Hunt asked the symphony for an explanation about Swalin's claims. Secretary and treasurer George E. Norman, Jr., responded to the lieutenant governor on July 16, 1973.

> Thank you for your letter of July 11 concerning your visit with Dr. Swalin.
>
> Naturally, we all regret that Dr. Swalin is expressing some unhappiness about his personal situation, and every reasonable effort is being made to try to reconcile some of his concerns.
>
> It would be too lengthy and difficult for me to write in detail about each of the matters that seem bothersome to Dr. Swalin, but basically they revolve around the fact that he has actually been replaced as the permanent Artistic Director/Conductor of the North Carolina Symphony Orchestra, and further, he no longer has any responsibility with respect to the programming or other routine features of the artistic side of the Symphony. Peripheral to this main point, however, are a number of others having to do with his questioning the authority of the Executive Committee to take these actions. I think some of these reflect his surprise at the speed with which the Search Committee was able to recommend a new Artistic Director/Conductor in October 1972, under the provisions of Paragraph (3) of the contract entered into with Dr. Swalin in August 1971. While I have never heard him comment on it, I believe he thought this would be much longer and more gradual than has occurred.
>
> Dr. Swalin has also stated he does not consider his contract a legal instrument, for a number of reasons, but at the same time, on the grounds that it is a personal and confidential document, he has been critical that the contents are widely known. An opposing view might be that it is in effect a public document, since it was entered into between the Society and Dr. Swalin, and discussed openly, and passed at the meeting of the Board of Trustees in Raleigh on August 5, 1971.[23]

Unable to accept defeat, Swalin continued his efforts to gain an audience with Governor Holshouser to plead his case. Finally, Phillip J. Kirk, Jr., administrative assistant to the governor, informed him that the state's chief executive was "swamped" with other important matters and did not have time to meet with him. Kirk requested that Swalin resolve his difficulties with the orchestra through Secretary Grace Rohrer and the Department of Cultural Resources.[24] Swalin's long years as the driving force behind the North Carolina Symphony Orchestra were over. He would serve out the rest of his five-year contract as emeritus conductor with little influence over the orchestra's activities, although he did serve as a member of the Symphony Society's board of trustees. And for years, he continued to express bitterness about being "forced" out as music director by the Symphony Society. In November 1975, for example, he wrote sympathetically to Schuyler Chapin, general manager of the Metropolitan Opera, who had recently suffered a similar "dismissal":

> In 1971, the Executive Committee, after secret meetings, forced a so-called "phase-out" contract on me which has been honored only in part. It was precipitated by labor

troubles in 1971, with a threatened strike relating to the signing of Union contracts for the following year. Then a small group of "amateurs" seized control of the operation and began to run it as they would a bank, and not as an institution *that belongs to the public.*[25]

Swalin nevertheless continued his interest in the comings and goings of the orchestra, venturing opinions and making inquiries about its finances and administration. In 1975, for instance, he expressed concern about its state funding when he wrote to Mercer Doty, director of the Fiscal Research Division of the General Assembly, asking specifically how certain monies were being used. He continued to attend meetings of the executive committee of the board of trustees and to speak out on issues before the committee. Perhaps hoping to exert direct influence on state government spending for music, Swalin became a candidate from Orange County in the Democratic primary for the state senate in 1974.[26] "Benjamin Swalin is a newcomer to politics," reported the Chapel Hill press, "and has not had much luck in getting his name or ideas known. He has made some effort to grab the student vote and says the right things, but without much depth. The fact that people don't feel they know him will hurt at the polls." That proved true, and Swalin's attempt at public office failed.[27]

Swalin still wanted to find regular work as a music director and conductor, and he hoped for a position with another orchestra. In 1981 he wrote to Thomas H. McGuire, then executive director of the Arkansas Symphony Orchestra, about a job as its conductor. McGuire, who subsequently became executive director of the North Carolina orchestra, responded that "It appears that there will not be any significant opportunity for a conductor, such as yourself, in the near future," but that he would keep Swalin's vita on file.[28]

Friends and colleagues who had known and worked with the Swalins for years became outraged when they learned of Ben's sudden "forced retirement." Longtime friend Johnsie Burnham was so annoyed and angry that she refused C. C. Hope's "offer of a lifetime honorary membership on the North Carolina Symphony Board of Trustees." She particularly directed her displeasure at the symphony's general manager, Guilford Daugherty, whom she blamed for hiring Gosling over Swalin. "This honor I must refuse," she answered Hope, "as long as the affairs of the Symphony Society are being run by Mr. Guilford Daugherty. His treatment of Benjamin Swalin after Dr. Swalin's years of dedicated services to the Symphony Society I consider outrageous and not to be condoned for any reason by the Board of Trustees of the North Carolina Symphony Society."[29] R. O. Huffman of Morganton resigned as a member of the society's board of trustees because "I cannot go along with what I consider the brutal treatment that has been accorded to the man without whom there would have been no N.C. Symphony, no million dollar grant."[30]

For years supporters of the Swalins persisted in their convictions that Benjamin's dismissal had been a summary injustice by the Symphony Society and that he did not receive the deserved credit and accolades for his contribution in establishing and maintaining the state orchestra. Many defenders felt that he had simply been put out to pasture and forgotten. In 1976 one annoyed Swalin advocate wrote:

> It is disturbing and puzzling to note that in recent publicity from the North Carolina Symphony there has been a noticeable omission of any mention of Dr. Swalin or acknowledgment given to him for the magnificent contribution he gave toward the firm establishment and development of the symphony spanning the years from the mid-thirties to the early seventies. Publicity has been omitted as though it was never a fact, though generations know it to be a fact....
>
> Without disparagement of contributions made by others, there can be honest and appropriate recognition accorded Dr. Swalin whose inspiration and vision solidly established for our state the North Carolina Symphony. It most assuredly would be a disgrace to our musical heritage in North Carolina to allow the name of Benjamin Swalin to be forgotten in this regard.
>
> Queries and protest rumblings are becoming more evident regarding this serious omission in symphony publicity and action should be taken promptly to right this obvious wrong of omission. Neglect in recent publicity of this outstanding musical leader of the symphony through the span of years is an ugly reflection upon the current symphony organization.[31]

The Swalins considered Ben's "forced retirement" a weakening blow to music and the arts in the state in general. They even saw his dismissal as part of a national "trend in the cultural and other organizations to displace directors with people who do not possess the expertise, thus divorcing knowledge from authority. The experts, scholars and intellectuals are being relegated to a 'servant's role.' It is an unearned insult."[32]

After their retirement from the symphony, the Swalins continued to enjoy traveling abroad for a number of years, visiting places in Europe including Austria, France, Italy, Norway, and Sweden.[33] But some summers they chose to remain in the United States. They wrote to friends in July 1977 that "Air-conditioning at home, in the office, and Libraries of Chapel Hill make it possible for us to type, practice, and carry on a work schedule. However, we did interrupt our routine late this June while attending the American Symphony League convention in New Orleans where the temperature was in humid 90's."[34] To another friend in November 1980 Maxine said, "For the first time in many years we spent the summer in the USA, and enjoyed the cool and beautiful Blue Ridge Mountains less than 100 miles away." Presently "We enjoy the freedom to write and travel and play, and pay pilg[r]images to the excellent libraries here."[35] Their sojourns included long drives to Minnesota to see acquaintances. But in September 1981, Maxine announced that the recent road trip to Ben's native state might be their last. "May we assure you," she wrote to Minnesota folks after a recent visit, "that after driving 1477 miles with that old car that we reached home safely and plan to retain the car as a third member in our garage. Since we live in the country we find it convenient in the event one car is disabled to still have transportation that gets us into town. We have no idea as to whether we can return to Northern Minnesota next summer for driving that distance again is not only very expensive multiplied by the number of days en route, but tiresome."[36]

Two years after leaving the orchestra, the Swalins undertook the task of writing a history of the North Carolina Symphony Orchestra that ultimately became the book *Hard Circus Road*. They began the project in the summer of 1974 in a rented room of a farmhouse overlooking a lake near Salzburg, Austria. "Always considerate of my mongrel shorthand," Maxine said, "Ben dictated slowly, and I rarely tangled in deciphering if I typed while the words were hot. My aim was to finish before lunch so that afternoons were free for lakeside or woodland hikes to our favorite kaffeehaus. At sunset we played softball on the shore with children whose father, the electrician at the Salzburg Festival, let us ride with him to the concerts."[37]

For his service in directing the North Carolina Symphony Orchestra for more than three decades, Benjamin Swalin received a number of awards: the North Carolina Award for Achievement in Fine Arts, honors from the National Federation of Music Clubs, and the Morrison Award for Achievement in Performing Arts in the 1960s. UNC presented him with an honorary doctorate in 1971, and Duke University in 1979. He authored two books, *The Violin Concerto: A Study in German Romanticism*, published in 1941, and *Hard Circus Road*, published in 1987. He was eighty-eight years old when he died on September 29, 1989, in Chapel Hill.[38]

Maxine Swalin also received several honors for her contributions to the symphony and the arts in North Carolina. In 1979 she too received an honorary doctorate from Duke, and ten years later the North Carolina Award for Public Service. On her hundredth birthday, in 2003, she was presented the North Caroliniana Society Award, given for outstanding contributions to the state's history, literature, and culture. Also in that year, the North Carolina Symphony established its annual Maxine Swalin Outstanding Music Educator Award to recognize "an individual who instills and inspires a love of music in North Carolina children." Two years later, she became one of three recipients of UNC's first annual Lifetime Achievement Award for the Performing Arts. In addition to the large role she played in helping her husband write *Hard Circus Road*, she published *An Ear to Myself*, her autobiography, in 1996.[39]

In October 2001, the new Meymandi Concert Hall—located adjacent to

Raleigh's Memorial Auditorium and named for the family of benefactor and major contributor Dr. Assad Meymandi—was dedicated as the headquarters of the North Carolina Symphony. At the same time, the lobby was dedicated as the Swalin Lobby, and a bronze sculpture of Benjamin and Maxine Swalin was unveiled. Dr. and Mrs. Albert M. Jenkins, Jr., of Raleigh, active donors and fund-raisers, were the primary advocates for acknowledging the Swalins and their contributions by naming the lobby in honor of Ben and Maxine and commissioning the sculpture. Lamar Stringfield's daughter, Meredith Stringfield Oates, attended the ceremony. Maxine Swalin was, of course, the honored guest at the dedication. She died on October 8, 2009, at the age of 106.[40]

Although the Swalins' replacement, John Gosling, had gotten off to a good start with some North Carolinians, not all critics were impressed with his initial efforts in getting the orchestra to perform well. One such critic was Adrian Scott, who attended a concert at UNC's Memorial Hall in February 1973.

> When John Gosling replaced Benjamin Swalin as conductor of the North Carolina Symphony Orchestra, one had great hopes that he would give the organization a new lease on life.
>
> After hearing last Wednesday's concert in Memorial Hall, all I can say is that I'm still living in hope.
>
> The sad truth is that there was little to commend about the orchestra all evening. The program opened with the Suite from "Der Rosenkavalier" by Richard Strauss ... and from the very start there was something wrong.
>
> The problem lay mainly with the strings, who were simply not paying attention to each other or to the conductor. The intonation was decidedly suspect at times, and there was absolutely no sense of direction or purpose to the music.
>
> Strauss writes broad, passionate music, and the orchestra had no passion whatsoever in what they were doing. There were moments when the winds did an excellent job, with some crisp brass chords and subtle woodwind phrases, but time and time again the strings stepped all over what Gosling was trying to achieve.
>
> Particularly abysmal was the way the strings handled one of those lovely little Viennese waltzes that Strauss throws in occasionally. The delicate, whispering opening, which should be played with almost melting sentiment and rubato, was given a stolid, listless rendition, despite Gosling's obvious attempts to stir up some enthusiasm.
>
> When Gosling led the orchestra into an accelerando, the winds responded magnificently but the strings took several measures to realize what was going on.
>
> Things improved radically with the next item on the program, a performance of the Aria "Marten [sic] aller Arten" from Mozart's "Seraglio." The soloist was Mattiwilda Dobbs, a most notable and able soprano who, while not on the same level as Sutherland, Callas or Schwartzkopf [sic], is a major talent.
>
> She has a lovely voice, with a full and resonant middle and bottom register and excellent clarity and definition at the top of her range.
>
> Alas, her excellence was not matched by the orchestra, who were as lifeless and unresponsive as ever.

Things were no different after the interval, when Miss Dobbs returned to sing arias by Donizetti, Bizet and Meyerbeer. Her voice was as attractive as it had been before, but the orchestra consistently worked at cross purposes.

In "Ombria [*sic*] Leggiera," from Meyerbeer's "Dinorah," first the horn and second the flute were guilty of simply not listening to what she was doing. They parted company, and it was not pleasant to listen to.

The concert ended with a performance of Mendelssohn's Italian Symphony. This, a most engaging and attractive work, was as disappointing as the rest of the program, in spite of some exciting playing from the winds. In the slow movement especially there was no soul or feeling at all.

One has to sympathize with John Gosling. He has a most difficult and daunting job, one which will take him some time to accomplish. The North Carolina Symphony Orchestra is having its problems at the moment, especially with personnel, and Gosling has not had enough time to do what he wants.

We wish him success in his endeavors. Judging by last Wednesday's showing, there is nowhere to go but up.[41]

As time went on, Gosling—who was launched into service quickly and amid controversy—generally received favorable receptions as the orchestra toured the state. Following the conductor's first year on the job, Bill Mebane of the *Asheville Citizen-Times* praised his success with the orchestra.

Taking the instrument created with love and inspiration by Dr. Swalin, he has given the orchestra new strength, precision and assurance.

Approximately half the players are new, and all the new ones are young. Scattered among the orchestra's seasoned veterans, they make for a becoming musical blend of youthful spirit and mature authority.

A new spirit, in fact, is audibly what Gosling has infused into the North Carolina Symphony. He has reshaped it to his own measure, and in doing it he has virtually created a new orchestra....

The symphony would be unique in any case, for its long schedule of concerts for North Carolina school children and the financial subsidy it receives from the legislature to carry them on. John Gosling already has a tradition to follow and a well-established foundation of interest and support from the public and the legislature.

But it looks very much as if Gosling will win a lot of new musical friends and influence great numbers of appreciative people with what he is doing for the North Carolina Symphony and what it is doing for him. This reciprocal aspect of their relationship is very important, because Gosling's orchestra reveals him as a musician of great intelligence, discriminating taste, discipline and imagination.[42]

During Gosling's tenure, the North Carolina Symphony Orchestra, with its "little" and full components, strove to maintain its longtime practice of taking classical music to communities throughout the state and even beyond its borders to neighbors such as Virginia, Georgia, South Carolina, and Alabama. "The North Carolina Symphony enters its 42nd season in 1973–74," announced the eastern North Carolina press in February 1974. "Under the direction of the new Artistic Director and Conductor, John Gosling, the 68-member orchestra will travel over 15,000 miles and perform for 300,000 school children and thousands of adults. In its 29th annual tour of North Carolina, the orchestra will perform approximately 180 concerts in schools, churches, civic auditoriums, and in such unique locations as the Jefferson First Union Plaza in downtown Charlotte and the Alvin C. York Theater in Fort Bragg."[43] The Little Symphony season lasted ten weeks, and the two contingents of thirty-five players each traveled to locations that included West Jefferson; Edenton; Boiling Springs; Sparta; Galax, Virginia; and Cheraw, South Carolina.[44]

The orchestra further developed the educational component begun by Adeline McCall. "Educational programs of the symphony have been expanded over the years, to the point where they now include orchestral concerts, informal 'Discovery' sessions by chamber ensembles, and clinics for high school instrumentalists," noted the press in April 1977.

> Educational programs play an integral part in the activities of the state's symphony. Each season, the 70 musicians who compose the orchestra perform a variety of educational services designed to enhance local school programs and to open the "world of music" to hundreds of thousands of youngsters throughout the state.
> Membership in the North Carolina Symphony Society helps support the orchestra's educational programs, which are planned under the guidance of Richard Walker, director of education and community services. The symphony gears its concert[s] to various age groups and classroom specifications and holds annual workshops for teachers to enable them to make full use of materials provided so as to integrate music into their school curriculum. Both the full complement of 70 musicians and the 35-member Little Symphonies perform concerts for elementary school students.[45]

The symphony launched its campaign to upgrade its image to that of a nationally recognized orchestra by featuring guest appearances by major artists. Among the renowned performers appearing in the 1970s were soprano Roberta Peters, pianist Van Cliburn, violinist Charles Treger, violinist Eugene Fodor, soprano Eileen Farrell, pianist John Ogdon, cellist Lynn Harrell, pianist Grant Johannesen, flutist Eugenia Zukerman, violinist Pinchas Zukerman, and violinist Ruggiero Ricci. Also featured were popular stars such as singer Ethel Merman and the Dizzy Gillespie Jazz Quintet. In cooperation with the North Carolina School of the Arts Ballet, Gosling conducted the orchestra in Tchaikovsky's *Nutcracker* in Memorial Auditorium. For the orchestra's 1978–1979 schedule, Gosling and associate conductor James Ogle shared duties, conducting the symphony or its new chamber orchestra component in concerts in at least sixty North Carolina towns.[46] When the orchestra was scheduled to perform Verdi's *Requiem*, Gosling boasted in the press that "We have a marvelous cast. Soprano Irene Jordan of the Met; Corinne Curry, who has performed at the City Center in New York and around the world, and Nicholas Divergilia [*sic*] from the Met. And Ara Berberian has one of the most beautiful bass sounds I've ever heard."[47]

As southern race relations improved following the civil rights movement of the 1960s, African American guest artists appeared with the orchestra during the Gosling era. On February 8, 1973, the nationally acclaimed soprano Mattiwilda Dobbs sang in Jones Auditorium at Meredith College in Raleigh. In the first half of the program, her arias were "So anch'io la virtù magica" from Donizetti's *Don Pasquale*; "Cavatine de Leila" from Bizet's *Les Pecheûrs de Perles*; and "Ombra leggiera" from Meyerbeer's *Dinorah*. For the second half of the program, she sang "Martern aller Arten" from *The Abduction from the Seraglio*, by Mozart. The orchestra, which began with the Suite from *Der Rosenkavalier* by Strauss, ended the concert with Symphony No. 4 in A Major, Op. 90 (*Italian*) by Mendelssohn. As noted earlier, Dobbs sang the same selections in another February performance at UNC. Her schedule for the 1974–1975 season included appearances in Durham, Burlington, and New Bern.[48]

Dobbs was born in Atlanta in 1925 and began her formal study of voice at Spelman College. In New York, she took further training with Lotte Leonard and received a Marian Anderson Award, a John Whitney Fellowship, and other scholarships that allowed her to continue her studies in Europe. She sang in Paris, in Vienna, at La Scala in Milan, and at Covent Garden in London. In 1955 she debuted in the United States with the San Francisco Opera, where she sang the lead female role in Rimsky-Korsakov's *The Golden Cockerel*. A year later, she debuted at the Metropolitan Opera, singing the role of Gilda in Verdi's *Rigoletto*. Dobbs became the first African American singer to sign a long-term contract with the Met, giving twenty-nine performances in six roles for more than eight seasons. Following her retirement from the stage in the 1970s, she became the first African American artist on the faculty at the University of Texas and served a year as artist-in-residence at Spelman College, where she and Marian Anderson received honorary doctorates in 1979. She died at age ninety in Atlanta in 2015. The magazine *Opera News* once opined that she would have enjoyed an even more renowned career had she not been appearing on the opera scene at the same time as such prominent white female voices as Maria Callas and Joan Sutherland. Nevertheless, she is regarded as having led the way for later black opera stars such as Leontyne Price, Shirley Verrett, Jessye Norman, and Kathleen Battle.[49]

Another African American soprano, and mezzo-soprano, of major reputation who performed with the Gosling orchestra was a native North Carolinian, Cynthia Clarey. She was born in Smithfield, grew up in Rocky Mount, and graduated from Howard University and from Juilliard in voice. She sang in Mozart's *The Magic Flute* with the Juilliard Opera Theater and toured Mississippi in Bizet's *Carmen* with Opera South. She also toured with the New York Quartet and soloed with the Greenwich Philharmonic and the Pro Arts Chorale and Orchestra. The twenty-four-year-old singer won the North Carolina Symphony's Young Artist Competition in 1974 and first sang with the

PROGRAM

NORTH CAROLINA SYMPHONY

JOHN GOSLING, *Conducting*

Jones Auditorium, Meredith College .... February 8, 1973

Raleigh, North Carolina .... Thursday, 8:15 p.m.

Suite from *Der Rosenkavalier* .... RICHARD STRAUSS
ARIAS:
   "Se anchio la virtu magica" (from *Don Pasquale*) .... DONIZETTI
   "Cavatine de Leila" (from *Les Pecheurs de Perles*) .... BIZET
   "Ombra leggiera" (from *Dinorah*) .... MEYERBEER
                Soloist: MATTIWILDA DOBBS

INTERMISSION

ARIA:
   "Marten aller Arten" (from *The Abduction from the Seraglio*) .... MOZART
                Soloist: MATTIWILDA DOBBS

Symphony No. 4, in A Major, Op. 90 *(Italian)* .... MENDELSSOHN

   Allegro vivace
   Andante con moto
   Con moto moderato
   Saltarello: Presto

JOHN GOSLING

John Gosling became the new Artistic Director and Conductor of the North Carolina Symphony on October 3, 1972. From 1967 to 1972 he was conductor and Music Director of the Erie Philharmonic Orchestra (Erie, Pa.) a fully-professional metropolitan orchestra. Mr. Gosling was one of five American conductors chosen for the International Conductors Competition and appeared with the Royal Liverpool Philharmonic Orchestra in England. He has made frequent guest appearances with major and metropolitan orchestras in Europe, Canada and the United States. Mr. Gosling studied on a scholarship at the Juilliard School of Music in New York and is also a graduate of the Catholic University of America in Washington, D. C. While in service, he was principal Trumpet of the U. S. Marine Band. Mr. Gosling is the father of a teen-age daughter, Susan, a freshman at Stephens College in Columbia, Missouri. His wife, Margaret, although an accomplished pianist, prefers painting. She has had exhibitions on both the East and West Coasts and has walked off with a few prizes.

The use of cameras or recording equipment during North Carolina Symphony Concerts is not permitted.

Program of a North Carolina Symphony concert featuring African American soprano Mattiwilda Dobbs at Meredith College in February 1973 (courtesy Roy C. Dicks).

orchestra at a concert in Rocky Mount in February 1975. The following day, she again appeared with the orchestra in the same program, which included her solo and the UNC Women's Glee Club in Debussy's *La Damoiselle élue*, at Memorial Hall in Chapel Hill.[50] Clarey subsequently gained fame as "an artist of a wide range of concert and operatic versatility, particularly known for her role as Carmen, which she sang in productions in the United States, Canada, Europe, Australia, and Japan. In the United States, she has performed with the opera companies of Chicago, Dallas, New York, Seattle, Santa Fe, Saint Louis, and the Tri-Cities in Binghamton, New York, as well as with such major orchestras as the Chicago Symphony, the Boston Symphony, and the New York Philharmonic, among others." She also appeared with the Los Angeles Philharmonic and made a number of recordings.[51]

The 1970s schedule also featured the well-known African American bass baritone William Warfield. Warfield was born in West Helena, Arkansas, in 1920 and grew up in Rochester, New York. He graduated from the Eastman School of Music. His recital debut took place in New York's Town Hall in 1950, and he went on concert tour in Australia. In 1952 he sang in *Porgy and Bess* on a European tour sponsored by the United States Department of State, when he performed with the renowned soprano Leontyne Price. They soon married and together recorded excerpts from *Porgy and Bess* in 1963. They divorced in 1972. Warfield made a number of solo recordings with major orchestras and appeared on television programs, in Hollywood films, and as narrator in a number of orchestral productions, including Aaron Copland's *Lincoln Portrait*. Most Americans perhaps remember him best for his "Ol' Man River" in the musical *Show Boat*. In 1975 Warfield became professor of music at the University of Illinois and then chairman of the voice department before moving to Northwestern University. A strong promoter of African American spirituals, he conducted voice workshops throughout the country for the LaRouche Youth Movement and served as president of the National Association of Negro Musicians. He was guest soloist at Reeves Auditorium at Methodist College in Fayetteville on December 3, 1974.[52]

Still another famous black soloist who debuted in North Carolina under the baton of Gosling was the pianist André Watts, who in the winter of 1976 played Beethoven's Concerto for Piano and Orchestra No. 5 with the symphony. He was born in Nuremburg, Germany, in 1946 to Maria Alexandra Gusmits, of Hungarian descent, and African American soldier Herman Watts. He received early instruction in piano from his mother, and the family moved to Philadelphia when he was eight years old. There he gained further training and won a competition to perform in a Philadelphia Orchestra Children's Concert. In 1963 he performed with Leonard Bernstein and the New York Philharmonic in its concert series for talented young artists. Soon afterward Bernstein had him substitute for the famous pianist Glenn Gould in a regular concert by the New York Philharmonic, an incident that enhanced the young Watts's reputation. That was followed the next year by his winning a Grammy as "best new classical artist" for his first recording. He quickly gained recognition as a major concert pianist and launched a busy schedule, including a London debut with the London Symphony Orchestra in 1966. Despite his demanding itinerary, Watts graduated in 1972 from Baltimore's Peabody Institute, where he studied under Leon Fleisher. In the 1970s, Watts was playing as many as 150 concerts a year. He appeared numerous times in the Lincoln Center's Great Performers series and on PBS's *Live from Lincoln Center*. He received an honorary doctoral degree from Yale and the coveted Avery Fisher Prize for American classical musicians. Watts would play with the North Carolina orchestra several times in the future, becoming the most frequent soloist in its classical series. In 2004 he filled the Jack I. and Dora B. Hamlin Chair in Piano at Indiana University.[53]

When the North Carolina Symphony began its pops series in the 1970s, African American jazz singer Sarah Vaughan performed as a guest artist. Born in Newark, New Jersey, in 1924, she studied piano and organ and sang in a church choir before winning an amateur contest singing "Body and Soul" at New York's Apollo Theater in 1942. She was hired as second pianist and vocalist with Earl (Fatha) Hines's big band, in which Billy Eckstine sang and Dizzy Gillespie and Charlie Parker were instrumentalists. When Eckstine founded his own band, Vaughan joined him, performing alongside jazz greats Gillespie, Parker, Art Blakey, and Miles Davis. In the late 1940s, she began making recordings, which established her reputation as a jazz singer. Several became popular hits, such as "Tenderly," "This Is Magic," "Make Yourself Comfortable," "Whatever Lola Wants," "Broken-Hearted Melody," and the album *How Long Has This Been Going On?* In 1982 she won a Grammy for best jazz vocal rendition for *Gershwin Live!* In her many stage appearances, the songs "Misty" and "Send In the Clowns" were favorite standards. The performances invariably won standing ovations. Upon Vaughan's death in 1990, singer Mel Torme said about her, "She had the single best vocal instrument of any singer working in the popular field. So much so that I used to call her the diva. At one point, I asked her why she never opted for an operatic career. She got huffy, and said 'Do you mean jazz isn't legit?' She was very defensive about being a jazz singer. Where someone like Benny Goodman was able to split his musical image and record Mozart, she wanted to perform precisely where she was."[54]

While Gosling was artistic director, the reputation of the North Carolina Symphony continued to grow. The symphony reached "major orchestra status," bestowed by the American Symphony Orchestra League, in 1976. The eastern North Carolina press reported the "Good news for Tar Heel music lovers," noting that "The designation was awarded to the symphony in recognition of its artistic development and budgetary levels of $1 million–plus for the past two years. In being named a major orchestra, the North Carolina Symphony joins the ranks of such prestigious orchestras as the New York and Los Angeles Philharmonic, Chicago Symphony and Philadelphia Orchestra. The lion's share of the credit for the orchestra's accomplishment goes to John Gosling for his commitment to artistic excellence."[55]

In addition to booking famous soloists to appear in its concerts, the symphony attempted to broaden its audience and attendance through its new pops series by staging joint performances with accomplished popular music artists who traditionally did not perform in the classical genre but had a large appeal to the general public. One early event that drew a large crowd was a concert played with the rock band Blood, Sweat and Tears in January 1974. In promoting the upcoming event with the band, Gosling declared: "This group has worked with symphony orchestras before. They are marvelous players, with marvelous arrangements. It will be an interesting experiment. You can't make a symphony out of a rock orchestra or a rock group out of a symphony. So we'll do our own music before combining forces."[56] "Does the North Carolina Symphony make you think of Bach, Beethoven and Brahams [*sic*]?" inquired one newspaper. "That classical image undergoes a radical chan[g]e Saturday at Dorton Arena in Raleigh when the symphony will appear in concert with the rock group Blood, Sweat and Tears. According to Conductor John Gosling, it is a frank attempt to appeal to the young music lovers in the state."[57] A correspondent for the *Daily Tar Heel* reviewed the concert.

When Blood, Sweat and Tears performed with the North Carolina Symphony Saturday in Raleigh, a musical and social phenomenon unique to this area occurred. Musically, the concert was a rare fusion of rock, jazz and classical music, tastefully put together.

As a social event, the concert brought together under the single roof of Dorton Arena two and three generations of listeners—for a single evening. The often stereotyped gap in musical tastes between them was bridged.

Watching the audiences' reactions to the performance was almost as enlightening as seeing, for the first time, a jazz-rock group on the same stage with a symphony orchestra. I use "audiences" in the plural because of the phenomenal variety of people at the concert.

There were the usual concert-goers, students from area colleges who came to see the band that meant so much to the early development of jazz-rock, different though the group's personnel may be from the band Al Kooper put together in 1967.

And then there was another audience. They came in coats and ties and gowns, that looked like formal wear in contrast to the casual attire of the younger audience.

The middle-aged and the senior citizens came to hear the symphony and conductor John Gosling, whom they know well. Gosling has been delighting audiences throughout North Carolina and surrounding states with increasing excellence and imaginative programming. He saved his farthest out for this orchestra's first joint rock concert....

Hundreds of teeny-bo[p]pers rushed the stage as John Gosling called Blood, Sweat and Tears back for an encore.

And the spotlight on the conductor revealed a broad grin, which was no stage facade. He was happy about a truly successful evening of real family entertainment—and not the G-rated movie kind.[58]

The *Asheville Citizen-Times* took note of Gosling and the success of the pops series. According to one of its editorials in December 1977,

John Gosling is quite a talented and determined man.

Six years ago, he determined to prove to North Carolinians that symphonic music and popular music go hand in hand.

In that short space, he has proven the point to his own satisfaction and to that of others, and he has taken the state's symphony orchestra on to even greater heights.

It is unfortunate that the word "symphony" turns many people off. The first thought of those who think they may not like it is that symphony music must be longhair, a notch or two above the average music lover, and therefore hard to understand.

That is the myth that John Gosling exploded when he left the Erie Philharmonic Orchestra six years ago and accepted the position of conductor/artistic director of the North Carolina Symphony.

He did it by combining symphony with pops in a most artistic and entertaining manner....

Gosling's use of popular musicians is an old show biz stunt. They attract the crowd that would never walk across the street to hear a symphony—and thousands of them have discovered, through the exposure to the North Carolina Symphony, that any music played well is good music.[59]

The conductor himself remained convinced that the North Carolina orchestra could expand its outreach and receipts with music to attract a popular audience without injuring its image as a symphony devoted to the classical genre. "We have never encountered a problem with artists from pops," he once said. "Most of them have played with symphonies enough to give great performances. It was Blood, Sweat and Tears first encounter with symphonic [music], but they got special material, and were really first rate musicians, and had no problems at all. In fact, they had a French horn player who'd been with the Metropolitan for several years. He went with Blood, Sweat and Tears because they could pay him more money. They were first class." During Gosling's tenure, the orchestra featured a variety of well-known popular artists such as guitarist Chet Atkins and jazz musician Dave Brubeck, in addition to the aforementioned Sarah Vaughan.[60]

The Gosling orchestra further extended its range during the heyday of the Friends of the College series, established in 1959 by North Carolina State College (later University) for performances in William Neal Reynolds Coliseum on the campus. It became the largest college-and-university series for classical music in the nation. Until its termination in 1994, Friends of the College attracted some of the world's best-known orchestras (including the "top five" in the United States), ballet troupes, and solo artists. And it provided another venue for the North Carolina Symphony to perform to large audiences. In 1976, for example, Gosling led the orchestra in Reynolds Coliseum on the same stage as the famous American composer Aaron Copland, who conducted his own music in a shared program. At a Friends concert in 1978, the symphony under the baton of Gosling performed Mahler's Eighth Symphony, joined by the university chorus and brass ensemble and a children's choir.[61]

Gosling and the musicians also performed in Reynolds Coliseum at the inaugural ball for Governor James B. Hunt, Jr., in January 1977. Gosling used the gubernatorial ball publicity for public exposure for the symphony and to express the orchestra's appreciation for state support. "We are the State's orchestra," he declared, "and I think it's splendid to be involved in tribute to the Governor and the many governmental officials who are responsible for the extensive financial support that the Symphony receives each year from the General Assembly."[62]

During his days in North Carolina, Gosling appeared as guest conductor of a number of orchestras including the Miami Philharmonic, the Oregon Symphony, the Symphony of Puerto Rico, and orchestras in Norway, Venezuela, and Mexico. On occasions when he did not conduct the concerts of the North Carolina Symphony, his capable associate conductor, James Edwin Ogle, Jr., took his place at the podium.[63]

Ogle was born in Virginia and developed an early affinity for the clarinet, receiving bachelor's and master's degrees in that instrument from the University of Michigan. He studied clarinet and conducting in France and competed in a conducting competition of the Danish National Radio Orchestra in Denmark. He joined the North Carolina Symphony in 1974 as an apprentice conductor, winning the symphony's first Young Conductors Competition, and stayed on for eighteen years, making a significant contribution as associate conductor of the orchestra, as over time he was permitted to direct increasingly important concerts. His tour with the symphony continued after Gosling's ended. Over the years, Ogle's concerts with the symphony encompassed educational and young people's programs; pops evenings, including Pops in the Park engagements; and summer events, as the orchestra's season was gradually expanded to provide longer employment for its musicians. He also conducted the *Nutcracker* with the North Carolina School of the Arts dance program, as well as productions with the American Dance Festival. He was involved in founding and substantial fund-raising for An Appalachian Summer Festival and the Cannon Music Camp at Appalachian State University in Boone. He also worked with Gosling at the Bear Valley Music Festival. Of Ogle's notable performances with the North Carolina Symphony, two stand out: a concert with band leader and renowned clarinetist Benny Goodman in 1982, and a program with one of North Carolina's distinguished artists, pianist Francis Whang of the UNC Department of Music, in 1983.

After successfully auditioning with the Boise Philharmonic in Idaho, Ogle shared conducting duties and commuted between North Carolina and Boise from 1989 until 1992. He then left the North Carolina Symphony and continued as music director of the Boise Philharmonic. Presently he is in charge of development in the College of Arts and Sciences at Boise State University and conducts the volunteer Meridian Symphony Orchestra, as well as annual performances of Handel's *Messiah* in New Bern, North Carolina.[64]

Under the leadership of Gosling, regular coverage of the symphony on radio exceeded that of his predecessor. In terms of outreach to the greater artistic community, too, he was an innovator with savvy marketing sense. In occasional choral programs, such as Beethoven's Ninth Symphony and Handel's *Messiah*, he engaged singers from the community in volunteer choruses formed by local choir directors. Many family members and friends of those singers purchased tickets to hear them perform with the orchestra.

In 1975 the symphony moved its headquarters from Chapel Hill and its rehearsal facilities from Durham to new headquarters in Raleigh's Memorial Auditorium. In May of the following year, the National Music Council presented a bicentennial plaque to the orchestra "acknowledging the contributions made by its founding conductor," Lamar Stringfield, and commemorating "the orchestra's first permanent home in its 45-year history."[65] Finally the North Carolina Symphony had found a lasting location, but conditions there were far from ideal for the rehearsal and performance of classical music. Like "clothes make the man," in the symphonic world, the venue in which an ensemble plays is very important. The orchestra's vagabond life had led its musicians to expect anything, but the new location in Raleigh left much to be desired. Memorial Auditorium, roughly as wide as it was deep, and with a balcony that severely diminished audibility beneath it, was a multipurpose relic of the Depression era. The WPA had helped construct the large stone building with Doric columns in 1932. One of many such halls built nationwide as war memorials, it was intended to commemorate North Carolina's war dead and to complement the Capitol at the other end of Fayetteville Street.[66] The building had served as a site for debutante balls, professional wrestling matches, lectures, rallies, and community concerts.

High on the agenda of the orchestra's management and on the to-do list of the city of Raleigh was a major upgrade of the hall. Therefore the first of several renovations took place during Gosling's tenure. The changes went beyond cosmetic improvements and involved the balcony's being raked down toward the stage, eliminating the overhang and thus reducing the number of acoustically impoverished seats. The room's width-to-depth ratio remained a major challenge, however. (The present-day wings of the building, which house Meymandi Concert Hall on one side and Fletcher Opera Theater on the other, were not part of this 1970s renovation but were added later. The

Duke Energy Center for the Performing Arts now comprises all the performance spaces.)

Of course, the symphony had to move out of Memorial Auditorium while the renovations took place. Raleigh's Civic Center, since demolished, was the only option for a temporary location, and that building made for a truly dismal period in the history of the orchestra. The acoustics and cavernous conditions were not conducive for classical music and the audiences it attracts. Attendance dwindled, and subscriptions fell. But the promise of returning to the orchestra's revamped home kept many patrons supportive of the symphony. It was a credit to the organization, as well as to Gosling and subsequent artistic directors and conductors, that the orchestra did relatively well under the circumstances. In the end, the symphony itself remained the attraction, especially as it featured fine soloists having name recognition.

In fact, although "The abysmal acoustics of the Civic Center worked constantly against the music," and "The amplification system destroyed balances and leveled dynamics," one of Gosling's most memorable concerts took place in the building in 1977. The evening featured Gosling and violinist Ruggiero Ricci in a program that offered Hindemith's *Symphonic Metamorphoses on Themes of Carl Maria von Weber*, completed in 1943 and thus comparatively new thirty-four years later. A review in the *News and Observer* praised the brisk tempi and the hauntingly beautiful *Turandot* movement. The orchestra's rendition of Mendelssohn's Violin Concerto was a model unsentimental performance. And in Rachmaninoff's Symphony No. 3, completed in 1936 and still relatively contemporary for the 1977 audience, the orchestra was heard to good advantage.[67]

The highlight of the Gosling era occurred when the symphony achieved its prestigious reputation as a state orchestra worthy of national recognition, a goal set by the Symphony Society when it phased out Swalin and hired Gosling. During that period, the orchestra not only introduced famous soloists to perform in North Carolina but also traveled out of state to perform in renowned concert halls in three major cities known for their high levels of cultural arts. The orchestra played in New York's Carnegie Hall in 1977 and Chicago's Symphony Hall and Washington's Kennedy Center in 1978. "This was a major step," recalled clarinetist Jimmy Gilmore, "in giving the orchestra some long deserved caché as the premiere performing arts organization in the state, and a chance to make the home folks aware that the orchestra had been designated by the American Symphony Orchestra League in 1976 as one of 31 'major orchestras' in the country."[68]

The symphony, state government, and press promoted the Carnegie Hall appearance as a milestone placing North Carolina on the national scene in the cultural arts. "New York, Here We Come," announced the *News and Observer* on Monday, March 6. "The state symphony is about to enter musical

Mecca, followed by a happy throng of North Carolina supporters who intend to show the Big Apple what a good time is." On Tuesday a chartered flight took the ninety-piece orchestra and a two-hundred-voice Duke University Chapel Choir and Chorale to New York. A contingent of five hundred state dignitaries and guests arrived the following day. According to the newspaper, they would attend "a round of parties and a post-premiere reception to be given by Gov. and Mrs. James B. Hunt, Jr. Many symphony members and guests will stay on in Manhattan for an evening at the Met Thursday and a weekend of Broadway shows and cabaret entertainment." In addition to Governor Hunt and his wife, former governors James E. Holshouser, Jr., Robert W. Scott, and Terry Sanford (then president of Duke University) planned to be present, as well as various state government department heads, university chancellors, and prominent business leaders. Other anticipated distinguished attendees included United States senator Robert Morgan; Juanita Kreps, the United States secretary of commerce on leave as vice president of Duke University; and Nancy Hanks, chairperson of the National Endowment for the Arts and a trustee of Duke. Back home listeners could hear the concert, with commentary by Martin Bookspan of the New York Philharmonic, on several radio stations.[69]

The day before the March 9 Carnegie Hall appearance, a writer for the *New York Times* posed the question "Why would the North Carolina Symphony, an orchestra whose major endeavor for years has been concert tours for 250,000 North Carolina schoolchildren, decide suddenly to appear at New York's Carnegie Hall in the most culturally competitive city in the country?" Elissa Josephson, spokesperson for the symphony and handling the advance publicity, answered: "It's part of the new image of the South. It's no longer the Sahara of the Bozarts." The orchestra's venture into the "big time" was part of a larger political and economic movement instigated by the first administration of Governor James B. Hunt, Jr. (1977–1985), to help bolster the growth and development of North Carolina through the promotion of its cultural resources—especially the North Carolina Symphony, the North Carolina Museum of Art, and the North Carolina School of the Arts.[70]

Having grown out of the state Art Society founded in 1924, the North Carolina Museum of Art was established in Raleigh in 1947 and funded by $1 million appropriated by the General Assembly, a sum matched by the Samuel H. Kress Foundation, largely through the efforts of legislator Robert Lee Humber. In the 1950s, the legislature provided money to renovate the State Highway Building in downtown Raleigh and locate the museum there. In 1983 the museum moved to its present location in a new facility on Blue Ridge Road in west Raleigh. Since that time, the institution—with private and public support—has grown significantly in its collections, galleries, work facilities, public services, and outdoor venues, with an additional building opening in 2010. It has hosted major national and international exhibits.[71]

The General Assembly founded the School of the Arts on a large campus in Winston-Salem in 1963. In cooperation with the UNC system, and now called the UNC School of the Arts, it "trains students for professional careers in the fields of dance, drama, filmmaking, music, the visual arts, and production and design." Half of those attending must be residents of North Carolina. A number of graduates have attained national fame in their fields.[72] But, as with the symphony and its "horn-tootin' bill," not all legislators favored state support for the school. When the bill for its creation came before the General Assembly, one conservative lawmaker rose to oppose wasting taxpayers' money "to teach these people to toe-dance, pick banjos and sing in foreign languages."

The Hunt administration, however, was committed to using the symphony and the state's other cultural resources to encourage and promote the development of North Carolina. The *New York Times* noted that while in the city, "the new Governor, Jim Hunt, ... will mix business with culture by reminding anybody who's interested that North Carolina is a good place to bring up the kids—and locate a business or industry."[73]

Among the musical celebrities attending the symphony's 1977 Carnegie Hall concert were "Eleanor Steber, former Metropolitan Opera soprano; Carlos Moseley, president of the New York Philharmonic and a Tar Heel native; Dr. Leon Thompson, education director of the New York Philharmonic; David Hall, former manager of the Philadelphia Orchestra; Roy Hemming, author of 'Discovering Music' and editor of Retirement Living magazine; conductor Mitch Miller of 'Sing Along with Mitch' fame; and Hugh Ross, conductor of New York's Schola Cantorum Chorus."[74] Prior to the concert, several receptions were held simultaneously in hotels a few blocks from Carnegie Hall. "More than 400 people attended a 6 p.m. reception given by Gov. Hunt and the North Carolina Department of Natural and Economic Resources. The University of North Carolina hosted a reception for alumni at the Essex House and a reception for N.C. State University Alumni was held in the nearby Dorset Hotel." But "Most of the action ... was on the second floor of the Essex House where a reception for alumni from Duke University" drew guests who congregated to meet David Hartman, host of ABC television's *Good Morning America* and a Duke alumnus.

After the receptions, many of the attendees walked to Carnegie Hall from the Essex House. But not everyone who showed up at the hall came to hear the orchestra. As the audience entered, a group of about fifty civil rights protestors gathered outside and called on Governor Hunt to release the prisoners known as the Wilmington Ten and the Charlotte Three. Those African Americans and one white woman had been tried and sentenced for their participation in racial unrest in the two cities that had erupted into violence and arson. Police cleared a path through the protestors for the concertgoers. After the performance, Governor and Mrs. Hunt, secretary of the Department of Cultural Resources Sara Hodgkins, and Mr. and Mrs. Mitchell Watson of the Symphony Society hosted a reception at The University Club to honor the orchestra and the choir and chorale.[75]

Reviews of the orchestra's performance appeared within a few days. *New York Times* critic Raymond Ericson called the Carnegie Hall concert "quite an event" and reviewed the performance.

> The orchestra was making the visit to celebrate its ascendance from a community ensemble in 1932 to a "major" symphony with a budget of $1.6 million. It is under the direction of John Gosling, who has headed it since 1972, and he has chosen a more enterprising program than New Yorkers often get from outside groups.
>
> Besides the standard "Carnival Overture" of Dvorak and Stravinsky's "Petrouchka" ballet score, there were Ned Rorem's "Assembly and Fall" and Poulenc's "Stabat Mater." The latter enlisted the services of some more North Carolinians, the Duke University Chapel Choir and Chorale, directed by J. Benjamin Smith, and Janice Harsanyi, soprano, who is on the faculty of the North Carolina School of the Arts.

> Considering its new status, it was not surprising that the orchestra was so smartly disciplined. The playing sounded as if every phrase had been honed to the finest degree. The attacks and releases were uniform. There was a precise clarity to everything.[76]

The symphony had commissioned Rorem's *Assembly and Fall* for the bicentennial celebration, and it had premiered in Raleigh in the fall of 1976.[77] Rorem, accompanied by Mrs. Serge Koussevitzky, widow of the former director of the Boston Symphony Orchestra, was in the audience in New York and stood for applause from the listeners. Former governor Sanford led a standing ovation for Dvořák's *Carnival* Overture. Governor Hunt expressed his admiration and pride for the orchestra at the New York premiere but also made the point that the concert was merely typical of what was customary at home in North Carolina. "I think this is a fantastic performance," he declared. But "We didn't come up here and put on the dog for New York

First as president of the North Carolina Symphony Society and then as secretary of the North Carolina Department of Cultural Resources, Sara W. Hodgkins was a strong supporter of the orchestra (photograph from 1977, courtesy State Archives of North Carolina).

City. I think it's great they performed the same numbers that they performed for our state."[78]

The orchestra's concerts in Chicago and Washington were similarly well received. "Our reviews in all these major venues were exceedingly positive," remembered Jimmy Gilmore. "No doubt, the North Carolina Symphony took everyone by surprise. We were so much better than anyone expected!"[79]

Back in North Carolina, critics generally continued to sing the praises of Gosling and the symphony. In October 1978, the Asheville press applauded him and the orchestra when a concert program featured a Bartók concerto in the mountain city.

> John Gosling, conductor of the North Carolina Symphony, [c]ould not have chosen a better work than the Bartok "Concerto for Orchestra" to demonstrate the conti[nu]ing prowess of his orchestra.
>
> The symphony's [performance] Wednesday night in the Thomas Wolfe Auditorium in Asheville also demonstrated th[at] Gosling, now in his sixth year with the orchestra, has put his individual artistic stamp on the group.
>
> Gosling's metier is a romantic one and he invests these works with a dramatic flash and energy that pleases his audiences. The technical accomplishment of the orchestra is such that when occasional minor mishaps intrude (the players are human and it happens in all major orchestras), there is a shudder of surprise.
>
> The "Concerto for Orchestra" by Bela Bartok is purposely constructed to show-off the various sections of the modern symphony orchestra in a work that has become a beloved twentieth century masterpiece.
>
> The expertly drilled musicians shined ... special cheers should go to the violas for some particularly fine solo passages.[80]

Gosling might have enjoyed even greater success during his time of rebuilding and expansion had there been funds to add more permanent members of the orchestra. As it was, he proved capable of creating attractive programs with some excellent solo artists. Despite negative opinions that developed among a number of the musicians, he was, according to most of the people who worked with him, a pleasant and sometimes engaging person. He made amateur singers feel welcome at his choral programs. He conveyed his interpretive notions to the musicians without much fuss or fanfare. And he was adept at supporting solo artists, generally willing to bend his artistic vision to that of his guests if the concepts were in conflict. But like Swalin before him, Gosling would end his days as artistic director/conductor with considerable controversy as the North Carolina Symphony faced new challenges.

6

Rancor and Recovery

By 1979—the year that signaled the end of John Gosling's tenure—the North Carolina Symphony found itself in dire financial straits. For Gosling's first year on the job (1972–1973), the Symphony Society had a budget of $666,014, all of which was expended during that period. Of that amount, $212,237 came from the state appropriation, $37,069 from the Ford Foundation fund, $155,350 from memberships, $145,408 from the sustaining fund, $52,000 from investment income, $41,650 from concert contracts, $12,000 through the Children's Division, and the rest from other sources such as recordings and miscellaneous. The artistic director/conductor's salary was $22,000, and salaries for the musicians totaled $339,081.[1]

But the symphony was in financial trouble, a situation resulting in large part from poor money management and fund-raising by the Symphony Society. In its report of June 30, 1973, the Office of the State Auditor condemned the society's record keeping. "During the course of this audit," the auditors declared, "we found the records of the Symphony Society to be incomplete and needing considerable improvement," particularly regarding the payroll and the general operating fund.

> We would also like to call attention to the seriousness of the financial condition of the North Carolina Symphony.... During Fiscal 1972, the symphony had to request [a] $52,000.00 additional state appropriation from the contingency and emergency fund and during Fiscal 1973 another $62,000.00 was requested in order to meet the required expenditures. Since the 1973 contingency and emergency funds were not approved until July 1973, which was after year end, the symphony had to resort to borrowing $50,000.00 from a local bank in order to meet its June obligations. Even if the symphony had received the additional state appropriation during June 1973 of $62,000.00 it would have still overexpended current receipts by $15,741.15.
>
> We have discussed the serious implications of the financial condition of the symphony with the General Manager and the Secretary of Cultural Resources. We would like to point out that unless additional financial aid sources can be found that the North Carolina Symphony will soon be unable to meet its current obligations.[2]

Despite the state auditor's call for more oversight and care in the symphony's handling of money and staying out of debt, the Symphony Society could not seem to overcome its financial difficulties, which existed largely because of the failure to create a responsible and professional management system for its funds. Although the symphony had close ties to the Department of Cultural Resources, including depositing its historical records with the State Archives in that department, the Symphony Society continued to resist the orchestra's becoming a full state agency under the jurisdiction of Cultural Resources and subject to its regulations and guidance. Nevertheless, the symphony continued to appeal for state grants and to rely increasingly on state assistance. When in September 1974 Senator Hamilton Horton of the General Assembly asked for a report on the sources and amounts of the symphony's revenues for three bienniums, he received the following figures from the legislature's Fiscal Research Division: for the biennium 1969–1971, total funds of $958,179, with $363,757 from state appropriations, $259,841 from membership fees, and $334,581 from other sources; for the biennium 1971–1973, total funds of $929,957, with $476,474 from state appropriations, $277,854 from membership fees, and $175,629 from other sources; for the biennium 1973–1975 (estimated), total funds of $1,453,224, with $971,151 from state appropriations, $316,069 from membership fees, and $166,004 from other sources.[3]

Some state officials looked to the Department of Cultural Resources to take full charge of the North Carolina Symphony and get its financial house in order. At its December 1974 meeting, secretary of Cultural Resources Grace Rohrer informed the executive committee of the Symphony Society's board of trustees that "when you come to the State Government for more and more money, you are asking for State control and intervention." In attendance on that occasion, Benjamin Swalin spoke out that "he never had any problems with the books while he was in office." He maintained that "the Symphony is better off as a Grant in Aid organization," and that the "Society needed a manager who was thoroughly familiar with bookkeeping and equipped with degrees from Wharton School of Finance or Harvard Business School." The Symphony Society should not ask for money from the state, he said (ironically, given his own appeals for government funds), but instead seek money from businesses such as Burlington Mills, which "should give $30,000.00 a year!"

Prior to the December gathering of the executive committee, Secretary Rohrer and the Symphony Society had "requested that the Attorney General give a ruling as to who had the authority of the management of the Symphony.—'Where does it lie?'—Department of Cultural Resources or Symphony Board?" The attorney general ruled that "it lies with the North Carolina Symphony Board of Trustees." In response to that decision, Mrs. Rohrer reminded the executive committee that if the growing symphony was going to handle its own operations, "management must be developed also" to deal with its pressing problems. The executive committee promised to do a better job of managing its finances. But, although it wanted to keep ties with the Department of Cultural Resources and comply with state laws, it would retain control of its own operations.[4]

Despite the vow to improve its business management, the Symphony Society remained in serious financial straits. As the 1970s drew to a close, little remained in the annual budget to pay salaries and support the day-to-day operations of the symphony. Building an orchestra of national reputation had proved costly. The contracts for paying major guest artists to appear in North Carolina had been expensive, as had the big concerts in New York, Chicago, and Washington. The problem of keeping an adequate budget was worsened by a drop in funds raised by the Symphony Society chapters. Unlike his predecessor, Gosling had not devoted much effort to fund-raising. The lack of a full-time, professional executive director with fund-raising and managerial expertise to maintain a sound fiscal and membership base had always been a problem for the Symphony Society. In fact, the organization probably would never have received the important Ford Foundation grant if it had not turned over fund-raising to the relentless Swalin, who—as described earlier—traveled from one end of the state to the other to obtain the necessary matching money from local chapters.[5]

In 1979 the Symphony Society approached the state legislature with hat in hand to beg for more special funding to maintain its operations. Putting particular emphasis on the important educational mission that the symphony provided for the state's public schools, the General Assembly passed a bill stating, "There is hereby appropriated from the General Fund to the Department of Cultural Resources for the purpose of supplemental grant-in-aid to the North Carolina Symphony Society, Incorporated, the sum of one hundred ninety-eight thousand dollars ($198,000) for the fiscal year 1979–80 and two hundred forty-eight thousand dollars ($248,000) for the fiscal year 1980–81."[6]

Local support for the symphony had been declining throughout the decade, which threatened the continuance of the children's concerts. In September 1976, for example, the *Statesville Record and Landmark* observed that "Unless the local symphony society manages to come up with about $5,000 this year, or nearly double what the drive produced last year, local schoolchildren may lose their chance to hear the symphony perform in Statesville.... In the current campaign ... the society needs to raise not only the $4,500 required to subsidize the schoolchildren['s] concerts, but also enough to make up for last year's deficit, which brings the total to about $7,000."[7]

The Ford Foundation money was fading fast by 1980. Amid the fiscal crisis, the musicians went on strike for a week in that year. Then, unable to pay the players' salaries, the Symphony Society cancelled the final five weeks of the concert season. Some orchestra supporters criticized Gosling for the symphony's financial problems, claiming that he had not done enough to raise money and that he had spent too much revenue contracting with expensive major guest artists and taking the orchestra to big cities to expand its reputation. Other difficulties also undermined his relationship with the symphony. Conflict grew between him and the musicians, who had become more vocal in their demands since forming the Orchestra Committee for collective bargaining rights. They particularly wanted more say in contract negotiations and in the hiring and firing of players, a duty Gosling, like his predecessor, carried out without their participation. The musicians' group also wanted a vote in the hiring of the artistic director/conductor. By the time of Gosling's third season, at least forty musicians had left the symphony. At one point, he even fired all the principals. He became increasingly unpopular with many of the musicians, who wanted to end his stint as artistic director/conductor.[8]

As conflict between the players and Gosling grew, he decided to submit his resignation to the board of trustees. "After seven years of accomplishment," he wrote to chairman George E. Norman, Jr., on May 25, 1979, "I feel that I have developed the orchestra to a high professional level and I now wish to seek new opportunities and challenges. Therefore, it is with regret that I submit my resignation as of the expiration date of my current contract, June 30, 1980." The orchestra's monetary problems during his years were his largest regret. "The fact that a firm financial base for the organization has not been achieved to keep pace with the high artistic level achieved has been of great concern to me," he lamented.[9] His resignation followed notice from the trustees that his contract would not be extended. The financial straits and labor problems with the players had convinced members of the Symphony Society's board not to extend the contract.[10]

Appearing with the orchestra in Gosling's last season as artistic director/conductor (September 25, 1979–May 30, 1980) were guest artists Jaime Laredo, violinist; André Watts, pianist; Alicia de Larrocha, pianist; Larry Adler, harmonica virtuoso; the Billy Taylor Trio jazz ensemble; Igor Oistrakh, violinist; Duane Hulbert, pianist; and Michele Djokic, cellist. The Beethoven Triple Concerto featured violinist Junko Ohtsu along with cellist Djokic and pianist Hulbert. The last performance was an all-orchestra concert on May 30. Gosling and associate conductor James Ogle shared conducting responsibilities for that series of appearances.[11]

Although Gosling's resignation letter of May 1979 seemed amicable enough, he later expressed considerable anger at not having his contract renewed. In 1981 he told the Raleigh *News and Observer* that "To this day, I've never been told why my contract was never renewed. My personal feeling was that I was a scapegoat … for [the society's] financial problems."[12] The extent of his bitterness was exhibited when he refused to return to the stage after his final concert and accept an award, flowers, and appreciation from secretary of Cultural Resources Sara Hodgkins, instead leaving her standing alone before a bewildered audience.

Upon leaving North Carolina, Gosling continued to appear as guest conductor with various orchestras and to lead the Bear Valley Music Festival, which he had founded in the High Sierra of California in the 1960s and had shared time with while working in North Carolina. At the festival, he "and a dedicated group of founders, musicians, and volunteers continued to make music in a variety of venues—the Lodge, under the open skies, and finally in a large circus tent. The repertoire expanded to include: Broadway show-tunes, opera, chamber music, educational programs, and guest artists from around the world." The festival was shown on television and featured on the *Today Show*. In 1985 Carter Nice, conductor of the Sacramento Symphony, succeeded Gosling as music director at Bear Valley.[13] Gosling went on to become music director and conductor of the Hilton Head Orchestra on the coast of South Carolina, a position he held from 1990 to 1997. He convened his first rehearsal with twenty unpaid musicians in the island's First Presbyterian Church. "It doesn't matter whether you went to Juilliard or P.S. 39," he told the orchestra. "And I really don't care whether or not you're paid. We're all here to make good music—so let's do it!" Gosling expressed an intention to perform a degree of "20th-century music" with the orchestra, and he committed to working with the Beaufort County school district by "leading a seminar in its program for gifted and talented children." He brought in nationally recognized musicians to perform at Hilton Head and raised the orchestra from amateur to full orchestra status.[14] In 1982 Gosling had moved to Savannah, Georgia, where he became principal guest conductor of the Savannah Symphony, performing many adult and children's concerts and giving preconcert lectures. He died and was buried in that city in October 2004.[15]

A number of Gosling's defenders in North Carolina had wanted him to stay on and, for some time after his departure from the state, maintained that the board refused to keep him largely because many of the musicians had come to dislike him. For instance, Mrs. B. R. Chamberlain, Jr., former executive vice president of the North Carolina Symphony Women's Association and former vice president of the Durham chapter of the Symphony Society, wrote to the *News and Observer* that

> The firing of former conductor John Gosling has left a moral wound in the relationship between the symphony and its audience that cannot be healed....
>
> The citizens of this state cannot accept the idea of the right of employees to select their own boss—a notion that the trustees accepted when they yielded to musicians' demands that Gosling be replaced. They also will not tolerate the firing of a good conductor and master showman who brought the respect of the tough music critics in New

York, Chicago and Washington to an orchestra that until that time was famous only for taking "kiddie concerts" to small towns....

The new conductor, whoever he may be, deserves our sympathy. I would advise him not to sell his present home and buy here, for we North Carolinians have proven ourselves ungrateful recipients of the priceless gift of musical talent and leadership.[16]

Mrs. Chamberlain was proved correct in her implication that Gosling's "firing" did not signal the end of the controversy about who should be hired as artistic director/conductor and who would make the selection.

At the time of the Gosling fiasco, the North Carolina Symphony was not the only state cultural institution experiencing personnel and organizational difficulties. The North Carolina Museum of Art also had its problems. The *News and Observer* took note of both agencies' internal tangles and quarrels.

The N.C. Symphony and the N.C. Museum of Art seem to have considerable difficulty achieving working relationships with their top artistic professionals. John Gosling's announcement that he was fired as conductor of the symphony—and his brusque refusal to accept the Governor's Award after his last performance—came hard on the heels of Moussa M. Domit's resignation under pressure as director of the art museum.

The symphony's chain of command is different from the museum's. The conductor works under contract with the private, non-profit symphony board of trustees. The museum director reports to the secretary of cultural resources and must deal with an array of governing boards and the N.C. Art Society.

But there are similarities between Gosling's departure and Domit's. Both men evidently can be temperamental, to judge by Domit's abrasiveness and Gosling's behavior after the final performance. Both men were involved in disputes over authority. A large part of Domit's failure was in his inability to maintain peace within the museum's hopelessly tangled chain of command.[17]

With Gosling's departure pending, the North Carolina Symphony had begun holding auditions for the position of artistic director/conductor. "The symphony's board of trustees is conducting an extensive search for Gosling's replacement," reported the *Asheville Citizen-Times* on March 16, 1980. "Among those to be considered are the six different conductors engaged for performances during this season.... The board probably will continue its search into next year, engaging additional guest conductors for the coming season, according to Tom Stanback, director of community services for the symphony." The newspaper further noted that "Isaiah Jackson, associate conductor of the Rochester Philharmonic Orchestra, ... is the only guest conductor scheduled to accompany the symphony during its Asheville performances."[18] But major problems with the orchestra remained and inhibited progress, as evidenced by the musicians' strike and the Symphony Society's cancellation of the last concerts of the 1980 season.[19] In July the musicians' committee finally won the concession of an equal vote in the selection of the symphony's artistic director/conductor. According to a contract covering 1980–1983 and agreed upon by the collective bargaining group and the society that month, "The selection of the Artistic Director will be mutually agreeable between the Board of Trustees of the Society and the Musicians."[20]

While the Symphony Society carried on a search for an artistic director/conductor, it made a temporary agreement with Laurence Leighton Smith to conduct the orchestra until a permanent appointment was made. Smith was born in Portland, Oregon, in 1936. With a bachelor of science degree from Portland State University and a bachelor of music from the Mannes College of Music in New York, he launched his career at Tanglewood as musical assistant to Erich Leinsdorf and at the Peabody School of Music. He won first prize in the Mitropoulos International Conducting Competition in New York in 1964 and then served as assistant conductor of the Metropolitan Opera until 1967, followed by two years as music director of the Westchester Symphony Orchestra and another year as guest conductor of the Phoenix Symphony Orchestra and then music director of the Austin Symphony Orchestra. In the 1970s and 1980s, he held positions as music director of the Oregon Symphony Orchestra and the San Antonio Symphony Orchestra, as well as making his guest appearances in North Carolina in 1980–1981. Smith became music director of the Louisville Orchestra and then taught in the conducting program at Yale.[21] In 1987 he traveled to Russia and shared the podium with Moscow Philharmonic conductor Dmitri Kitayenko. Smith's portion of the Moscow program included selections from Copland's *Appalachian Spring*, Gershwin's "Lullaby," and Charles Ives's "The Unanswered Question." Apparently he was the first American to conduct the Moscow Philharmonic, an event that led to recordings known as the Moscow Sessions. Smith also served as music director of the Colorado Springs orchestra and as guest conductor at others including the New Jersey Symphony Orchestra and the Indianapolis Symphony Orchestra. In addition to his career as a conductor, Smith often appeared as a pianist, particularly an accompanist. He died in 2013.[22]

When in the summer of 1981 the North Carolina Symphony Society's board of trustees decided to hire experienced conductor Patrick Flynn as the new artistic director/conductor, a firestorm of controversy erupted involving the musicians, the board, music critics, and the public. To find a principal conductor, the board—with Symphony Society president Nancy B. Faircloth, wife of future Republican United States senator Lauch Faircloth, as chairperson—had created a search committee. The musicians had no part in the selection process, which had fallen exclusively to the committee appointed by Faircloth. Outraged that they were not involved in choosing the next conductor as stipulated in the contract agreed upon by the board of trustees and their union, the musicians denounced Flynn's appointment. "It would be a direct and intolerable violation of the good faith agreement," they claimed when they first heard that Flynn might be their next conductor.[23] Apparently at least in part as a concession to the players, Flynn's contract was for a trial period of only one year.[24]

On July 2, the *News and Observer* reported that "Over the strong objections of orchestra members, the N.C. Symphony Board of Trustees voted unanimously ... to offer its conductor's position to Patrick Flynn." President Faircloth "said the decision was based on the recommendation of the trustees' conductor search committee," and Flynn's credentials were excellent. But Robert K. Anderson, double bassist and chairman of the musicians' collective bargaining committee, threatened, "It's very unlikely that we're going to start next season as scheduled."[25] Upon hearing of the new contract, the wife of one of the players wrote to the newspaper: "Readers who may be following the saga of the N.C. Symphony Board versus the symphony musicians should realize that the conflict involves more than just the hiring of a new conductor. The issue involves a state-supported organization whose board has cancelled a contract between management and its employees.... All of us employees in North Carolina should be wary of this situation." One society trustee, however, publicly defended the board's action in hiring Flynn, claiming that it was supported by some of the older, veteran players: "They're glad to see him lower the boom on some of these kids, who've been pretty well spoiled."[26]

"For a time," declared an Asheville editor in September 1981, "it appeared that the symphony might not have a season this year, but a compromise between the directors and the objecting musicians was reached. So Flynn is permanent guest conductor and not conductor and music director." The compromise resulted in the board's offer to Flynn of only a one-year commitment. When asked whether "in time the friction between him and some of the musicians will evaporate," Flynn answered:

No, probably not.

But it's not important. As long as they continue to produce beautiful sounds, I'll continue to conduct and that's what this business is all about.

When I was much younger I recall feeling hurt or offended if I discovered that a musician didn't like me. But that was a long time ago.

I am not disparaging the musicians in the orchestra. They are talented, skilled professionals. But they are very conservative people, too, most of them. And it is not at all unusual for some of the musicians in a symphony orchestra to want to get rid of their conductor. It happens to most conductors at one time or another.[27]

Patrick Flynn was born in Birmingham, England, in 1936. He studied piano at the Royal Academy of Music and received a Cassel Prize for his playing. His teachers included Sir John Barbirolli and Julius Katchen. In the 1960s, Flynn became an associate of the Royal College of Music in piano performance and, after serving in the army, received his licentiate in conducting from the Royal Academy of Music. He worked in New Zealand and then Australia. In 1970 he became conductor of the Australian Opera, a position he held until 1977, conducting performances of *The Tales of Hoffmann, Rigoletto,* and Bertolt Brecht's *Rise and Fall of the City of Mahagonny.* Other productions under his baton included *Hair, Jesus Christ Superstar,* and *Joseph and the Amazing Technicolor Dreamcoat.* Flynn left Australia for New York, where he worked as conductor with the American Ballet Theatre and the Dance Theatre of Harlem before coming to North Carolina.[28]

Under Flynn's direction, the North Carolina Symphony had played two pops concerts in the summer of 1981, one in Raleigh and the other in Fayetteville. With the musicians' displeasure over Flynn's hiring, even with the one-year contract, still evident, the orchestra formally opened its 1981 season at Raleigh's Memorial Auditorium on October 3, with Flynn conducting. By that time, critics and the public alike had taken sides in the dispute over his hiring, with some supporting the players and others backing Flynn and the society's decision to employ him. The musicians did not hesitate to express overtly their dislike of Flynn, his talent as a conductor, and the way he was selected. One critic panned the opening concert and Flynn's debut performance. Another writer rose to his defense, offering "My apologies to Mr. Flynn, and my regrets that some members of the orchestra, whose talents are abundant, as those of Mr. Flynn, allowed themselves to, unprofessionally, show anything but loyalty and total support to their conductor."[29] As the season progressed, the animosity between the two factions grew, with Flynn caught in the middle.

Simultaneously, severe financial problems continued to plague the orchestra, which was forced to cancel concerts and contracts with guest soloists. A number of patrons expressed anger and surprise at the dire fiscal straits in which the symphony found itself, and they accused the board of trustees of mismanaging the funds. Former board member Margot Richter expressed her displeasure in a letter to the *News and Observer* in September 1981.

The N.C. Symphony Society Board of Trustees is totally irresponsible. It has spent a large percentage of their $1 million Ford Foundation endowment on operating expenses.

The board has mismanaged the symphony and its funds. It has undermined the confidence of the people of North Carolina and the orchestra. It's obvious the board is not competent to continue managing the affairs of the symphony.

Secretary of Cultural Resources Sara Hodgkins stated ... that "the history of the N.C. Symphony Society fund-raising has been from crisis to crisis, rather than a systematic approach. But when you aren't paying people, you aren't in a position to criticize."

When tax money is involved, she has every right as a representative of the people of North Carolina to criticize and to see at least that the state's money is properly managed.

I was a member of the symphony society board for several years during the Ford Foundation grant. How would you like to work under the present conditions? The board can cancel the contract it signed today as fast as the last one.[30]

In another letter to the newspaper, a new arrival to North Carolina wrote of her disappointment at the cancellation of the appearances of guest soloists. "I speak," she declared, of the tricky shenanigans pulled off by the board of directors of the N.C. Symphony, namely the cancellation of most of the soloists scheduled to appear in the coming season.

My husband and I moved to Raleigh within the past year, not only to share in the lives of my son and his family, but also to partake in some of the culture expected of a capital city.

Having bought season tickets for the coming year to the N.C. Symphony's performances, we looked forward to attending. I must admit the featured soloists played a big part in our decision to join.

After reading that all the artists appearing in our chosen series were cancelled, it is now apparent to me why the symphony has had its problems and cannot generate any enthusiasm from local residents. Waiting until opening day to notify the ticket holders through the newspapers is not my idea of good business practice—surely not the kind that builds confidence with the public.[31]

To deal with the financial collapse and get the organization back on a sound operating basis, the Symphony Society decided to employ its first professional executive director, whose salary would be paid by the society. In early 1981, Henry Bowers of the board of trustees approached Thomas H. McGuire about taking that position, subsequently known as president and CEO. McGuire had the essential musical and business background for the job. Born in Georgia, he had studied music at UNC, where he received a PhD in 1975. Soon rejecting a career in teaching, he returned to UNC and earned an MBA. He started an employment service but shortly returned to music, joining the American Symphony Orchestra League. In 1978 the Arkansas Symphony Orchestra hired him as its executive director. McGuire welcomed the chance to return to North Carolina and work for a larger orchestra. He accepted the society's offer, which followed his interview with board members Bowers and Banks Talley, Jr., as well as conductor Flynn.

Thomas H. McGuire became the North Carolina Symphony's first executive director (later designated president and CEO) in 1981 and served until 1984 (courtesy A. J. Fletcher Foundation).

In cooperation with the board of trustees and Chairperson Faircloth, McGuire undertook the task of putting the orchestra back on sound financial footing.[32] It was obvious to everyone involved that the task of getting out of debt and establishing a firm fiscal foundation would not be quick or easy. The immediate challenge was severe enough that "in the fall of 1981, management locked the players out for four weeks. Almost immediately the orchestra lost 11 musicians, bringing the roster down from 73 to 62 full-time players. And so began the long, arduous process of rebuilding the financial base of the organization, and the *esprit de corps* of the players."[33]

Amid its fiscal woes, the Symphony Society's board still had to deal with the growing conflict between the musicians and the conductor. When Flynn's contract expired in the spring of 1982, the board decided not to renew the agreement and instead to hire another candidate as artistic director/conductor. News of that decision ignited a firestorm of protest from supporters of Flynn, who felt that his artistic sensibilities and his ability as a conductor made him the right choice for the job, and that he had been unfairly maligned by the musicians, specifically six members of the orchestra. Longtime patrons who had been disappointed at how the board dealt with former music director Benjamin Swalin in the early 1970s perceived a parallel and felt particularly angry at Flynn's fate. They pointed out that under his leadership the orchestra had sounded especially good, and that his astute programming and use of local and regional solo artists had helped the symphony begin to recover from its financial distress.

The decision not to renew Flynn's contract led to public demonstrations of unhappiness with the board, its leadership, and its perceived lack of artistic vision. Pickets in downtown Raleigh called for the board to "Fire McGuire" and "Keep Flynn In." A local radio talk-show host who approved of the conductor broadcast discussions about the controversy. A representative of the Raleigh Oratorio Society, which had worked with Flynn, and a former program director of the Friends of the College, which had hired the orchestra for its series, wrote letters and met with Nancy Faircloth to express their unhappiness. Among the well-established symphony supporters who joined the public protests were subscribers and donors Albert and Susan Jenkins.[34]

One disgruntled symphony enthusiast and Flynn defender wrote to the Raleigh press:

> Apparently the symphony players have again got their way.
>
> I am speaking about the rejection of Principal Guest Conductor Patrick Flynn in the search for a permanent conductor for the symphony. Though many North Carolina concert-goers may be puzzled by this untoward event, we may well ask ourselves why we have allowed this to happen.
>
> Is it possible that New York, London and Paris can acknowledge Flynn's superb musicianship and North Carolina cannot? Anyone present at his concerts this year no doubt came away exhilarated, but perhaps we witnesses remained silent when we should have spread the word.
>
> Spreading the word takes time, and Flynn was given only one year for us laggards to sit up and shout. This is unfair.
>
> Why, after we lured him here, have we treated Flynn as so much flotsam swept up on our shores only to be swept out again? The message in the bottle is that we could have had something rarer than gold, had we picked up our ears.[35]

Another enraged protest came from John W. Lambert, a local music critic and theretofore strong supporter of the symphony, who wrote a blistering letter to President Faircloth attacking her for her role in the dismissal of Flynn and calling for her to resign. He also wrote a heated discourse to members of the state legislature denouncing Faircloth and McGuire and requesting that the lawmakers cease to allocate state funds for the symphony.[36]

In interviews with the *Raleigh Times*, Flynn himself described how he had been badly treated by a "half-dozen or so" players who "did such things as run poison-pen ads against him in the personals section of the Spectator, a weekly newspaper; snickered during a concert in which he played a piano solo; and made 'vomiting noises outside my dressing room.'" He accused those "just plain sickos" of attempting "to damage his professional reputation and discredit him by giving false information to Billboard and Variety, the leading music trade publications, and by contacting his agent and the American Ballet Theatre, his chief contract employer, saying that the musicians would not play for Flynn." He felt that the musicians' attacks on him had "damaged my career rather badly. The appearance is that I did one year here in North Carolina, that it didn't work out and that I was fired." He said that "Of course, I'm angry and in many ways bitter." But "I've had far more success as a conductor than this orchestra has had as an orchestra.... I've put programs in this year which have in fact tripled sales. The receipts are there if anyone cares to look. I have had many, many people—critics and others who know music—say to me this orchestra has never sounded better." He admitted, however, that he "was never in the running" for an extended contract with the symphony, and he "took the job as principal guest conductor with the understanding that he wouldn't accept a permanent job, even if it were offered, as long as the musicians remained opposed to him."[37]

In rebuttal of Flynn's claims of mistreatment by the musicians, Ronald Weddle, spokesman for the Orchestra Committee, explained the players' version of the controversy to the Raleigh press. "It's unfortunate that (Flynn) has chosen to do this sort of thing," he said. "It's a classic case of sour grapes." He maintained that the only one of Flynn's charges against the musicians that was true was that of placing advertisements in the *Spectator* ridiculing and criticizing the conductor. And "As soon as the leadership of the orchestra found out about it, it was stopped. The orchestra immediately apologized to Patrick and to (board chairman) Nancy Faircloth about that." Furthermore, "If a childish prank like that, running limericks in a classified ad section, can ruin his career, he doesn't have much of a career to ruin." Weddle regretted that "there were a few people who pulled pranks ... but the fact that Patrick was found unacceptable was a professional judgment by the musicians totally apart from that." In fact, he insisted, "If Patrick was able to achieve on the podium (as conductor) the same kind of success he's had in public relations—

in keeping the orchestra in the public eye—we would have been glad to have made him music director."

Instead, the players in secret ballot had voted 59 to 0, with several abstaining, against retaining Flynn as artistic director/conductor. According to Weddle, the musicians did not like some of Flynn's interpretations of musical selections and the fact that on occasions he publicly criticized and belittled the orchestra. They also considered him egotistical and too self-promoting, feeling that "Patrick Flynn is a lot more concerned about selling Patrick Flynn than he is about this orchestra." They did not, however, deny his talent. "Nobody has ever said that he was untalented," admitted Weddle. "What we have said is that he is not the right person for this orchestra. His inconsistency, the way he contradicts himself, carried through in all of his efforts, including his conducting…. What this orchestra needs is someone who is extremely sound and consistent, someone who has an organized approach."[38]

With accusations and rancor flung back and forth, Flynn's year with the symphony came to an end. Around mid–April 1982, he acknowledged that he was sure his contract would not be renewed and withdrew "his own name from consideration because he did not expect to be approved by the musicians, who have the authority to veto the board's selection."[39] His last formal concert in Raleigh took place at Memorial Auditorium on April 24. According to critic John W. Lambert, the program was a "stately performance" of Brahms's *A German Requiem*, Op. 45. Flynn "was assisted by two fine young soloists, soprano Nina Kay Lowe and baritone Bruce Hall, and by the Raleigh Oratorio Society, which had been carefully prepared by Director James M. Marshall. The performance was the fulfillment of a year-old agreement between the Symphony and the Oratorio Society; this event had been scheduled for last spring but fell victim to the budget-cutting axe which was wielded then. Heard now under Maestro Flynn's inspired direction," the soloists were superb, and "The orchestra played as if its life depended on it and sounded even better than it has under other, less inspired circumstances. The audience sensed that this was a very special event and rewarded the performers with a well-deserved standing ovation." Lambert continued with praise for Flynn:

> The reason for this sublime musicianship is not hard to comprehend; it is to Principal Guest Conductor Patrick Flynn and to him alone that credit for the unity, cohesiveness, and overall superlative playing heard in his concerts this year must be given, and this final, formal Raleigh performance of the 1981–82 season was a perfect example of this artistry. To the very end, his graciousness and self-effacingness have been pronounced; all season long Flynn has consistently deferred to the orchestra, rarely bowing on his own, always insisting that the musicians share the applause with him, and his response to the standing ovation reflected no exception to this policy.

The Raleigh concert was followed by the orchestra's last formal performances under Flynn's baton in Kinston on April 27 and then in Charlotte. The program consisted of music by Gershwin and featured Flynn himself as piano soloist in *Rhapsody in Blue*. "Thus ended," concluded Lambert, "another chapter in the checkered history of the North Carolina Symphony. What happens from here on out will depend upon the public, the board, and the musicians—not necessarily in that order."[40] The season's last concert without Flynn at the podium was a performance on May 5 at the Thomas Wolfe Auditorium in Asheville led by principal pops conductor Eric Knight. It featured "arrangements of familiar songs with titles which play on the words 'knight' or 'night.'"[41]

The players' complaints about Flynn did follow him after his departure from North Carolina and impede his professional work. However, he ultimately served successful tenures with orchestras in Pueblo, Colorado; Lubbock, Texas; Riverside County, California; and Saginaw Bay, Michigan. Before his sudden death in 2008, he could look back on an illustrious career of work with the BBC, the Paris Opera, the Spoleto and Varna international festivals, and various symphonies and dance companies in Europe and South America as well as the United States, New Zealand, and Australia. He composed scores for documentaries, television, and films. Critics have called him "the complete conductor, the podium equivalent of a polymath," "a masterly artist ... a conductor to treasure," and "a bizarre conductor of enormous talent."[42]

The person chosen to become the next artistic director/conductor of the North Carolina Symphony was Gerhardt Zimmermann, who for the past several years had been first assistant conductor and then associate conductor of the St. Louis Symphony. He was born in Van Wert, Ohio, in 1945. He adopted the trumpet as his instrument of choice and received a bachelor of music degree from Bowling Green State University and a master of fine arts in musical conducting from the University of Iowa. His most influential teacher at Iowa was James Dixon, whom Zimmermann later credited with teaching him much about the composition, pacing, and tempo of musical scores, as well as conducting. He was especially impressed with Dixon's conducting of Mahler, a composer for whom Zimmermann had a special affinity, and whom he often featured in concerts. Zimmermann first taught music in public schools in Ohio and then conducted the orchestra of Augustana College in Rock Island, Illinois, and the Clinton Symphony Orchestra in Iowa. He went on to become assistant professor of music and conductor of the university orchestra at Western Illinois University before joining the St. Louis Symphony. In April 1973, he shared the second-place prize in the Georg Solti Competition for conductors in Chicago. Solti was music director of the Chicago Symphony Orchestra.[43]

Zimmermann signed a one-year contract with the North Carolina Symphony with an option to renew, and he retained an existing position as conductor of the Canton, Ohio, Symphony, directing both orchestras. In publicly

Gerhardt Zimmermann led the symphony as artistic director/conductor from 1982 until 2003 (photograph by Michael Zirkle, courtesy North Carolina Symphony).

announcing his appointment on May 3, 1982, chairperson Nancy Faircloth noted—with understatement—that "The search at times has been rocky." She told the press that "the board chose Zimmermann about two weeks ago, but an annou[n]cement was delayed because it was difficult to communicate with him while he was on tour," and that "she didn't know when Zimmermann would begin work, but he would be in North Carolina long before the symphony's season-opening concert on Sept. 16." The *Asheville Citizen-Times* reminded its readers that "The North Carolina Symphony has been plagued by financial problems, a 1980 strike and opposition among many musicians on 'artistic grounds' to principal guest conductor Patrick Flynn. But musicians' representatives, who participated in the search for a permanent conductor, said ... they were 'delighted' with the selection of Zimmermann."[44]

Zimmermann's first concerts in North Carolina met with general critical approval. His initial appearances were programs in celebration of the orchestra's fiftieth anniversary of its original performance in 1932. The anniversary concerts featured the same music that had been played fifty years earlier, and Benjamin Swalin was invited to conduct part of the program. The main commemorative concert took place in Raleigh on September 16, but it was preceded by the same program in Greensboro a week earlier in an attempt to make the concert available to a wider audience. A humorous episode occurred onstage in Greensboro just before the orchestra began to play. Swalin forgot that he was not supposed to be first to conduct on the program, and confusion ensued. Principal clarinetist Jimmy Gilmore later described the incident.

> Before the program started, Gerhardt [Zimmermann] was waiting in the wings chatting with Dr. Swalin. After the "A" sounded, Gerhardt straightened his tie and prepared to walk onstage. Suddenly, before he could take a step, Doc [the musicians' nickname for Swalin] was on stage, headed for the podium. Gerhardt cried out desperately, "Ben, come back!," "Ben, come back!" But Ben ... kept walking to the podium. Doc bowed genteelly to the audience and turned to a completely stupefied orchestra. He was all set to conduct the Beethoven "Symphony No. 1," but the orchestra was ready to play "Rienzi Overture" by Wagner. There was a pause, and then, as if on signal, there were musicians scurrying all over the stage trying to set up for the Beethoven. Doc calmly waited for things to settle down and gave the down beat. Everyone played the Symphony as if nothing had happened. However, some in the audience were left to ponder how amazing it was that a composition listed in the program as Wagner could sound so much like Beethoven.

The new conductor made light of the awkward situation. Maxine Swalin later recalled that "Before conducting the overture, Mr. Zimmermann announced in a casual way that 'tonight, the overture follows rather than precedes the symphony.'"[45]

On September 15, the orchestra played the same program at UNC's Memorial Hall, this time in the proper order. Critic Jeff Grove described the performance.

> Zimmermann began the evening with a scintillating reading of the overture to Wagner's early opera *Rienzi*. The conductor took advantage of the work's general grand-opera style, but also allowed mellower moments to come through.
>
> Benjamin Swalin, the Symphony's conductor from 1939 to 1971, took over the helm for Beethoven's *Symphony No. 1 in C major*, opus 21. Beethoven's first outing in symphonic writing is modeled on the work of Mozart and Haydn, but underneath the conventional is something new begging to be set free. The 81-year-old conductor let that something loose with a youthful aplomb seldom matched by conductors half his age.
>
> After intermission, Herbert Hazelman's *Danse Moronique* brought comic relief to

the program. Hazelman, an oboist in the original N.C. Symphony, was on hand to lead the work. He received generous applause for his early but polished composition.

Zimmermann returned to conduct "La Media Noche," a serenade forming the second movement of Albert Stoessel's suite *Hispania*. It did not sound like a serenade at times, when the basses pounded out the tango accompaniment too loudly, but the overall effect saw the violins' contribution shine anyway.

Zimmermann next conducted Borodin's *In the Steppes of Central Asia* in a performance marred somewhat by the violins' inability to agree on the exact pitch of their sustained high notes.

Swalin rounded out the official program with Tchaikovsky's eloquent miniature tone poem, *Marche Slave*, opus 31. His poignant reading drew a standing ovation from the audience, which had already given Swalin one ovation earlier in the concert.

Zimmermann then led three encores—a trio of Dvorak's *Slavonic Dances*—for a fiery ending that earned Zimmermann his own standing ovation.

Wednesday's sold-out and passionate performance indicated that Zimmermann's tenure probably will pay off handsomely for the N.C. Symphony.[46]

Zimmermann followed the fiftieth anniversary commemorations with concerts earning other favorable reviews. Critic David McHugh gave the following complimentary assessment of the symphony's performance of Beethoven's Ninth Symphony in Raleigh's Memorial Auditorium on October 20.

> You can't miss with Beethoven's Ninth Symphony; no matter how badly you play it, people still stand up and yell....
>
> But if an indifferent performance pleases, a good one thrills, and Gerhardt Zimmermann and the North Carolina Symphony gave a good performance Wednesday night in Memorial Auditorium.
>
> The Ninth is difficult to conduct, requiring a large orchestra, four soloists and a big choir. And the more performers, the more things can go wrong. Just getting everything balanced and cued in at the right time is a headache.
>
> But Zimmermann, whose affinity for Mahler and Strauss equips him perfectly for such tasks, handled the details with aplomb.
>
> Control and discipline marked the entire performance, and the orchestra sounded unusually well-rehearsed. Tempo choice was appropriate throughout, especially in the Adagio, which must be played very slowly but not be allowed to slacken musically. Zimmermann's tight control of phrasing kept the long, slow melodic lines taut and vital.
>
> The string playing sounded rich and polished, most noticeably in the low strings. The violins played crisply, even in the tricky second movement. Entrances were sharp, and the sound thick with vibrato.
>
> But Zimmermann did more than just direct traffic. His conducting showed warmth and good humor, over and above technical polish. This symphony is filled with large gestures, like the thundering timpani in the second movement and the repeated anticlimaxes of the last movement. Zimmermann made the most of them, letting the timpani hammer away fortississimo and exaggerating the dramatic pause before the bassoon drolly heralds a march-like parody of the last movement's main theme.
>
> The singing was at least adequate in all respects, and occasionally very good.

McHugh found some flaws in the concert. "But nothing could spoil the evening's primary revelation: Gerhardt Zimmermann, in his short tenure, has already gone a long way toward molding the North Carolina Symphony into a respectable, professional-sounding orchestra."[47]

A few days later, Zimmermann conducted the symphony in an "all–Beethoven concert" in Asheville, where "The highlight of the program was the Beethoven Ninth Symphony, in which the director and orchestra achieved a perfection that would be hard to surpass. The four soloists and three Asheville-area choruses united with director and orchestra in a performance that delighted the most appreciative audience."[48]

Zimmermann continued to enjoy success and favorable reviews in North Carolina, and after the initial one-year commitment, the symphony consistently renewed his contracts until his retirement in 2003. With twenty-one years at the helm of the orchestra as artistic director/conductor, he has served the longest term to date since the Swalin era. During his tour, the orchestra maintained its fundamental mission of taking music to the state's schoolchildren through its Little Symphony program.

In the early 1980s, Adeline McCall retired as director of education. In her final months, she worked closely with Jackson Parkhurst. Parkhurst had been an assistant conductor under Swalin and then returned in 1980 to revitalize the children's program and serve as Zimmermann's assistant conductor after Ogle departed. Both business manager Hiram Black and the musicians welcomed his return. Parkhurst instigated, wrote, and produced the symphony's Saturday morning Young People's Series concerts. He also founded the Brevard Chamber Orchestra and helped establish the Lexington Park String Ensemble. As a member of the Brevard Music Center staff, he conducted its Repertory Training Orchestra and coordinated its educational programs. Parkhurst served as a guest conductor in Iowa, New York, South Carolina, and Massachusetts. For two years, he was chairman of the education committee for the American Symphony Orchestra League. His work expanded to embrace social activism, including such projects as a series of concerts in support of the AIDS ministry at Raleigh's Christ Episcopal Church. Because of health problems, he retired from the symphony in 1998. In 2006 principal clarinetist Gilmore said of him: "His 18-year tenure as Director of Education was a benchmark of quality, integrity, and passion for the mission. To this day, he is a dear friend of the orchestra."[49]

For its 1983–1984 season, the symphony scheduled Zimmermann to conduct such accomplished guest artists as violinists Charles Treger and Eugene Fodor, violist Sol Greitzer, mezzo-soprano Donna Banks Dease, and percussionist John Kasica. Zimmermann's concert selections included *American Symphonette* No. 2 by Morton Gould, Berlioz's *Symphonie Fantastique*, Howard Hanson's Elegy for Orchestra, Dvořák's Symphony No. 7, Messiaen's *L'Ascension*, and Beethoven's Symphony No. 7. The season's program announced that associate conductor James Ogle and principal pops conductor Eric

Knight would lead pops concerts, and the orchestra would play for the *Nutcracker* ballet, the Young People's Series, "a season-long celebration of Brahms' 150th birthday, the magnificent Verdi *Requiem* [with the combined Durham Civic Choral Society and the Carolina Choir], an evening with jazz legend Oscar Peterson ... and much more."[50] The Saturday morning Young People's Series, led by Parkhurst in Raleigh's Memorial Auditorium, included "Visions of Sugarplums," a November 26 program of carol sing-alongs with the orchestra; "Meet the Orchestra" on February 18, a performance of Benjamin Britten's introduction to musical instruments with an appearance by actor Ira David Wood III as Sir Oswald Pangbourn Fairfax, a character portrayed as the oldest living conductor; and, on April 14, a production of Prokofiev's *Peter and the Wolf*, "choreographed by Ann Vorus [Parkhurst's wife] and Antonia Beh, and performed by some of the area's most talented young dancers."[51] Columnist Nell Hirschberg of the *News and Observer* wrote about one of Parkhurst's concerts: "From the moment Parkhurst burst onto the stage and struck up the band ... he turned on a sparkling performance of words, wit, dance and music.... What a wonderful way to learn about music."[52]

Like other music directors, Zimmermann appeared as guest conductor at a number of orchestras during his years with the North Carolina Symphony, and he usually received high praise from local critics. In July of 1983, for instance, John von Rhein, music critic for the *Chicago Tribune*, said of his success in summer concerts in Chicago's Grant Park:

> There are many worse places at which to renew old acquaintances and start new ones than Grant Park on a cool summer evening.
>
> Wednesday night's concert, for example, brought two Petrillo Music Shell debuts, that of conductor Gerhardt Zimmermann and pianist Detlef Kraus. Some will recall Zimmermann as having appeared briefly in Chicago a little more than 10 years ago as one of the podium hopefuls in the Solti conductors competition later won by Guido Ajmone-Marsan. Losing that contest apparently did not hinder his career progress, for he went on to become assistant conductor of the St. Louis Symphony for five years. He now directs the orchestras of North Carolina and Canton, Ohio.
>
> To judge by the quality of his initial Grant Park Symphony program, Zimmermann is one of the better talents at work on the regional American orchestra scene. He wields his baton with an authority that never seems willfully imposed on the players or the music. Everything is clear, controlled and flexible under him. There is a productive sense of give-and-take. He has good musical ideas and he carries them out with conviction. More than that one cannot expect of a first-timer under the rigid rehearsal conditions that govern such concerts.[53]

Guest conducting appearances with the American, Cleveland, Atlanta, Pittsburgh, Columbus, Long Beach, and Phoenix symphonies followed. In the 1990s, Zimmermann again conducted the Chicago Symphony, as well as André Watts and the National Symphony in an all-Beethoven festival at the Kennedy Center. The *Washington Post* said of his performance with the

National Symphony: "One of the marvels of Maestro Zimmermann's baton was the subtlety of the rubato. When tempos fluctuated, they did so naturally, almost imperceptibly. The full power of the National Symphony Orchestra— a sound Beethoven never heard in his lifetime but surely longed for with all of his soul—arrived gravely, magnificently under Maestro Zimmermann's guidance." He also recorded three violin concertos with the Warsaw Philharmonic in Poland.[54]

Zimmermann brought a new focus to the North Carolina Symphony in style and ensemble. He emphasized the German repertoire influenced by Haydn, Mozart, Strauss, and Mahler and scheduled large, demanding programs that called for extra musicians. He also introduced new works by contemporary composers, which did not please all the orchestra's ticket holders, some of whom found departure from the old masters too innovative.[55] He countered that "The problem with new music is the same as in Beethoven's day. People living then did not enjoy hearing Beethoven's symphonies premiered. People are afraid of something new and different. But this is not a dead music and it is important to program some music from our times."[56]

Financial stringency and recovery placed some restrictions on the number and nature of the concerts, and staying out of debt remained a persistent problem for the symphony. In 1984 Thomas McGuire left to take a position as director of the new A. J. Fletcher Foundation. His successor as the orchestra's executive director was Banks C. Talley, Jr. Talley had just retired as vice chancellor for student affairs at North Carolina State University, where he had worked for thirty-three years and been active in the establishment and promotion of the Friends of the College series, the university theaters, the Craft Center, and the Gregg Museum of Art. In 1977 he had taken a leave of absence from the university to become chief of staff for Governor James B. Hunt, Jr., and in 1983 to serve as executive vice president of the National Trust for Historic Preservation in Washington, D.C. Throughout his eleven years as the symphony's executive director, he labored to establish and maintain an endowment and a sound fiscal footing for the orchestra. Talley at times faced difficult

Banks Talley, Jr., CEO of the North Carolina Symphony from 1984 to 1995 (photograph from 1995, courtesy State Archives of North Carolina).

economic cutbacks and downturns, such as when he had to announce in 1990 that the Symphony Society had a deficit of $1.2 million.[57]

But in that same year, Memorial Auditorium underwent a second and major overhaul at a cost of $9 million, funded by $7 million resulting from a voter referendum and $2 million from the state. The auditorium required extensive renovations to meet the needs of the symphony and the North Carolina Theatre, which also staged its productions there. "Specifically, the building was dilapidated, the stage was vaudevillian, sound and lighting systems were inadequate, and the public spaces and restrooms were incapable of handling the demands placed on them by the public during performances." Except for a leaking roof, the edifice was in sound condition structurally. The architectural firm Haskins, Rice, Savage & Pearce received the contract to design and supervise the alterations. "Due to the immediate needs of the symphony for rehearsal space, a $3.5 million stage-house addition, with an acoustically correct rehearsal hall wrapped around the existing stage, was designed and built. The initial work allowed for permanent symphony rehearsal space while construction was underway to renovate the existing auditorium."

The renovations included expanding the public lobby "by adding a grand front lobby with a contemporary glass atrium surrounded by a Doric-columned pavilion of the same limestone material and Neo-classical style of the existing building." A grand staircase and balcony enlarged the small upper lobby, and a skylight was placed between the new addition and the old façade. "The other existing lobbies were visually enlarged by opening them up to adjacent spaces and adding lighting and classical detailing to the ceilings. The existing restrooms, grossly inadequate, were renovated, and new restrooms were added, virtually tripling the number of facilities for both men and women." Workmen gutted the main auditorium and removed the crumbling plaster ceiling. "A new gypsum wallboard ceiling with fiberglass coffered beams, acoustical panels, and plaster tiles replaced the old ceiling at a higher elevation to improve the hall's reverberation time from 1.4 seconds to a more symphonic time of 1.7 seconds. Both the new ceiling and proscenium were acoustically designed to optimize the space for the particular sound of the North Carolina symphony." The North Carolina Theatre received a new sound system, which permitted the theater to make greater use of "the space for Broadway plays even though the hall is tuned to symphonic music. In addition, a major renovation to the existing stage rigging, lighting, and dimming system was completed to accommodate the most elaborate sets available for 'truck-and-bus' Broadway plays." The newly renovated building garnered accolades for its design and aesthetics from the public and design experts alike. Haskins, Rice, Savage & Pearce won first place for rehabilitation/restoration in the 1991 Renovation Awards competition sponsored by the publication *Commercial Renovation*.[58]

Under the direction of Zimmermann, the symphony made its second appearance at New York's Carnegie Hall. On October 4, 1987, the orchestra performed works by composer Robert Ward, honoring him on his seventieth birthday. The selections included the revised Symphony No. 4 and excerpts from the operas *Minutes Till Midnight* and *The Lady from Colorado*. The soloists were saxophonist James Houlik, mezzo-soprano Victoria Livengood, and baritone Eugene Perry. Ward conducted the vocal part of the program. The composer had strong ties to North Carolina. He was born in Cleveland, Ohio, in 1917; received a bachelor's degree from the Eastman School of Music in Rochester, New York; and studied with composer Howard Hanson and with Aaron Copland at Tanglewood. In the 1950s, he was music director of the Third Street Music School Settlement in New York. In 1967 he took a position as president, then chancellor, of the North Carolina School of the Arts. He later joined the faculty at Duke University, where he stayed for many years and helped start an opera company. His best-known work, an operatic setting for Arthur Miller's *The Crucible*, won a Pulitzer Prize in 1962. Ward died at his Durham home in April 2013.[59]

The symphony's trip to Carnegie Hall for Ward's birthday was not the same type of expensive and elaborate extravaganza that its debut there in the 1970s had been. In an effort to limit expenditures and adhere to a tight budget, the orchestra traveled to New York and back the same day. Prior to the New York event, the orchestra had celebrated Ward's birthday with a concert in Dana Auditorium at Queens College in Charlotte on September 23. After the New York visit, it did so again in Page Auditorium at Duke University on October 7.[60]

The decade of the 1980s was also marked by the debut of the orchestra's Pops in the Park outdoor Labor Day concerts. With financial support, and television and radio coverage, provided by Capitol Broadcasting Company, the annual performances drew large crowds to Raleigh's Pullen Park in 1981 and to the Meredith College campus thereafter. The audiences continued to grow, and by the year 2000, an estimated 40,000 people attended Pops in the Park.

Encouraged by the success of the Labor Day performances, a committee of musicians instigated Summerfest, a yearly series of outdoor concerts. According to principal clarinetist Gilmore, "Our first proposal to the Board in 1983 fell flat. No one wanted to sign on for what seemed a potentially risky enterprise after so much recent financial trouble. In 1984 we made the Board an offer they couldn't refuse: let us use the music from the Symphony library, the truck, the stands and chairs and we will handle the rest. The musicians agreed to play and be paid for an equal share of the money we received at the gate. Mr. Zimmermann, when asked by the board what he thought of the project said, 'You have a group of musicians who are willing to play for free.

You would be crazy not to take them up on it!' Because of his endorsement and with no obligation to pay salary and benefits, the Symphony Society agreed to let us proceed." The first series of four concerts took place at Meredith, after the musician committee "lined up the orchestra, named the series *Summerfest*, organized programs and repertoire, arranged for a sound system, booked sponsors, and handled the myriad details involved in producing a full-scale outdoor event." In 1986 Edward Woolner, developer of Cary's Regency Park, provided the summer concerts a permanent venue there. The Koka Booth Amphitheatre was completed with a permanent pavilion in 2001, and the orchestra continues to play to large crowds at the park every summer.[61]

Despite the financial strain that often challenged the North Carolina Symphony in the 1980s and 1990s, it seemed somehow to find enough funds, and its concert seasons, with well-known guest artists, expanded. A constant throughout Zimmermann's tenure was his friend and frequent solo collaborator pianist André Watts. Among the memorable concerts were evenings of Mahler's music (a favorite of Zimmermann), during which the late-romantic master's large scores were presented in the region, many for the first time. Among the best were Mahler's *Kindertotenlieder*, with mezzo-soprano Donna Dease, in 1983; a stunning Symphony No. 5, the *Resurrection* Symphony, played three times in 1985; and the massive Symphony No. 8, the *Symphony of a Thousand*, in 1989. Other memorable large scores included Shostakovich's *Leningrad* Symphony in 1995 and his Symphony No. 5 in 2001.

The orchestra acquired a significant asset with the arrival of its first African American associate conductor, William Henry Curry, in 1996. He replaced Michael Jinbo, who had held the position of assistant conductor for four seasons. Curry was born in Pittsburgh in 1954. Along with his brother, who became a cellist, he developed an early interest in classical music as a violist, and he first conducted at the age of fourteen. He studied conducting at Oberlin Conservatory but left in 1975 to accept a position as assistant conductor with the Richmond Symphony Chamber Orchestra and then the Richmond Symphony Orchestra. He went on to become resident conductor of the Baltimore Symphony and then the St. Paul Chamber Orchestra. While in the latter position, he became associate conductor of the Indianapolis Symphony, serving there from 1983 to 1988. In 1988 Curry won the Leopold Stokowski Conducting Competition and performed in Carnegie Hall. He subsequently conducted for the tour of Anthony Davis's opera *X: The Life and Times of Malcolm X* and a stage production of *The Mother of Three Sons*, by Leroy Jenkins. Curry made a professional recording of *X* that was nominated for a Grammy award. In 1990 he accepted an appointment as resident conductor of the New Orleans Symphony, before joining the North Carolina Symphony as associate conductor six years later. Curry conducted the orchestra numerous times in its classical series but became perhaps best known and most popular for his effective direction of Summerfest, of which he became artistic director. Curry also took the podium as music director/conductor of the Durham Symphony in 2009, a position he has continued to hold since his retirement from the North Carolina Symphony in 2016. His successors were associate conductors David Glover and then Wesley Schulz.

While with the North Carolina Symphony, Curry acquired the title "resident conductor," a distinction that was retired at the time of his departure. His last concert as resident conductor with the state orchestra was a Sunday performance in New Bern in the spring of 2016, which was preceded by concerts in Raleigh and Chapel Hill. The program featured Tchaikovsky's Fifth Symphony and Curry's own composition "Eulogy for a Dream." Announcing his retirement from the symphony, he reminisced that "My 20-year tenure with the North Carolina Symphony included some of the most satisfying experiences of my life. My musical collaborations with this world-class and personable orchestra were inspired by the joy of music. For those happy 20 years, my gratitude knows no bounds. My audiences appreciated the best of my efforts and the NCS administration was supportive of my desire to

In 1996 William Henry Curry became associate conductor of the North Carolina Symphony—the first African American to hold that position and the only associate conductor to receive the title of resident conductor (photograph by Michael Zirkle, courtesy North Carolina Symphony).

broaden the orchestra's repertoire." He specifically referred to symphonies by Sibelius, Bruckner, Liszt, and Tchaikovsky.

During his long career, Curry has appeared as guest conductor with numerous orchestras in the United States and abroad. At the invitation of the United States Department of State, he spent three weeks in Taiwan in the fall of 2009 teaching master classes and leading concerts of American music.[62] As the first and only African American associate, and then resident, conductor of the North Carolina Symphony, he remembers with pride his career in classical music, despite having been rejected for certain positions because of his race. He once said that as a black artist, "There are a lot of sacrifices that I have made. Go to the North Carolina Symphony. Look in the orchestra. Are there any black people there besides me? The answer is no. Look in the audience[.] [A]re there any black people besides me? Two? I am estranged from my people by having chosen this career.... So if you go into this as a black person be prepared to be by yourself in a sense."[63]

Nevertheless, Curry's appointment as a distinguished African American artist with a southern orchestra helped support a call for diversity and equality in the field of classical music. That he remained with the North Carolina Symphony for twenty years is likewise significant. His passions include romantic music by Tchaikovsky and Rachmaninoff as well as American scores by Copland, Ives, and others. Curry brought many new listeners to music and the symphony during his years as artistic director/conductor of Summerfest. He became one of the orchestra's most popular conductors, earning the admiration and affection of both the musicians and the public. As resident conductor, he actually lived in Raleigh and engaged with the community, giving presentations at local bookstores, participating in panel discussions, teaching privately and at William Peace University, and conducting youth orchestras. Curry is also a composer, and several of his works have been performed in North Carolina to favorable reviews. As music director of the Durham Symphony, he continues to lead full seasons as well as recurring programs celebrating Martin Luther King, Jr. Day.

During the recovery and expansion period of the late Zimmermann years, the orchestra finally acquired a respectable concert venue exclusively its own, which came to be called Meymandi Concert Hall. When the hall opened in a wing on the west side of Raleigh's Memorial Auditorium in February 2001, it displayed a "shoe box design (the walls slightly asymmetric for acoustical purposes)." That and "its modest capacity (1,700 seats, 1,550 if singers occupy the gallery behind the stage) reconfigure the intersection of public place and intimate exchange that was largely lost in the wave of gigantism that swept theater building a century ago." For years the symphony had endured the bad acoustics of the cavernous Memorial Auditorium, in which the 2,300 seats were seldom filled. Unlike its predecessor, the Meymandi facility "is not a multipurpose hall. There is no proscenium; the orchestra stage seems to reach out into the audience. What people see has a great effect on how they hear, and there is here the sense of openness and social contact." Lawrence Kirkegaard & Associates designed the acoustical qualities. As a result, there "is a warm and living sound environment. One hears the orchestra's constituents individually and clearly." That firm had recently planned the sound attributes for Ozawa Hall at the Tanglewood Music Center in Massachusetts, Carnegie Hall in New York, and Orchestra Hall in Chicago.

Architects Irvin Pearce, Jeffrey Lee, and David Francis (of the firm of Pearce Brinkley Cease + Lee) successfully blended the Meymandi wing and the new east wing, housing the 600-seat A. J. Fletcher Opera Theater, with the central auditorium, characterized by its Doric façade. The result was "three theaters together with a connecting gallery of glass walls and the Indiana limestone used on the original building." The complex was designed to be suitable for hosting Broadway shows. One approving observer declared that "The Meymandi Concert Hall is a 21st-century rebirth of an early 19th-century theater, the kind of space for which so much of the symphonic repertory was intended and where it thrives. Ambitious cultural planners for American cities are advised to put delusions of civic grandeur aside, come down to Raleigh and have a look."[64]

The symphony's musicians expressed their delight with the acoustics of the new facility. "In the new hall we can move to a new level," said principal horn player Andrew McAfee. "In a sense, we have been playing only for the audience until now. In Meymandi, we can begin playing for ourselves as well. We will be able to communicate more intimately with each other and greatly improve the final product." Timpanist John Fedderson noted that "In Memorial, I often have to rein in the force of my playing or, alternatively, overcompensate to be heard. In Meymandi, we can start playing as we are trained to do. We can begin to play comfortably within the scale of each piece." Conductor Zimmermann anticipated considerable improvement in the clarity of certain compositions. "The articulation in Bach, Haydn and Rossini does not come through in Memorial. I want to have the intimacy and clarity of chamber music, even in [the] biggest sections of Mahler or Shostakovich." Furthermore, in the new facility, he wanted to "do some concert operas that feature the orchestra—'Turandot,' 'Rosenkavalier,' 'Salome.' I would love to do works that have theatricality—Berlioz's 'Lelio,' which has a narrator[,] or Corigliano's Promenade Overture, in which the players walk in one by one to join the orchestra." He also wanted to revisit choral works such as Mahler's Eighth Symphony and the Berlioz *Requiem* and *Te Deum*. Associate conductor William Curry thought that "the new hall will give the orchestra a boost in self-esteem as the musicians begin hearing themselves in a better way, pushing them to greater heights."

However, the three-part complex—originally named the BTI Center for the Performing Arts and now the Duke Energy Center for the Performing Arts—did not come cheap. It was completed at a cost of $39 million, raised from various appropriations, grants, patrons, and donors. For the right to name the complex for BTI (Business Telecom Inc.), company founder Peter Loftin contributed $3.1 million. In return for his contribution, the symphony offered him a choice of seats in Meymandi Concert Hall. He chose front row center. In exchange for pledging $2 million, Assad Meymandi claimed the right to name the symphony hall and select seats in "the box overlooking the left side of the stage—a perch often reserved for royalty in Europe." The City of Raleigh, which contributed substantially to the cost, owns the entire multipart facility. Memorial Auditorium is now home to the North Carolina Theatre and Broadway Series South. The A. J. Fletcher Opera Theater—named for the late A. J. Fletcher, an opera enthusiast, attorney, and founder of Capitol Broadcasting Company in Raleigh—hosts the Carolina Ballet, as does Memorial Auditorium. The smaller Kennedy Theatre, located at the rear of the complex with a Salisbury Street entrance, was named for the BTI Center's major fund-raiser, K. D. Kennedy, Jr., and his wife, Sara Lynn. The black-box experimental theater is the home of Theatre Raleigh and offers space for innovative performances.[65]

Reflecting on the new facility, architect Pearce remarked, "The BTI Center for the Performing Arts is a building of exceptions rather than of rules. We were pushed to do things we had never done before." He called for precast concrete panels, because "We needed massive walls that would not vibrate." The architects designed the center to enable people to move easily from Fletcher Theater to Meymandi Hall through a central glass lobby. They made the most of space in Meymandi by including two levels of private boxes and utilizing the choir loft—located behind the orchestra—for audience seating

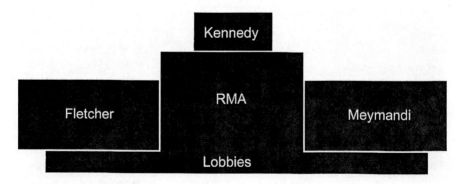

Arrangement of the BTI Center for the Performing Arts (now the Duke Energy Center for the Performing Arts) (courtesy Irvin A. Pearce).

Principal architect Irvin A. Pearce during construction of the BTI Center in December 2000 (courtesy Irvin A. Pearce).

when no choir was performing. "With no proscenium to contend with," noted Pearce, "and with state-of-the-art acoustics, we have an incredible connection between the musicians and the audience." In the architects' vision, Meymandi was "to be designed for the ears, while Fletcher Hall was to be designed for the eyes."[66]

Following the completion of the complex, the United States Institute for Theatre Technology gave a 2002 Merit Award to the BTI Center for the Performing Arts. The award was made to the City of Raleigh as owner of the complex, the architectural firm Pearce Brinkley Cease + Lee, the acoustical consultant Kirkegaard & Associates, and the theater consultant Robert Davis. The project also benefited from the expertise of structural engineer T. Y. Chang of Lasater Hopkins Chang, and the mechanical and electrical services of the Wooten Company.[67] Writing for the *News and Observer* in 2002, columnist Dennis Rogers declared that "The newly-refurbished BTI Center for the Performing Arts is as close to perfect as you could want in a public building." He deplored, however, that the view down Fayetteville Street from the historic State Capitol to the attractive new complex was obscured by Raleigh's unsightly Civic Center.[68] The Civic Center was subsequently demolished and replaced by a Convention Center on South Salisbury Street that does not hide the performing arts complex.

The initial effort to build the new concert hall owed much to the business skill and personality of Richard R. Hoffert, who became executive director of the symphony when Banks Talley retired in 1995 to serve as a consultant and fund-raiser for Preservation North Carolina. Hoffert was a native of Bethlehem, Pennsylvania, and a graduate of Indiana University School of Music. Before coming to North Carolina, he had been for a number of years vice president of marketing and development for the St. Louis Symphony. His earlier career had included being a high school music teacher, assistant manager of Miller Auditorium at Western Michigan University, and director of development and marketing for the Indiana Symphony Orchestra. Drawing on his experience at St. Louis, he set a goal of building the North Carolina Symphony's endowment and raising $5 million for the new concert hall. He also launched negotiations with city officials who favored funding the project: city manager Dempsey Benton, a strong proponent of a center for the performing arts; Roger Krupa, future director of the Raleigh Convention Center complex and an initial supporter of the idea; and mayor Tom Fetzer, less enthusiastic but ultimately cooperative.[69] Hoffert's musical background gave him an affinity with the musicians, and he "brought a real sense of professionalism to the business side of the operation and was very popular with just about everyone." However, he did not remain in North Carolina to see the completion of Meymandi Concert Hall but instead left to take a position as president and CEO of the Indianapolis Symphony Orchestra.[70]

In 1999 he was succeeded by David Chambless Worters, who as president and CEO of the symphony would oversee the completion and opening of Meymandi Concert Hall. Worters grew up in Newton, Massachusetts, near Boston. He began studying piano under the instruction of his mother, who had studied at Juilliard, and then attended the New England Conservatory Preparatory School, where he won the Frances B. Lanier Award at graduation. In 1989 he received a BA degree in economics from Harvard, where he sang in the Harvard Glee Club and served as its student manager. Worters began his professional career with the ensemble Boston Musica Viva and received a fellowship in orchestra management from the American Symphony Orchestra League (presently the League of American Orchestras) for the season 1991–1992. The fel-

Richard Hoffert, CEO of the North Carolina Symphony from 1995 to 1999 (courtesy Richard Hoffert).

lowship enabled him to understudy with orchestra executives in Chicago, San Francisco, and Spokane, and he transitioned from chamber music to music management. At the Chicago Symphony, he met and was particularly influenced by that orchestra's president, Henry Fogel. Worters then managed the Northwestern Indiana Symphony Orchestra and the Syracuse Symphony Orchestra before coming to North Carolina. In 2010 he left the Tar Heel State to take a position as president and CEO for the Van Cliburn Foundation in Texas. The famed pianist Cliburn said of his appointment: "David is a cultured gentleman who brings with him academic credentials in the tangible world of economics coupled with a lifetime of knowledge and genuine love for the Art of Great Music."[71] Worters subsequently returned to the Tar Heel State.

While CEO of the North Carolina Symphony, Worters strove to implement the $13.5 million "Building on Excellence" campaign to complete the new concert hall and fund symphony programs. According to him, "The money raised in this campaign will finance the completion of Meymandi Concert

Hall, outfit the orchestra with the instruments and equipment befitting an orchestra of such high quality, and provide the Symphony with a strong endowment. A permanent endowment including the establishment of a Music Education Fund is critical to the Symphony's mission of statewide service and music education to thousands upon thousands of school children each year."[72]

Around the time that Worters arrived and construction of Meymandi Concert Hall was underway, business manager Hiram Black retired, so Worters began the search for a replacement. The person selected to succeed Black was Scott Freck from the Oregon Symphony. He was given the title "general manager and vice president for artistic operations." He proved effective in administering contracts, scheduling concerts and guest artists, and introducing innovative programming.[73]

As the new concert hall neared completion, Zimmermann used the opportunity to announce publicly his plans for a diverse and innovative program of concerts in the future.

> The excitement that we feel about moving into Meymandi Concert Hall and beginning a new period in the orchestra's history is reflected in the music I have selected for this season [2001–2002]. Continuing the two-year musical retrospective that we began last year, I have programmed music which highlights great compositions of the past centuries as well as important composers and works of the past 20th century....
>
> I have divided this retrospective into three categories....
>
> The first encompasses those composers like Bach and Mozart who had a great influence on composers who followed them, and composers such as Beethoven (the musical giant of all), Debussy and Stravinsky who virtually shook the foundations of the musical world during their lifetimes. I refer to these five as Millennium Composers.
>
> The second category, Influential Composers, comprises those who were influential in the development of certain areas of orchestral music. Brahms, for example[,] changed the function of the soloist and the importance of the orchestra in his piano and violin concerti. Liszt, of course, was the first artist to have his own set of "groupies" and the music of Tchaikovsky was of great significance to Stravinsky.
>
> The final category is made up of 20th Century Composers, from many nationalities, who have bridged the path of music to the 21st Century.... For example, Ravel took the lead from American

David Chambless Worters, CEO of the North Carolina Symphony from 1999 to 2010 (courtesy David Chambless Worters).

jazz and made it into his own unique personal style. John Adams is usually associated with the creation of "minimalism" (along with Steve Reich and Phillip [*sic*] Glass).

This season also celebrates the 100th anniversary of the great American composer, the late Aaron Copland.

We will also showcase some innovative newer works this season, including *Dead Elvis* by Michael Daugherty and the world premiere of Peter Schickele's Concerto for Saxophone Quartet and Orchestra.[74]

On the evening that the Meymandi Concert Hall opened, February 21, 2001, "A good-looking crowd of dressed-up patrons made their way between generous sprays of magnolia blossoms and Champagne bars ... having paid up to $500 a head for the concert and celebrations before and after." Prior to the performance, Assad Meymandi took to the stage to predict optimistically that the orchestra would ultimately reach a size of one hundred musicians and have a $1 million endowment.[75]

The program for the evening began with Shostakovich's *Festive* Overture, Op. 96, followed by Bernstein's *On the Town* and the Liszt Concerto No. 2 in A Major for Piano and Orchestra. Piano soloist André Watts performed the Liszt. After a champagne intermission, Zimmermann led the orchestra in Bernstein's *A Musical Toast*, Nathaniel Stookey's *Big Bang* (a world premiere), and Stravinsky's Suite from *The Firebird* (the 1919 version).[76] According to a *New York Times* critic, "The opening program was more festive than profound. The orchestra did well with Shostakovich's boisterous 'Festive' Overture and with exceedingly complicated music from Leonard Bernstein's 'On the Town.' Nathaniel Stookey's 'Big Bang' was a cheerful little exercise in fragmentation, silence and audience participation. The familiar 'Firebird' Suite by Stravinsky was competently done."

The acoustics in the new hall did not disappoint. *News and Observer* music and theater critic Roy C. Dicks answered the question "Does the North Carolina Symphony sound significantly better in the new Meymandi Symphony Hall?" with "(a resounding) *yes*. Although it was pretty much a given that Meymandi would be better than Memorial Auditorium acoustically, actually the situation is very near the phrase 'like night and day' that the symphony administration has been touting." He went on to praise the "luxurious resonance," "clarity," and "all-encompassing warmth" that the new space afforded.[77]

The gala opening of Meymandi Hall was followed on February 23 and 24 by sold-out performances featuring violinist Nadja Salerno-Sonnenberg. The spring classical series also included pianist Muza Rubackyte on March 16 and 17, the Raleigh Oratorio Society on April 6 and 7, and pianist Angela Cheng on May 11 and 12. The pops series presented Banu Gibson and the New Orleans Hot Jazz on March 2 and 3, Big Band Swing with guest conductor Jeff Tyzik on April 27 and 28, and singer and composer Michael Feinstein on May 18 and 19.[78]

Throughout his career in North Carolina, Zimmermann kept his commitment to include the works of contemporary composers. Under his baton, the symphony performed compositions by Claude Baker, John Corigliano, Michael Daugherty, John Harbison, Lowell Liebermann, Steven Mellilo, Stephen Paulus, Jan Sandström, Joseph Schwantner, and Ellen Taaffe Zwilich. Some of the North Carolina composers featured were Roger Hannay, Hunter Johnson, Daniel Locklair, Russell Peck, Robert Suderburg, and Robert Ward. Among the nineteenth-century works rarely heard by modern audiences but that Zimmermann had the orchestra play were "both Berlioz's *Lelio* and his monumental *Requiem*; Beethoven's complete incidental music to *Egmont*; Liszt's *From the Cradle to the Grave* and *Festklänge*; *Hamlet* and *Le Voyévode* by Tchaikovsky; and Franck's *Le Chasseur Maudit*." From the seldom-heard works of twentieth-century composers, the orchestra performed "Prokofiev's *Alexander Nevsky* (complete with film); Poulenc's *Les Biches*; Messaien's *L'Ascension*; *Fanfares Liturgiques* by Henri Tomasi; Bohuslav Martinu's *The Epic of Gilgamesh*; Reinhold Glière's Symphony No. 3 ('Ilya Murometz'); two major works by Leos Janácek: *Glagolitic Mass* and *Sinfonietta*; Kodály's *Peacock Variations*; Walter Piston's … Suite from *The Incredible Flutist*; Debussy's *Printemps*[;] Anton Webern's Symphonie, Op. 21; *The Perfect Fool* by Holst; a pair of rare Rachmaninoff gems, *Capriccio Bohemien* and *Prince Rostislav*; Copland's *Orchestral Variations*; and the original jazz version of Gershwin's *Rhapsody in Blue*."[79]

In keeping with his appreciation for Mahler, Zimmermann recalled with special pride conducting in the 1988–1989 season an impressive production of the composer's Eighth Symphony—the *Symphony of a Thousand*—at North Carolina State University's Friends of the College series, which had also hosted the work with Gosling conducting in the 1977–1978 season. "We got together 975 performers, 750 in the chorus itself," Zimmermann recalled. "The orchestra was huge. We did two performances of that on a platform on the floor of North Carolina State's basketball arena. The chorus went up all the way in the bleachers, and we had an audience of about 10,000 at each performance. It was such a thrill."[80]

In Zimmermann's last year with the symphony, the organization reported an "approximately $9 million budget … from ticket sales, contract sales, individual contributions and corporate sponsorships, as well as from a generous grant-in-aid from the North Carolina General Assembly…. Among other government grants are those from the National Endowment for the Arts, the City of Raleigh, the County of Wake and the Town of Cary." It proudly claimed "one of the most extensive music education programs of any U.S. orchestra," which gave more than fifty concerts per year to North Carolina schoolchildren.[81]

Upon Zimmermann's announced retirement, the symphony scheduled nine guest conductors for the 2002–2003 season to compete for the vacant position. "This should prove to be an incredibly exciting season in every way," it proclaimed to its patrons and ticket buyers. "Nine stupendously talented conductors will be our guests; each will lead the orchestra in performing beloved classical favorites. Watch how each of these Maestros 'plays' your own North Carolina Symphony. You won't want to miss their performances. One of them may be our next Music Director!" The nationally and internationally known guest conductors in the competition were Peter Oundjian, Giancarlo Guerrero, Andrea Quinn, Jeffrey Kahane, Roberto Minczuk, Michael Christie, Fabio Mechetti, Jahja Ling, and Grant Llewellyn. Zimmermann's farewell concerts took place on May 2 and 3 in Meymandi Hall and featured guest pianist Norman Krieger. The program consisted of Brahms's *Gesang der Parzen*, Stookey's *Out of the Everywhere* (a world premiere), Beethoven's *Choral Fantasy*, and Lutoslawski's Concerto for Orchestra.[82]

After his resignation from the North Carolina Symphony, Zimmermann continued to direct the Canton Symphony Orchestra, accepted invitations to appear on the podiums of numerous orchestras in the United States and abroad, and served a term as North Carolina's conductor laureate, returning several times as guest conductor. He maintained summer stints as music director and principal conductor at the Breckenridge Music Festival in Colorado. He debuted with the Cleveland Opera in 2006 and became director of orchestral activities at the University of Texas at Austin's Butler School of Music.[83]

The appointment of Gerhardt Zimmermann as the orchestra's fourth music director had fit the mood and politics of the state at the time, and particularly in the wake of the internal turmoil generated during the long search. There was more than a bit of relief at the idea of a young, calm, steady new leader, and indeed predictions that he would stay for a very long time were fulfilled. Zimmermann came with strong endorsements, and during his years of leadership, he hired many musicians, putting his stamp on the orchestra in a lasting way. His name is German, and he clearly preferred the German romantic repertory. But he is American, and there were a good many American works in his programs, including more than a few premieres. His work was facilitated and supported at the outset by associate conductor James Ogle, who had established a strong presence under Gosling. Ogle's work in dance programs, educational concerts, and fund-raising and development provided significant adjuncts during Zimmermann's early years, as the contributions of resident conductor William Henry Curry would do later in Zimmermann's tenure and then during the transition to his successor, Grant Llewellyn.

Zimmermann brought steady and secure growth during his tour in North Carolina. The symphony resumed broadcasting on local public radio stations and occasionally on television; made a few recordings; significantly expanded its season; returned to Carnegie Hall; developed additional venues, including a summer home at Cary's Regency Park; and acquired the new Meymandi Concert Hall in Raleigh. It increased its revenues, which facilitated a comparable increase in the number of classical and pops concerts in the home region, as well as enhancements in the quality and frequency of appearances of significant guest artists in the orchestra's many series. Growth would slow after Zimmermann's departure. In retrospect, he served in North Carolina during some of the orchestra's best times, and he made the most of the opportunities presented to him. The performances of works he admired and composers he championed were often excellent. But at times he was less inspired, with results that did not uniformly spark enthusiasm among his audiences. Toward the end of his long term, it became clear to a number of the orchestra's advocates that a change in artistic leadership was in order, with a concurrent broadening of the repertoire. A rising music talent from Wales would prove to be the change that the North Carolina Symphony sought as it moved into another era.

7

In the Limelight

After a more-than-two-year search and thorough consideration of the qualifications and performances of all the conductors competing to become its new music director, the North Carolina Symphony offered the position to Grant Llewellyn, who accepted. "Grant Llewellyn has been named music director of the N.C. Symphony by symphony President and CEO David Chambless Worters," reported the local press in January 2004. According to Worters, "Grant simply captured the interest and imagination of everyone he encountered here. He has the talent, the passion, the charisma, the eloquence and the vision to lead this orchestra to unprecedented new heights, artistically and organizationally."[1] The committee that selected Llewellyn was composed of four musicians from the orchestra, Symphony Society board members James Moeser and Ed Woolner, general manager Scott Freck, and CEO Worters. It appointed Bruce Ridge as chairman. The committee determined which conductors to consider for the North Carolina opening, whom to invite to perform before North Carolina audiences, and whom to ask back for a second look before making the final choice.[2]

Of the previously mentioned first nine conductors competing, Peter Oundjian, noted particularly for his talent as a violinist, made his trial appearance in September 2002. Critics, the musicians, and members of the administration remarked on how good the string section sounded under his baton, and a number of them considered him to be the top contender. But he accepted a position as music director and conductor of the Toronto Symphony and withdrew from the North Carolina competition. He was followed in October by Nicaraguan Giancarlo Guerrero, then associate conductor of the Minnesota Orchestra. In November Andrea Quinn, music director of New York City Ballet, gave her trial performance, and she was followed in that same month by Jeffrey Kahane, music director of the Los Angeles Chamber Orchestra and the Santa Rosa Symphony. Roberto Minczuk, associate conductor of the New York Philharmonic, then performed in January 2003, as did the young

Michael Christie. Next came Brazilian Fabio Mechetti, music director of the Jacksonville Symphony Orchestra, in February; and then in March, Grant Llewellyn, from Boston's Handel and Haydn Society, and Jahja Ling, music director of the San Diego Symphony. Two new candidates, Alastair Willis and Anne Manson, were slated to appear for trial concerts in September and October respectively, bringing the total number of conductors considered for the vacant position to eleven. Four of those were scheduled as finalists to return and give performances to determine the final selection—Llewellyn in November 2003, Quinn in February 2004, and Ling and Minczuk in March. (In addition, associate conductor Curry, assistant conductor Kenneth Raskin, and conductor laureate Zimmermann led the orchestra during the winter and spring season.)

Before the last three finalists made their dates, the symphony offered the position to Llewellyn. The task of making the offer fell to Worters, who traveled to Boston and approached Llewellyn after an evening concert at Symphony Hall conducted by the maestro, who apparently was not aware that the CEO had come to offer him the position. Llewellyn invited Worters to join a postconcert gathering at the nearby Pizzeria Uno restaurant. There, amid a noisy crowd of diners, Worters informed Llewellyn that he was the North Carolina Symphony's choice as its next music director.[3]

Llewellyn came to North Carolina with considerable credentials as a conductor. He was born in 1960 in Tenby, Wales, and attended Chethams School of Music, the Conservatorio di Musica Francesco Morlacchi in Italy, and Cambridge University. He received a conducting scholarship to study at the Royal College of Music with Norman Del Mar, followed by a conducting fellowship at Tanglewood in 1985. There he came under the influence of such artists as Bernstein, Ozawa, Masur, and Previn. From 1990 to 1997, Llewellyn served as assistant conductor of the Boston Symphony Orchestra, presiding over concerts at the Tanglewood Festival, the Boston subscription series, and the Boston Pops events. He then became music director of the Handel and Haydn Society and returned to conduct the Boston subscription series for 2003–2004. Also prior to coming to North Carolina, he worked with three European orchestras: the BBC National Orchestra of Wales (associate conductor, 1990–1995); the Stavanger Symphony Orchestra (principal guest conductor, 1993–1996); and the Royal Flanders Philharmonic (principal conductor, 1995–1998). He had particularly strong ongoing ties to the BBC National Orchestra of Wales, where he received the title of conductor-in-residence and cooperated in a number of radio, compact disc, and television projects. Along with his service to North Carolina, his itinerary for the future included several repeat and new engagements with orchestras elsewhere in the United States and abroad.[4]

When he came to North Carolina in 2004 to become the symphony's fifth music director, Llewellyn met with considerable public fanfare. His photograph was displayed on banners throughout Raleigh, and the publicity generated was virtually unprecedented in the capital's cultural history. He was the first of the orchestra's music directors who was not born American and the first not to maintain a residence in the state. His permanent address was in Wales, where he lived with his family. But he was young and dashing, a cellist, and a leader with his feet firmly planted in both the orchestral and early-music worlds. His career with the North Carolina Symphony would prove to be an illustrious one, as the classical music community applauded his talent.

Prior to his arrival in North Carolina, Llewellyn generally had won acco-

In 2004 Grant Llewellyn joined the North Carolina Symphony as music director/conductor (photograph by Nicholas Joubard, courtesy Hazard Chase).

lades throughout his appearances. But, as with all conductors, the critics were not always kind. In July 2002, John von Rhein of the *Chicago Tribune* said of him and the Opera Theatre of St. Louis's production of Mozart's *The Magic Flute*:

> Routine was the word for the season's "Magic Flute," OTSL's first foray into Mozart's masterpiece since 1984. Nobody apparently told director Darko Tresnjak there is more to "Zauberfloete" than knockabout farce and pretty stage pictures. Here, alas, the farce wasn't particularly funny nor the pictures particularly pretty.
>
> There were some promising young singers in principal roles.... But they never fully came together as an ensemble. Grant Llewellyn's erratic conducting did neither Mozart nor the performers any favors. Another Eden lost.[5]

Llewellyn opened the North Carolina orchestra's fall 2004 season with his first appearance as the new music director on September 15 in Meymandi Concert Hall. The program featured Haydn's Symphony No. 104 in D Major (*London*) and Mahler's Symphony No. 1 in D Major (*Titan*). The symphony played the same program on September 16 in Lee Auditorium at Pinecrest High School in Southern Pines, and then again in Meymandi on September 17 and 18.[6]

Under the new maestro's guidance, the symphony undertook a full schedule of concerts in Meymandi Hall and on the road at various sites throughout the state. The orchestra's program for February to May 2006, for example, had Llewellyn conducting twenty concerts—eleven in Meymandi—featuring such artists as violinists Dovid Friedlander and concertmaster Brian Reagin, principal cello player Bonnie Thron, percussionist Evelyn Glennie, and pianists André Watts and Richard Goode, as well as the Choral Society of Durham and the North Carolina Master Chorale. The same schedule listed assistant conductor Carolyn Kuan as leader of the orchestra in five performances, including one with popular pianist Burt Bacharach in Meymandi and two with violinist Amy Fetherolf, one in Southern Pines and the other in Salisbury. The itinerary for resident conductor Curry had him taking the podium for nine concerts. Among those were performances by guest artist Branford Marsalis (saxophone) in Meymandi Hall on February 17 and 18 and by principal trombone John Ilika in Durham on May 18, New Bern on May 19, Chapel Hill on May 20, and Meymandi on May 21. Among the music selections for the season were works by such composers as Mozart, Mahler, Beethoven, Brahms, Bach, Berlioz, Debussy, Ravel, Rachmaninoff, Elgar, Stravinsky, John Williams, Arthur Honegger, Darius Milhaud, and James MacMillan.[7]

The September 2006–January 2007 program provided the same level of concerts and renowned artists and saw Llewellyn at the podium on numerous occasions in Meymandi Hall and at other locations in the state. It also featured Joan Landry—one of the few women thus far—as assistant conductor, as well as Curry's many concerts as resident conductor and a guest appearance by conductor laureate Zimmermann.[8] In addition, that season marked the seventy-fifth anniversary of the orchestra, which commemorated the event with performances and promotion of a new special presentation—*Schubert's Farewell: The Miraculous Final Year*, a project based on Schubert's chamber music from the last year of his life. *Schubert's Farewell* was conceived by pianist Ignat Solzhenitsyn, who described how the idea came to fruition.

> Like many ambitious ideas, it originated on the back of a humble cocktail napkin. North Carolina Symphony General Manager and V.P. for Artistic Operations Scott Freck and I were reflecting on the Mozart-and-Brahms celebration we had just concluded with the Symphony (November 2003), and Scott asked me, over a drink: "Well, so what do you want to do next? How do we top this?" Scott talked inspiringly about

how well received that first festival had been, and how next time we could plan something on an even bigger scale, both grander in sweep and even less beholden to the usual blueprints that all of us—conductors, soloists and administrators—tend to use over and over again from one season to the next. Listening to him speak so freely and eloquently, I immediately thought of my long-cherished Schubert idea which had remained dormant for some years, dormant precisely due to the daunting practical complexities of presenting a highly unorthodox festival within the basic framework of a symphony orchestra subscription season. So I said, "Scott, next time, let's not only narrow the focus to one composer, but let's *really* concentrate, and examine, as under a microscope, just twelve months in that man's life: the miraculous final year of Franz Schubert." Scott's face lit up with intrigue and interest, and we immediately engaged the subject right there at the bar. As time went on, we went back and forth on the general concept, and also on some of the details, and were also fortunate to benefit from the invaluable advice and inspiration of then-incoming Music Director Grant Llewellyn....

So what makes this music so great? In a series of four programs, each focusing on a different facet of Schubert's creativity, we ... show ... why these works belong not *near*, but indeed *at*, the very summit of the Western canon.[9]

Llewellyn's immediate and ongoing success in North Carolina led to an early extension of his original four-year contract. Two years after his arrival, the press reported in the fall of 2006 that

Two seasons of enthusiastic performances, charm and strong ticket sales have resulted in an unexpected contract extension for the North Carolina Symphony's music director.

Grant Llewellyn's contract expires in 2008, and symphony leaders said they wanted to lock him in before other orchestras tried to lure him away. Knowing Llewellyn will be here through 2012 also opens up new musical possibilities, they said.

Llewellyn, who lives in Wales with his family and stays at a Raleigh condo when he's in the state, has been credited with reinvigorating the 74-year-old symphony.

Since he started in 2004, donors have been giving more money. Major donors wanted to know how long the state would be able to keep Llewellyn, which helped extend his contract.

Worters would not disclose Llewellyn's salary in the new agreement. The conductor received $92,000 in his first, partial season in 2004–05, when he conducted only six weeks' worth of concerts, according to the most recent federal tax records.[10]

Llewellyn had proved to be all the symphony had hoped for in leading the orchestra. Critics, concertgoers, and the musicians all agreed that he was taking the orchestra to a new level in the quality of its performances. After a February 2010 presentation of Shostakovich's Cello Concerto No. 1 and Brahms's Symphony No. 4, critic Roy C. Dicks wrote that the "concert was one of those nights you dream about, with performances that grab you up, shake you around, and leave you in a daze afterwards. Music director Grant Llewellyn and the orchestra were white-hot, aided by a world-class soloist, in an evening unquestionably demonstrating the cathartic power of music."

Reviewing an April 2011 concert in Meymandi Hall, Steve Row declared that "Llewellyn has crafted a string section that can whisper with the best, bringing a fine sense of delicacy without any thinness." After a 2013 performance featuring the music of Sibelius, critic Ken Hoover wrote: "The North Carolina Symphony with Llewellyn at the helm is the equal of any orchestra I know in interpreting the music of Sibelius. This performance was rhapsodic, intense and superbly guided." Critics also voiced approval of the recordings made by Llewellyn. In a June 2009 issue of *Gramophone* magazine, David Gutman opined that Llewellyn's compact disc *American Spectrum*, featuring saxophonist Branford Marsalis, was "more than just enthusiastic, with discipline remarkably tight … the result is a winner." In a December 2009 *International Record Review*, Nicholas Salwey said of Llewellyn and pianist Yevgeny Sudbin's disc of Rachmaninoff and Medtner piano concertos: "[T]he intensity of the collaboration results in performances which withstand competition from the finest."[11]

Audiences also voiced their good opinions about the maestro and the quality of the orchestra under his direction. Nancy Olson, a loyal concert attendee and owner of Raleigh's popular independent bookstore Quail Ridge Books, noted on one occasion that "I began attending concerts in 1981 and have been amazed at the orchestra's tremendous, steady improvement every season, culminating in the brilliance of Grant's leadership." The orchestra's musicians also approved of Llewellyn and the high level to which he had raised their performances. "When Llewellyn came, the atmosphere changed," violist Jeffry Moyer once remarked. "He allowed us a freer musical expression. He demanded high standards but was very supportive. The skills and the cohesion of the orchestra have definitely risen during his tenure." Moyer noted particularly the conductor's introduction of more baroque music. "We didn't play much Baroque before Grant and when we did, we played it awfully," he recalled. "But during the course of Grant's rehearsals an incredible change occurred. He got us playing in Baroque style without really telling us how. It was just through his sensitivity and skill."[12]

Thus the first decade with Llewellyn as music director proved successful and garnered praise from critics, audiences, and the orchestra's musicians alike and brought a renewal of the maestro's contract through 2017–2018. In September 2013, Roy Dicks wrote the following complimentary critique of the symphony's past ten years.

> Ten years into a relationship is a good time to stop and take stock. For Grant Llewellyn, music director of the North Carolina Symphony since January 2004, the assessments from all sides (himself, the orchestra, the management, the audience and the critics) seem to be the same: it's been a roaring success. That's a heck of a honeymoon, one that's likely to continue through the 2017–2018 season, Llewellyn's latest contract renewal end date. Meanwhile, Llewellyn is concentrating on the 2013–14 season, which

he opened on September 19, 2013, in Raleigh with Beethoven's Ninth Symphony and several Robert Ward pieces. Two additional Raleigh performances and one in Chapel Hill all played to positive reviews.

It's easy to understand these assessments once you've seen and heard Llewellyn. He's not the old-school stereotype of the reclusive, dictatorial conductor. His affable, down-to-earth personality, combined with his enthusiastic, deeply-felt musical interpretations, make him an instantly likable, accessible artist. The dashing and energetic 52 year-old Welshman is charming and charismatic, whether explaining upcoming programs in TV interviews or speaking from the podium during concerts....

One of Llewellyn's key contributions has been the addition of more Baroque and Classical period compositions....

Llewellyn has initiated a number of special projects, ... and he has been particularly interested in collaborative efforts. One of his favorites was the December 2010 staging of Peter Shaffer's play, "Amadeus," co-produced with Chapel Hill's professional theater, PlayMakers Repertory Company. Costumed actors performed in front of the on-stage orchestra, which supplied appropriate Mozart pieces interspersed throughout.[13]

In a practice that began with music director Stringfield, the symphony continued with Llewellyn its custom of taking its music on the road to pay homage to North Carolina's folk and other traditional music. On January 30, 2007, the *Asheville Citizen-Times* announced:

The N.C. Symphony will stop in Asheville, Murphy, Cullowhee, Rutherfordton and Hickory as part of its "Capital Bank Blue Skies and Red Earth Tour" in May.

Musicians from across the state, including eighth-generation Madison County ballad singer Donna Ray Norton, will share the stage with the symphony during the tour, a celebration that showcases the richness of the traditional music of North Carolina.

"In a way, we're sewing a musical quilt," Scott Freck, the symphony's general manager, said at the Asheville Area Chamber of Commerce on Monday. "A patch of blues, a patch of gospel, a patch of jazz and classical—in the end we'll have a quilt that covers all of North Carolina." Freck characterized the program as a "survey of what music has meant to North Carolina."

Originally presented as a concert in September in Raleigh, the tour is traveling the state with funding by Capital Bank.

Presenting partners of the tour's stops include the Western Piedmont Symphony, Western Carolina University, Tri-County Community College, the Asheville Symphony and KidSenses Children's Interactive Museum and Rutherford County Community Concert Association. The partners will keep all the ticket revenue from the performances.

Grant Llewellyn, music director of the state orchestra, said the tour should do much to dispel the notion that symphonic performances are "formal and fussy."

"To be asked to share so many of North Carolina's musical idioms is a thrill for me," he said at the chamber of commerce Monday.

"My family were dirt-poor farmers. Music was what we did for fun," said Donna Ray Norton, who performed with the orchestra during the September concert. "I'm so excited to have this come to my part of North Carolina."[14]

During the tenure of CEO Worters, the symphony—with Suzanne Rousso as director of education—continued its important mission to reach the state's schoolchildren with classical music. In 2005–2006 the Symphony Society's fourteen chapters, with four hundred volunteers, helped fund twenty-two school concerts, as well as thirty evening concerts and five free outdoor performances, in their local communities.[15]

When a major economic recession struck the United States and the world in 2008, the North Carolina Symphony suffered a significant downturn in private and public funding. In such financial crises as the recession, cultural institutions especially experience the effects of widespread fiscal decline as support for their programs diminishes. The symphony found itself in debt by several million dollars and launched a major effort to attack that problem. In May 2010, the musicians' committee, or collective bargaining group, voted to take a 15 percent pay cut for two years, which reduced the basic salary for a player from $59,400 to $47,956 annually. "No one likes to take a 15 percent pay cut," announced John Ilika, principal trombone and chairman of the committee. "But we felt like it was a necessary thing to do, and we are doing it with our heads held up high." That was the second time since the financial crisis hit that the players had "agreed to reopen their contract. Last year, they took a one-year cut … of 17 percent for the 2009–10 season, mainly by reducing their contracts from 43 weeks to 37 weeks." Music director Llewellyn also agreed to a reduction of his annual salary from $206,975 to $186,278. According to a newspaper report in May 2010, CEO Worters predicted that the orchestra would "break even for the first time in several years for the fiscal year that ends June 30…. But he said the organization still has more than $3 million in debt borrowed from its line of credit to operate during the past several years." More cuts were made by cancelling concert plans, tours, and expensive guest artists, and the symphony had substantially reduced its debt within two years. At the time, the orchestra acquired about 40 percent of its budget from individual and corporate donations, 30 percent from the sale of tickets, 20 percent from the state legislature, and 10 percent from such sources as the endowment and grants from local governments. It had managed to raise "$6.6 million of its $8 million goal that it needs to claim $1.5 million in matching state money." Acquiring sufficient funds to maintain the high level of artistry that had come to characterize the North Carolina Symphony remained, and continues to remain, a persistent challenge.[16]

When Worters resigned in 2010 and the Symphony Society conducted a search for his replacement, it chose Sandi Macdonald as the new (and present-day) CEO. She arrived in Raleigh in 2011. Macdonald was born in Toronto and studied at the Royal Conservatory of Music there. She received a bachelor's degree in business marketing and a master's degree in business administration from the University of Phoenix and studied arts management at the Banff School of Management and George Brown College in Toronto. Her career began as management trainee for the Canadian Opera Company and the

National Ballet of Canada. She then worked in marketing and communications in opera and orchestra in Toronto and Detroit. She held positions with the Toronto Symphony Orchestra, including marketing and communications director, and was senior director of strategic planning and audience development for the Seattle Symphony. She worked for the Cleveland Orchestra from 2003 to 2011 as director of marketing and public relations and then as director of its Miami, Florida, residency prior to coming to North Carolina. Macdonald is chair of the Greater Raleigh Convention and Visitors Bureau and an advisory member of the Raleigh Chamber of Commerce. She also serves on the board of advisors of Kidznotes, an El Sistema–style organization committed to enhancing children's lives through music training, and is a

Sandi Macdonald became the first female CEO of the symphony in 2011 (photograph by Michael Zirkle, courtesy North Carolina Symphony).

PRESTO mentor for El Sistema USA. Macdonald was named *Triangle Business Journal*'s 2018 CEO of the Year.[17]

With the administrative leadership of first Worters and then Macdonald, the performances and reputation of the North Carolina Symphony as a world-class orchestra under the baton of Maestro Llewellyn continued to rise. From the beginning of his tenure, the conductor delivered excellent results in terms of renewed vigor among the players as he broadened the symphony's programs to include works of not only British but also French origin that had been to some extent ignored during his predecessor's lengthy tenure. Nor did he overlook new music and American works in general. He rebalanced the orchestra and refreshed its ranks with new and generally much younger members. He led the ensemble to new heights of artistic and technical accomplishment, bringing it new recognitions at home and elsewhere. Commercial recordings and regular broadcasts of subscription programs extended the reach of the symphony. The selection of the orchestra to perform at the first SHIFT Festival at the Kennedy Center in 2017 was indicative of its rising national importance. The weeklong event spotlights North American orchestras of all sizes.

Llewellyn's talent and leadership led to the growing quality and appeal of the subscription concert programs. After several years, he settled on a single choir in Raleigh as his principal choral partner: the North Carolina Master Chorale, directed by Alfred E. Sturgis, choral director at North Carolina State

University. Llewellyn proved a master of Mahler, despite the predilection of his predecessor for that composer's large-scale symphonies. He was masterful also with Shostakovich, but the performances that most significantly expanded the orchestra's horizons and earned it the most widespread praise were the collaborative efforts with PlayMakers Repertory Company and the UNC School of the Arts.

Llewellyn retains a permanent residence in Wales and commutes to perform with the North Carolina orchestra and numerous others in the United States and abroad. September 2017 marked his third season as music director of the Orchestre Symphonique de Bretagne. He maintains his close relationship with the BBC Orchestra of Wales, conducting a number of concerts and leading it on tour in South America. With that orchestra in 2017, he led "a concert specially designed for those with autism, sensory and communication impairments, and learning disabilities." Among his recent recordings are discs of Prokofiev's violin concerti with Matthew Trusler and the BBC Orchestra of Wales and of Lowell Liebermann's orchestral compositions with the BBC Symphony Orchestra. With the North Carolina Symphony, he has recorded discs of Britten's *Cello Symphony* and Prokofiev's *Sinfonia Concertante* with cellist Zuill Bailey.[18] In December 2018, Llewellyn announced that the 2019–2020 season would be his last as the symphony's full-time music director.

Although the North Carolina Symphony has gained a national reputation as a first-class state orchestra, racial diversity remains a challenge for the organization. From its beginnings to the present day, only a few African American artists have performed at its concerts. Currently there are no black musicians in the orchestra, although over the years some have filled in as supply or temporary players. However, in addition to African American guest artists such as André Watts, at least three black guest conductors (two of which are native North Carolinians) have appeared at the podium with the symphony.

In its 2004 season, the symphony contracted with African American conductor André Raphel Smith to conduct three concerts. The first two featured guest violinist Soovin Kim as the soloist in a program of Brahms, Prokofiev, and Dvořák. They were scheduled for the Carolina Theatre in Durham on May 20 and Kenan Auditorium in Wilmington on May 21. The third concert, which included guest artist Yo-Yo Ma, cello, took place in Meymandi Concert Hall on May 22 with a program of Brahms, Haydn, and Dvořák. Smith was born in Durham, North Carolina, in 1962 and undertook musical training at age eleven. He was awarded a bachelor of music degree at the University of Miami and a master's degree from Yale University. While at Yale, he studied conducting with Otto-Werner Mueller, with whom he continued training at the Curtis Institute of Music, from which he earned a diploma in conducting. He also trained at Juilliard, where he received the Bruno Walter Memorial Scholarship and an advanced certificate in conducting. With the support of the National Endowment for the Arts, Smith served for three years as assistant conductor of the St. Louis Symphony. Then from 1994 to 2000, he was assistant conductor of the Philadelphia Orchestra. He debuted in Carnegie Hall in 1997, where he led the Orchestra of St. Luke's in celebration of black singer Marian Anderson's centennial. Throughout his career, Smith appeared with numerous orchestras in the United States, including the New York Philharmonic and the symphonies of Cleveland, Chicago, and Minnesota, as well as in New Zealand and Brazil.[19]

Another black guest conductor—who led a Saturday morning concert with the North Carolina Symphony in October 2012—was Chelsea Tipton II, a native of Greensboro. He received a bachelor's degree from the Eastman School of Music and a master's from Northern Illinois University and took further training at the University of Cincinnati's College-Conservatory of Music. Tipton has appeared with a number of major orchestras throughout the United States and Europe and served as principal pops conductor of the New Haven Symphony and for nine seasons as music director of the Southeast Texas Symphony in Beaumont. He conducted that orchestra in the Sphinx Competition Showcase at Carnegie Hall, "the culmination of a ten-city tour with the orchestra." In the summer of 2011, he toured Europe with the popular musician Sting. Two years later, the Atlanta Symphony Orchestra bestowed on him its first annual Aspire Award, which honors professional musicians who are African American or Latino. One of his career highlights came when he served as a last-minute replacement for Robert Spano to conduct a Gershwin season finale with the Brooklyn Philharmonic, and the *New York Times* applauded him for "leading sweeping and vibrant performances of 'Rhapsody' and 'An American in Paris.'"[20]

The black guest conductor at the North Carolina Symphony's New Year's Eve concert in 2017 was Thomas Wilkins, music director of the Omaha Symphony, principal conductor of the Hollywood Bowl Orchestra, and conductor of the Boston Symphony's youth concert series. Born in Norfolk, Virginia, he graduated from the Shenandoah Conservatory of Music and the New England Conservatory of Music. His career has included stints as resident conductor of the Detroit Symphony and the Florida Orchestra in Tampa Bay and as associate conductor of the Richmond Symphony. Wilkins has appeared as guest conductor with many of the major orchestras in the nation, including the Philadelphia and Cleveland orchestras, the New York Philharmonic, and the National Symphony. He also has held positions on the music faculties of North Park University in Chicago, the University of Tennessee in Chattanooga, and Virginia Commonwealth University in Richmond. He has served on the boards of a number of arts, charitable, and public organizations and in 2014 received the Outstanding Artist award at the Nebraska Governor's Awards presentation. Having been the Omaha Symphony's longest-serving music director, he has announced his retirement from that organization and will become music director emeritus.[21]

Women (except those who are black) have fared better than African Americans in their representation in the North Carolina orchestra. They now make up about 50 percent of the musicians, and Sandi Macdonald is serving as the first female CEO. In recent years, the symphony hired three female assistant or associate conductors: Carolyn Kuan, Joan Landry, and Sarah Hicks.

A native of Taiwan, Carolyn Kuan became assistant conductor in the spring season of 2006. She graduated cum laude from Smith College and received a performance diploma from the Peabody Conservatory and a master's degree from the University of Illinois. She is the first woman to win the Herbert von Karajan Conducting Fellowship, which led to a residency at the 2004 Salzburg Festival. Her conducting experience includes numerous engagements with major orchestras, operas, and ballets in North America and throughout the world, as well as for recordings. She is particularly noted for her direction of contemporary and Asian music. In 2011 Kuan became music director of the Hartford Symphony Orchestra and has an extended contract to 2022.[22]

Joan Landry came to the North Carolina Symphony during the 2006–2007 season as assistant conductor, having just completed three seasons as associate conductor with the Honolulu Symphony. She was born in Massachusetts and earned a bachelor of music degree from the New England Conservatory of Music and a master's degree and an artist diploma in orchestral conducting from the Hartt School of Music, where she also received an honors award in instrumental conducting. She has been apprentice conductor with the Oregon Symphony and music director of the Lewis and Clark Symphony Orchestra. In addition to guest conducting numerous orchestras in the United States, she appeared with the Bach Festival and the Karlsbad and Marienbad symphonies in the Czech Republic and served as cover conductor for the National Symphony and the Boston Pops, as well as music director of the Bay Youth Symphony and the Cape Cod Symphony. She is noted for her work with young audiences and youth orchestras. In November 2013, Landry was appointed music director of the Arlington Philharmonic Orchestra.[23]

Born in Tokyo and raised in Honolulu, Sarah Hicks joined the North Carolina Symphony in 2010 for a number of seasons as associate conductor. Both a pianist and a violist, she won prizes for performance while in her early teens. She received a bachelor of arts degree in composition magna cum laude from Harvard and a degree in conducting from the Curtis Institute of Music. She has received a number of awards and scholarships and has appeared as guest conductor with numerous major orchestras in the nation and abroad, at times with such popular artists as Jaime Laredo, Hilary Hahn, Josh Groban, and Smokey Robinson. For two months in the summer of 2011, she toured as conductor with Sting. She has been associate conductor of the Richmond

Symphony, resident conductor of the Florida Philharmonic, assistant conductor of the Philadelphia Singers (the chorus of the Philadelphia Orchestra), and music director of the Hawaii Summer Symphony, which she established in 1991. She taught at the Curtis Institute of Music and subsequently became staff conductor there. Hicks is noted for her abilities as a conductor of pops performances, as well as her expertise in the classical repertoire. The *New York Times* placed her among "a new wave of female conductors."[24]

A division in the Office of Arts and Libraries of the Department of Natural and Cultural Resources, under the administrative leadership of CEO Macdonald, the North Carolina Symphony currently has an annual operating budget of about $15 million. Of that amount, 36 percent comes from contributions, 31 percent from ticket sales and performances, 29 percent from the State of North Carolina, and 4 percent from investments in the endowment. State government's yearly contribution of $2 million is allotted once the symphony acquires $9 million through ticket sales and fund-raising. The symphony's endowment stands at around $20 million, having grown significantly since 2012. The average annual salary for a musician is about $50,000. When Macdonald arrived in 2011, the debt of the symphony was $1.7 million. Now, in 2018, it is $210,000. She insists that financial sustainability is a major priority and that the endowment is an essential source for maintaining that sustainability. The expanding audience is closely related to the state's demographics; "40% of ticket-buying households are now Gen X-ers and Millennials."

In the 2016–2017 fiscal year, the orchestra traveled 18,500 miles in North Carolina and beyond, presenting around 180 concerts and 120 community engagement events. More than 250,000 people heard it play. Four concerts took place before a national audience in Washington, D.C., where the symphony's performance at the SHIFT Festival was reviewed by the *Washington Post* and the *New York Times*. The symphony gives about 40 school concerts annually, and in the past year, 55,000 fourth and fifth graders attended its music education programs. In addition, orchestra members held 30 free music discovery events at preschools and libraries. As it has from its earliest days, the educational mission remains a high priority for the symphony, which strives to reach schools in 91 counties within an eighteen-to-twenty-four-month period.[25]

The North Carolina Symphony ended its spring classical season of 2018 in Meymandi Concert Hall on May 18 and 19, when Llewellyn conducted Schoenberg's *Verklärte Nacht* and Strauss's *Ein Heldenleben*. For the opening of its annual Summerfest series at the Koka Booth Amphitheatre on May 26, associate conductor Wesley Schulz led the orchestra in Mussorgsky's *Pictures at an Exhibition* as part of the popular program.[26] For opening night of the 2018–2019 season in Meymandi on September 21, the symphony scheduled a Beethoven concert featuring *The Consecration of the House*, Rondo for

The orchestra performing in Meymandi Concert Hall (photograph by Michael Zirkle, courtesy North Carolina Symphony).

Piano and Orchestra, *Choral Fantasy*, and Symphony No. 5. With Llewellyn conducting, the guest artists were pianist Andrew Tyson and the North Carolina Master Chorale.[27]

Calling special attention to fund-raising to maintain support for the symphony's mission of school concerts, columnist Jim Jenkins of the *News and Observer* recently wrote that "The North Carolina Symphony is the finest organization of its kind in America—not just for the skill of its musicians or the creativity of its programs, or its versatility. Rather, it rises above others because of a solemn commitment made in the 1940s to serve the state, from school houses to concert halls, and it keeps that promise to this day."[28]

Indeed, the North Carolina Symphony has enjoyed a long and accomplished career, from its beginning to the present. It was born of a rising progressive call for the development of art, literature, history, and music in the early twentieth century. It has grown to be a leading orchestra and cultural icon not only in the South, where it has maintained a close relationship with the region's musical tradition, but also in the entire nation. The symphony's story has not unfolded without controversy, financial setbacks, internal quarrels, and other difficulties. But if its past history is any indication of its future, the orchestra will meet its challenges and continue to bring the best of musical performance to the people of the Old North State and beyond.

Chapter Notes

Introduction

1. John H. Mueller, *The American Symphony Orchestra: A Social History of Musical Taste* (Bloomington: Indiana University Press, 1951), 31.

2. John Warthen Struble, *The History of American Classical Music* (New York: Facts on File, 1995), xvi–xvii.

Chapter 1

1. Bill C. Malone and David Stricklin, *Southern Music/American Music*, rev. ed. (Lexington: University Press of Kentucky, 2003), 13.

2. Ronald L. Davis, "Classical Music and Opera," in Bill C. Malone, ed., *Music*, vol. 12 of *The New Encyclopedia of Southern Culture*, ed. Charles Reagan Wilson (Chapel Hill: University of North Carolina Press, 2008), 43; William Byrd, *Histories of the Dividing Line betwixt Virginia and North Carolina* (New York: Dover, 1967), 282–284.

3. Dumas Malone, *Jefferson the Virginian* (Boston: Little, Brown, 1948), 78–80.

4. Dumas Malone, *Jefferson and the Rights of Man* (Boston: Little, Brown, 1951), 14, 87–88.

5. Davis, "Classical Music and Opera," 43; Malone and Stricklin, *Southern Music/American Music*, 13–14 (quotation).

6. A. Roger Ekirch, *"Poor Carolina": Politics and Society in Colonial North Carolina* (Chapel Hill: University of North Carolina Press, 1981), 14–17.

7. William S. Price, Jr., *"There Ought to Be a Bill of Rights": North Carolina Enters a New Nation* (Raleigh: North Carolina Office of Archives and History, 1991), 13.

8. William S. Powell, ed., *The Correspondence of William Tryon and Selected Papers*, 2 vols. (Raleigh: North Carolina Office of Archives and History, 1980–1981), 1:577–578.

9. Thomas Jefferson to Giovanni Fabbroni, June 8, 1778, in Jefferson, *Writings*, ed. Merrill D. Peterson (New York: Library of America, 1984), 760–762.

10. Elizabeth Reid Murray and K. Todd Johnson, *Wake: Capital County of North Carolina*, 2 vols. (Raleigh: Capital Publishing and Wake County, 1983–2008), 1:193.

11. Margaret Supplee Smith and Emily Herring Wilson, *North Carolina Women Making History* (Chapel Hill: University of North Carolina Press, 1999), 90; Clement Eaton, *The Growth of Southern Civilization, 1790–1860* (New York: Harper and Row, 1961), 117.

12. Guion Griffis Johnson, *Ante-bellum North Carolina: A Social History* (Chapel Hill: University of North Carolina Press, 1937), 306.

13. Murray and Johnson, *Wake: Capital County*, 1:193–194.

14. *Ibid.*, 1:341.

15. *Daily Tar Heel* (Chapel Hill), October 31, November 30, 1933. In the fall of 1933, the composition was resurrected and played at a university sporting event.

16. *Buffalo* (NY) *Daily Courier*, January 20, 23, 1846, January 5, June 18, 1850; *Brooklyn* (NY) *Daily Eagle*, November 8, 1847; "Gustav Blessner (1800–1888)," IMSLP Petrucci Music Library, imslp.org/wiki/Category:Blessner,_Gustav.

17. *Raleigh Register*, March 20, 1846.

18. *Brookville* (PA) *Republican*, October 30, 1867, March 21, 1870; "Gustav Blessner," IMSLP Petrucci Music Library.

19. Clement Eaton, *The Waning of the Old South Civilization, 1860–1880* (Athens: University of Georgia Press, 1968), 30–31.

20. Sarah McCulloh Lemmon, ed., *The Pettigrew Papers*, 2 vols. (Raleigh: North Carolina Office of Archives and History, 1971–1988), 1:463.

21. Margaret Foote and Wiley J. Williams, "Classical Music," in William S. Powell, ed., *Encyclopedia of North Carolina* (Chapel Hill: University of North Carolina Press, 2006), 242.

22. Murray and Johnson, *Wake: Capital County*, 1:195.

23. Alan D. Watson, *Wilmington, North Carolina, to 1861* (Jefferson, NC: McFarland, 2003), 181–182.

24. Murray and Johnson, *Wake: Capital County*, 1:339.

25. Davis, "Classical Music and Opera," 43.

26. Malone and Stricklin, *Southern Music/American Music*, 17.

27. *Ibid.*, 16.

28. Davis, "Classical Music and Opera," 43–47.

29. Watson, *Wilmington*, 182.

30. Murray and Johnson, *Wake: Capital County*, 1:339.

31. C. Daniel Crews, "Moravians," in Powell, *Encyclopedia of North Carolina*, 764–765.

32. John H. Hutcheson, Jr., "Moravian Music," in Powell, *Encyclopedia of North Carolina*, 763–764.

33. *Ibid.*, 763.

34. Donald M. McCorkle, "The Moravian Contribution to American Music," *Music Library Association* 13 (September 1956): 598. See also McCorkle, "The *Collegium Musicum Salem*: Its Music, Musicians, and Importance," *North Carolina Historical Review* 33 (October 1956): 483–498.

35. *Winston-Salem Music Festival* (brochure) (Winston-Salem: Salem Academy and College, 1907), copy in Joffre Bunker Collection, Private Collections, State Archives, North Carolina Office of Archives and History, Raleigh.

36. Hutcheson, "Moravian Music," 764.

37. Watson, *Wilmington*, 182.

38. Bill Barlow, "Minstrelsy," in Malone, *Music*, 89–90.

39. Struble, *History of American Classical Music*, 12–13.

40. Davis, "Classical Music and Opera," 47.

41. Murray and Johnson, *Wake: Capital County*, 1:338–339.

42. Johnson, *Ante-bellum North Carolina*, 174.

43. Murray and Johnson, *Wake: Capital County*, 1:340.

44. Richard Crawford, *America's Musical Life: A History* (New York: W. W. Norton, 2001), 275–277 (quotations on 275).

45. Johnson, *Ante-bellum North Carolina*, 175.

46. Struble, *History of American Classical Music*, 21.

47. Eaton, *Waning of the Old South Civilization*, 100–102. For Lanier see Jane S. Gabin, *A Living Minstrelsy: The Poetry and Music of Sidney Lanier* (Macon, GA: Mercer University Press, 1985). For Gottschalk see Ronald L. Davis, "Gottschalk, Louis Moreau," in Malone, *Music*, 234–235.

48. Eaton, *Waning of the Old South Civilization*, 100–102; Mary Elizabeth Massey, *Refugee Life in the Confederacy* (Baton Rouge: Louisiana State University Press, 1964), 201–202.

49. Murray and Johnson, *Wake: Capital County*, 1:493.

50. Bell Irvin Wiley, *The Life of Johnny Reb: The Common Soldier of the Confederacy* (Baton Rouge: Louisiana State University Press, 2004), 151, 152, 156.

51. Clyde N. Wilson, *Carolina Cavalier: The Life of James Johnston Pettigrew* (Athens: University of Georgia Press, 1990), 40.

52. Wiley, *Life of Johnny Reb*, 154–157 (quotation on 157).

53. Rod Gragg, *Covered with Glory: The 26th North Carolina Infantry at the Battle of Gettysburg* (New York: HarperCollins, 2000), 22–23, 57–58; Harry H. Hall, *A Johnny Reb Band from Salem: The Pride of Tarheelia* (Raleigh: North Carolina Office of Archives and History, 2006); Glenn Tucker, *Zeb Vance: Champion of Personal Freedom* (New York: Bobbs-Merrill, 1965), 157.

54. Struble, *History of American Classical Music*, 21.

55. E. Merton Coulter, *The South During Reconstruction, 1865–1877* (Baton Rouge: Louisiana State University Press, 1947), 292.

56. *Pamlico Enterprise,* quoted in Joe A. Mobley, *Pamlico County: A Brief History* (Raleigh: North Carolina Office of Archives and History, 1991), 83.

57. Kate Lewis Scales to "Darling Papa," February 6, 1877, Alfred Moore Scales Papers, Private Collections, State Archives.

58. Kate Lewis Scales to "Precious Mama," January 13, June 2, 1877, May 11, 1878, Scales Papers, State Archives.

59. *News and Observer* (Raleigh), February 5, 1889.

60. *Ibid.,* April 17, 1889.

61. *Ibid.,* October 25, 1889.

62. *Ibid.,* May 29, 1889.

63. Paul F. Wilson, "Opera Houses," in Powell, *Encyclopedia of North Carolina*, 851–852.

64. Murray and Johnson, *Wake: Capital County*, 1:581, 584.

65. Joe A. Mobley, *Raleigh, North Carolina: A Brief History* (Charleston, SC: History Press, 2009), 90, 92; Murray and Johnson, *Wake: Capital County*, 2:438.

66. *News and Observer*, March 1, 3, 5, 6, 1889.

67. *Ibid.,* March 1, 1889.

68. Charles P. Mitchell, *The Great Composers Portrayed on Film, 1913 through 2002* (Jefferson, NC: McFarland, 2004), 93–96.

69. *News and Observer*, March 1, 1889.

70. *Ibid.,* March 7, 1889.

71. *State Chronicle* (Raleigh), November 25, 29, 1889.

72. *News and Observer*, November 30, 1889.

73. *Ibid.,* November 3, 7, 27, 1889.

74. *State Chronicle*, December 16, 1890.

75. William A. Link, *North Carolina: Change and Tradition in a Southern State* (Wheeling, IL: Harlan Davidson, 2009), 248–257. For the New South, see C. Vann Woodward, *Origins of the New South, 1877–1913* (Baton Rouge: Louisiana State University Press, 1951), and Edward L. Ayers, *The Promise of the New South: Life After Reconstruction* (New York: Oxford University Press, 1992).

76. Murray and Johnson, *Wake: Capital County*, 2:438–439.

77. *News and Observer*, January 31, February 2, 5, 8, 1902; Murray and Johnson, *Wake: Capital County*, 2:439; Mitchell, *Great Composers on Film*, 218.

78. Link, *North Carolina*, 268–280, 287–299.

79. William S. Powell, ed., *Dictionary of North Carolina Biography*, 6 vols. (Chapel Hill: University of North Carolina Press, 1979–1996), s.vv. "Boyd, James," "Chesnutt, Charles Waddell," "Green, Paul Eliot," "Porter, William Sydney (O. Henry)," and "Wolfe, Thomas Clayton."

80. H. G. Jones, "Literary and Historical Association," in Powell, *Encyclopedia of North Carolina*, 681–682.

81. Wiley J. Williams, "State Art Society," in Powell, *Encyclopedia of North Carolina*, 1071; Powell, *Dictionary of North Carolina Biography*, s.vv. "Phifer, Robert Fulenwider," and "Poe, Clarence Hamilton."

82. David Louis Sterrett Brook, *A Lasting Gift of Heritage: A History of the North Carolina Society for the Preservation of Antiquities, 1939–1974* (Raleigh: North Carolina Office of Archives and History, 1997), 4 (quotation).

83. Ansley Herring Wegner, *History for All the People: One Hundred Years of Public History in North Carolina* (Raleigh: North Carolina Office of Archives and History, 2003).

84. *Winston-Salem Music Festival.*

85. Foote and Williams, "Classical Music," 242–243 (quotation on 242); Maxine Eleanor Taylor Fountain, ed., *Enthusiasts All: A Story of the Impact Made by the North Carolina Federation of Music Clubs upon the State of North Carolina, 1917–1974* (Chapel Hill: Creative Printers, 1974), 25–26.

86. H. L. Mencken, "The Sahara of the Bozart," in *The American Scene: A Reader*, ed. Huntington Cairns (New York: Alfred A. Knopf, 1977), 157–168. For a full discussion of Mencken and southern culture, see Fred C. Hobson, *Serpent in Eden: H. L. Mencken and the South* (Chapel Hill: University of North Carolina Press, 1974).

87. Davis, "Classical Music and Opera," 45.

88. Malone and Stricklin, *Southern Music/American Music*, 13.

Chapter 2

1. Douglas R. Nelson, "The Life and Works of Lamar Stringfield (1897–1959)" (PhD diss., University of North Carolina at Chapel Hill, 1971), 4; Powell, *Dictionary of North Carolina Biography*, s.v. "Stringfield, Lamar"; Michael Hill, ed., *Guide to North Carolina Highway Historical Markers* (Raleigh: North Carolina Office of Archives and History, 2001), 203.

2. Nelson, "Life and Works of Lamar Stringfield," 6–7 (quotations from the *Asheville Citizen-Times* on 6).

3. Powell, *Dictionary of North Carolina Biography*, s.v. "Stringfield, Lamar."

4. Nelson, "Life and Works of Lamar Stringfield," 15; Powell, *Dictionary of North Carolina Biography*, s.v. "Stringfield, Lamar"; Peter C. Hager, "Lamar Stringfield (1897–1959)" (2011), *Encyclopedia of Appalachia*, http://www.encyclopediaofappalachia.com/entry.php?rec=201.

5. Howard Turner Pearsall, "The North Carolina Symphony Orchestra from 1932 to 1962: Its Founding, Musical Growth, and Musical Activities" (PhD diss., Indiana University, 1969), 7–8.

6. Benjamin Swalin, *Hard Circus Road: The Odyssey of the North Carolina Symphony* (Raleigh: North Carolina Symphony Society, 1987), 2.

7. Pearsall, "North Carolina Symphony Orchestra," 7–10.

8. Nelson, "Life and Works of Lamar Stringfield," 16–18; Pearsall, "North Carolina Symphony Orchestra," 10–12; Powell, *Dictionary of North Carolina Biography*, s.v. "Stringfield, Lamar"; Christa Anne Bentley, "Finding *The Lost Colony* (1937): Paul Green, Symphonic Drama, and the History of a Collaboration" (MA thesis, University of North Carolina at Chapel Hill, 2012), 22–24.

9. *New York Times*, December 23, 1934.

10. Pearsall, "North Carolina Symphony Orchestra," 11–14; Nelson, "Life and Works of Lamar Stringfield," 17–19, 23–24; Bentley, "Finding *The Lost Colony*," 24; Powell, *Dictionary of North Carolina Biography*, s.v. "Stringfield, Lamar."

11. Nelson, "Life and Works of Lamar Stringfield," 23–24.

12. Pearsall, "North Carolina Symphony Orchestra," 14–16; Powell, *Dictionary of North Carolina Biography*, s.v. "Pratt, Joseph Hyde"; *News and Observer*, April 3, 1932. Mrs. Reuben Roberson of Canton and John Small of Charlotte became honorary vice presidents. Felix Grisette of the steering committee was elected secretary-treasurer. Nine persons served as an executive committee and seven as the steering committee.

13. John W. Lambert, "North Carolina Symphony," in Robert R. Craven, ed., *Symphony Orchestras of the United States: Selected Profiles* (New York: Greenwood, 1986), 288; Pearsall, "North Carolina Symphony Orchestra," 18, 21–24.

14. *Greensboro Daily News,* October 30, 1932.

15. *Daily Tar Heel,* November 30, 1932.

16. *Greensboro Daily News,* November 26, 1932.

17. *Chapel Hill Weekly,* December 2, 1932.

18. *Dictionary of National Biography,* s.v. "Grainger, Percy Aldridge," http://www.oxforddnb.com/.

19. Pearsall, "North Carolina Symphony Orchestra," 24–25.

20. Pearsall, "North Carolina Symphony Orchestra," 26–28, 308.

21. L. Moody Simms, Jr., "Powell, John," in Malone, *Music,* 325–326.

22. *News and Observer,* July 23, 1933; Rosalyn M. Story, *And So I Sing: African-American Divas of Opera and Concert* (New York: Warner, 1990), 53, 54, 62, 92, 98; Eileen Southern, *The Music of Black Americans: A History* (New York: W. W. Norton, 1971), 290, 292, 426, 439, 500–501; "Jarboro, Caterina (1903–1986)," *Online Encyclopedia of Significant People and Places in African American History,* BlackPast.org, www.blackpast.org/aah/jarboro-caterina-1903-1986.

23. *New York Times,* July 23, 1933.

24. *New York Times,* July 25, 1933.

25. *News and Observer,* November 24, 1934.

26. "Jarboro, Caterina," *Online Encyclopedia,* BlackPast.org; Story, *And So I Sing,* 97; *New York Times,* August 14, 1986.

27. David M. Kennedy, *Freedom from Fear: The American People in Depression and War, 1929–1945* (New York: Oxford University Press, 1999), 145, 170–172 (quotation on 145).

28. Link, *North Carolina,* 354–355; Smith and Wilson, *North Carolina Women Making History,* 222.

29. *New York Times,* May 18, 1934.

30. Benjamin Swalin, *Hard Circus Road,* 136.

31. Malone and Stricklin, *Southern Music/American Music,* 71.

32. Joe A. Mobley, *Weary of War: Life on the Confederate Home Front* (Westport, CT: Praeger, 2008), 121–123; Malone and Stricklin, *Southern Music/American /Music,* 39–89.

33. Pearsall, "North Carolina Symphony Orchestra," 29–31; George J. Ferencz, ed., *"The Broadway Sound": The Autobiography and Selected Essays of Robert Russell Bennett* (Rochester, NY: University of Rochester Press, 1999), 1–5, 43, and passim; *Asheville Advocate,* August 24, 1934.

34. *Asheville Advocate,* July 20, 1934.

35. *Asheville Advocate,* August 3, 1934. For a brief reference to Whitborne, see the *New York Times,* December 6, 1923.

36. Pearsall, "North Carolina Symphony Orchestra," 308–309; *Asheville Advocate,* August 3, 10, 1934. For sources on Donaldson, see research by Bill Edwards at Ragpiano.com. For Still see William Grant Still, *My Life, My Words: The Autobiography of William Grant Still, American Master Composer* (Flagstaff, AZ: Master-Player Library, 2011).

37. *Asheville Advocate,* August 24, 1934.

38. Pearsall, "North Carolina Symphony Orchestra," 32.

39. *Asheville Advocate,* September 14, 1934.

40. Pearsall, "North Carolina Symphony Orchestra," 32–33.

41. *New York Times,* December 23, 1934; Pearsall, "North Carolina Symphony Orchestra," 310.

42. Pearsall, "North Carolina Symphony Orchestra," 33–36, 54, 310–311.

43. *New York Times,* June 16, 1935.

44. Pearsall, "North Carolina Symphony Orchestra," 37–39 (quotation on 39).

45. *Durham Herald,* November 20, 1943.

46. Pearsall, "North Carolina Symphony Orchestra," 39–41.

47. *New York Times,* December 15, 1935.

48. Maxine Swalin, *Coming of Age in North Carolina's Fifth Century,* pt. 1 (Chapel Hill: North Caroliniana Society, 2003), 7; Pearsall, "North Carolina Symphony Orchestra," 41.

49. *New York Times*, December 15, 1935.

50. Pearsall, "North Carolina Symphony Orchestra," 41–43; Benjamin Swalin, *Hard Circus Road*, 6–8; John L. Humber, "The North Carolina Symphony, the People's Orchestra: A Brief History," pt. 3 of Maxine Swalin, *Coming of Age*, 25. According to Pearsall, p. 46, "There is some controversy over the causes of the orchestra's discontinuance. Some people contend the group merged with a similar organization in Virginia. Facts are evident that a W.P.A. band remained in Greensboro until 1940."

51. Nelson, "Life and Works of Lamar Stringfield," 34–41; Bentley, "Finding *The Lost Colony*," 48, 52–55; Powell, *Dictionary of North Carolina Biography*, s.v. "Stringfield, Lamar."

52. *News and Observer*, May 22, 1949.

53. Powell, *Dictionary of North Carolina Biography*, s.v. "Stringfield, Lamar"; Leonardo De Lorenzo, *My Complete Story of the Flute: The Instrument, the Performers, the Music*, rev. ed. (Lubbock: Texas Tech University Press, 1992), 375.

54. Nelson, "Life and Works of Lamar Stringfield," 9–10, 62.

55. Powell, *Dictionary of North Carolina Biography*, s.v. "Stringfield, Lamar"; Fountain, *Enthusiasts All*, 41–42; Jimmy J. Gilmore, "Lamar Stringfield: Piper of Dreams," *Opus Magazine*, Fall 2007, 27–30; Hill, *Guide to North Carolina Highway Historical Markers*, 203; *New York Times*, January 23, 1959.

56. Bruce E. Baker, Carole Watterson Troxler, and Wiley J. Williams, "Folk Music," in Powell, *Encyclopedia of North Carolina*," 447–449; Malone and Stricklin, *Southern Music/American Music*, 35–36; Crawford, *America's Musical Life*, 600–601.

57. Struble, *History of American Classical Music*, xix.

Chapter 3

1. Maxine Swalin, *Coming of Age*, 6; Benjamin Swalin, *Hard Circus Road*, xvii–xx.

2. UNC Libraries, "Swalin, Benjamin Franklin" (2010; 2017), *NCpedia*, https://www.ncpedia.org/swalin-benjamin-franklin; Maxine Swalin, *Coming of Age*, 5–6; Maxine Swalin, *An Ear to Myself* (Chapel Hill: by the author, 1996), 65.

3. *Willmar* (MN) *Tribune*, September 18, 1918.

4. *Ibid.*, August 13, 1919.

5. *Star Tribune* (Minneapolis), April 10, 1919.

6. Benjamin Swalin, *Hard Circus Road*, xviii.

7. Maxine Swalin, *Coming of Age*, 6; Benjamin Swalin, *Hard Circus Road*, xviii–xix; *Star Tribune*, July 9, 1922; *Willmar Tribune*, November 16, 1921.

8. Benjamin Swalin, *Hard Circus Road*, xix.

9. *New York Times*, August 10, 1930.

10. Benjamin Swalin, *Hard Circus Road*, xix–xx.

11. Maxine Swalin, *An Ear to Myself*, 1, 11 (quotation); "Maxine McMahon Swalin," *CVNC: An Online Arts Journal in North Carolina*, October 8, 2009, https://www.cvnc.org/article.cfm?articleId=1181.

12. Maxine Swalin, *Coming of Age*, 3.

13. Maxine Swalin, *An Ear to Myself*, 15–16.

14. Maxine Swalin, *Coming of Age*, 4.

15. Maxine Swalin, *An Ear to Myself*, 19.

16. *Ibid.*, 28–32 (quotations on 32).

17. *Ibid.*, 35–36.

18. Maxine Swalin, *Coming of Age*, 4–5.

19. Maxine Swalin, *An Ear to Myself*, 53–54.

20. *Ibid.*, 54–57 (quotation on 55).

21. *Ibid.*, 59, 83, 105.

22. *Ibid.*, 60–67 (quotations on 67).

23. *Ibid.*, 68–73 (quotations on 68).

24. Benjamin Swalin, *Hard Circus Road*, xvii–xviii.

25. Maxine Swalin, *An Ear to Myself*, 74–80 (quotations on 74, 79, and 80); Folders 261–262 (Maxeben 1929–1990s), Series 4: Subject Files 1915–1986, Benjamin F. and Maxine M. Swalin Papers, Southern Historical Collection, Wilson Library, University of North Carolina at Chapel Hill. The Swalins' home outside town was on Jones Ferry Road. *News of Orange County* (Hillsborough, NC), May 30, 1963.

26. Maxine Swalin, *An Ear to Myself*, 83.

27. Benjamin Swalin, *Hard Circus Road*, 9.

28. Pearsall, "North Carolina Symphony Orchestra," 42, 44, 45 (quotation); Benjamin Swalin, *Hard Circus Road*, 9–10.

29. Benjamin Swalin, *Hard Circus Road*, 1, 10–11.

30. *Daily Times-News* (Burlington, NC), May 4, 1937; *Chicago Tribune*, August 14, 1938; Pearsall, "North Carolina Symphony Orchestra," 46–47; Benjamin Swalin, *Hard Circus Road*, 8, 12.

31. Benjamin Swalin, *Hard Circus Road*, 13. For a brief biography of Green, see Powell, *Dictionary of North Carolina Biography*, s.v. "Green, Paul Eliot."

32. Benjamin Swalin, *Hard Circus Road*, 13; *Daily Tar Heel*, January 14, 1939.

33. Maxine Swalin, *An Ear to Myself*, 90.

34. Benjamin Swalin, *Hard Circus Road*, 13.

35. Lambert, "North Carolina Symphony," 289; Pearsall, "North Carolina Symphony Orchestra," 57–58.

36. Pearsall, "North Carolina Symphony Orchestra," 59–60.

37. Benjamin Swalin, *Hard Circus Road*, 15–16.

38. Pearsall, "North Carolina Symphony Orchestra," 60; *Daily Tar Heel*, May 5, 1940.

39. *Daily Tar Heel*, May 5, 1940.

40. Pearsall, "North Carolina Symphony Orchestra," 60–63; Benjamin Swalin, *Hard Circus Road*, 16.

41. Benjamin Swalin, *Hard Circus Road*, 17; Pearsall, "North Carolina Symphony Orchestra," 62–64.

42. Benjamin Swalin, *Hard Circus Road*, 17–18.

43. Maxine Swalin, *An Ear to Myself*, 82.

44. Benjamin Swalin, *Hard Circus Road*, 23–24; Pearsall, "North Carolina Symphony Orchestra," 70.

45. Benjamin Swalin, *Hard Circus Road*, 24.

46. Pearsall, "North Carolina Symphony Orchestra," 96.

47. Pearsall, "North Carolina Symphony Orchestra," 64–65, 68–71; Benjamin Swalin, *Hard Circus Road*, 19, 23; *New York Times*, August 9, 2012.

48. Pearsall, "North Carolina Symphony Orchestra," 72; Benjamin Swalin, *Hard Circus Road*, 19–20.

49. Benjamin Swalin, *Hard Circus Road*, 20.

50. Session Laws of North Carolina 1943, S.B. 248, c. 755.

51. Benjamin Swalin, *Hard Circus Road*, 21.

52. Pearsall, "North Carolina Symphony Orchestra," 79–80.

53. *Daily Tar Heel*, December 5, 1944.

54. Pearsall, "North Carolina Symphony Orchestra," 382.

55. *Ibid.*, 80–82.

56. Benjamin Swalin, *Hard Circus Road*, 30–31, 33; Pearsall, "North Carolina Symphony Orchestra," 83–89.

57. Benjamin Swalin, *Hard Circus Road*, 30.

58. Pearsall, "North Carolina Symphony Orchestra," 88–90.

59. Maxine Swalin, *An Ear to Myself*, 84.

60. Benjamin Swalin, *Hard Circus Road*, 27–28.

61. *Ibid.*, 35–36.

62. Pearsall, "North Carolina Symphony Orchestra," 86–87; Benjamin Swalin, *Hard*

Circus Road, 35–36. Another musician, George Haley of Asheville, also a double bassist, was killed at the Battle of Guadalcanal.

63. Benjamin Swalin, *Hard Circus Road*, 51.
64. Pearsall, "North Carolina Symphony Orchestra," 100–102; Humber, "North Carolina Symphony," 29–30; Benjamin Swalin, *Hard Circus Road*, 51–62; *Robesonian* (Lumberton, NC), September 23, 1936; *Daily Times-News*, February 7, 1938.
65. Maxine Swalin, *An Ear to Myself*, 90.
66. Pearsall, "North Carolina Symphony Orchestra," 98.
67. Benjamin Swalin, *Hard Circus Road*, xx.
68. Pearsall, "North Carolina Symphony Orchestra," 103.

Chapter 4

1. Pearsall, "North Carolina Symphony Orchestra," 103–108; Maxine Swalin, *An Ear to Myself*, 119.
2. Benjamin Swalin, *Hard Circus Road*, 37.
3. Pearsall, "North Carolina Symphony Orchestra," 108–109; Benjamin Swalin, *Hard Circus Road*, 39–41.
4. Benjamin Swalin, *Hard Circus Road*, 41–42.
5. Pearsall, "North Carolina Symphony Orchestra," 111–115; Benjamin Swalin, *Hard Circus Road*, 42–43, 48.
6. *New York Times*, March 2, 1947.
7. Pearsall, "North Carolina Symphony Orchestra," 110–111; Benjamin Swalin, *Hard Circus Road*, 45; *High Point* (NC) *Enterprise*, April 8, 1951.
8. Pearsall, "North Carolina Symphony Orchestra," 190, 196.
9. *Daily Tar Heel*, June 26, 1953.
10. Benjamin Swalin, *Hard Circus Road*, 55–56, 57–59 (quotation on 55–56).
11. Pearsall, "North Carolina Symphony Orchestra," 110–111, 116, 126; *New York Times*, August 15, 1949, April 15, 1951.
12. Pearsall, "North Carolina Symphony Orchestra," 132, 197, 232.
13. Ibid., 152–159, 174, 220.
14. Benjamin Swalin, *Hard Circus Road*, 66; *Democrat and Chronicle* (Rochester, NY), April 20, 1945; *Robesonian*, April 1, 1948, December 24, 1956, July 3, 1958; *Bee* (Danville, VA), April 9, 1953; *Asheville Citizen-Times*, August 21, 1954.
15. Pearsall, "North Carolina Symphony Orchestra," 132–146, 377–380.
16. *New York Times*, October 19, 1952.
17. *Waco* (TX) *News-Tribune*, May 10, 1955.
18. Pearsall, "North Carolina Symphony Orchestra," 168, 182; *Daily Tar Heel*, November 11, 1956; *Ottawa* (ON) *Journal*, April 19, 1975.
19. Sandra Cook Stuart, "A Biography of John Cook," Organ Works of John Cook, Raven Compact Disks, https://ravencd.com/merchantmanager/product_info.php?products_id=6; *Lancaster* (OH) *Eagle-Gazette*, July 14, 1960; Pearsall, "North Carolina Symphony Orchestra," 190.
20. *Daily Tar Heel*, November 15, 1936; *Daily Times-News*, January 18, 1959; *Asheville Citizen-Times*, March 19, 1950; *Bee*, March 28, 1975.
21. Marco Shirodkar, "Alan Hovhaness Biographical Summary," The Alan Hovhaness Web Site, http://www.hovhaness.com/biography.html; Pearsall, "North Carolina Symphony Orchestra," 203.
22. *Statesville* (NC) *Record and Landmark*, May 11, 18, 1963; *Greensboro Daily News*, May 9, 1963.
23. Pearsall, "North Carolina Symphony Orchestra," 146, 159, 183, 190, 197, 231; Benjamin Swalin, *Hard Circus Road*, 47–50.
24. Benjamin Swalin, *Hard Circus Road*, 47–50 (quotations on 47).

25. *Daily Times-News*, November 6, 1952.

26. Pearsall, "North Carolina Symphony Orchestra," 153, 231; Benjamin Swalin, *Hard Circus Road*, 49, 69; Powell, *Dictionary of North Carolina Biography*, s.v. "Love, James Spencer."

27. "On the Move," *Time*, May 9, 1949, 69–70.

28. *New York Times*, April 15, 1951.

29. Sey Chassler, "Symphony on Wheels," *Collier's*, February 23, 1952, 30–31.

30. "Tarheel Symphony," *Newsweek*, June 9, 1952, 86.

31. Maxine Swalin to G. Gold of Don Loper Inc., September 5, 19, 1968, Correspondence 1968, North Carolina Symphony Society Records, State Archives.

32. Benjamin Swalin, *Hard Circus Road*, ix.

33. Vincent F. Simonetti, interview with the authors, December 19, 2017, Durham.

34. Ronald Weddle, interview with the authors, December 21, 2017, Raleigh.

35. *Asheville Citizen-Times*, April 30, 1969.

36. *Statesville Record and Landmark*, July 25, 1962.

37. Benjamin Swalin, *Hard Circus Road*, 121.

38. *Asheville Citizen-Times*, May 22, 1959.

39. *Charlotte Observer*, as printed in the *Iredell Morning News* (Statesville, NC), May 28, 1959.

40. *Greensboro Daily News*, May 24, 1959, reproduced in Benjamin Swalin, *Hard Circus Road*, 71. The cartoonist was William Sanders.

41. Benjamin Swalin, *Hard Circus Road*, 69–73; Pearsall, "North Carolina Symphony Orchestra," 202.

42. Benjamin Swalin, *Hard Circus Road*, 74, 96–97 (quotations on 74).

43. *Ibid.*, 90, 95–97.

44. Pearsall, "North Carolina Symphony Orchestra," 227; Benjamin Swalin, *Hard Circus Road*, 89–94; *Statesville Record and Landmark*, May 11, 1962; *Robesonian*, April 7, 1977.

45. *New York Times*, June 21, 1964.

46. Benjamin Swalin, *Hard Circus Road*, 123–124.

47. *Ibid.*, 124–128.

48. *Ibid.*, 128–129.

49. *Ibid.*, 132–133.

50. *Ibid.*, 129–132.

51. Benjamin Swalin, *Hard Circus Road*, 94–95; Simonetti interview.

52. Hiram B. Black to Travis H. Tomlinson, September 20, 1968, Correspondence 1968, North Carolina Symphony Society Records, State Archives.

53. Benjamin Swalin, *Hard Circus Road*, 95.

54. Jimmy J. Gilmore, "The Long Road Home: A Musician's Story," *Opus Magazine*, Fall 2006, 37.

55. Benjamin Swalin, *Hard Circus Road*, 61, 76–88 (quotations on 61 and 76–77).

56. *New York Times*, January 4, 1959.

57. Benjamin Swalin to Warren Benfield, September 10, 1968, to Mr. and Mrs. Schoenbrun, September 4, 1968, and to Joseph Silverstein, September 10, 1968, Correspondence 1968, North Carolina Symphony Society Records, State Archives.

58. Hiram B. Black to Enrique Raudales and to Katsuko Esaki, September 26, 1968, Correspondence 1968, North Carolina Symphony Society Records, State Archives; Weddle interview; Benjamin Swalin, *Hard Circus Road*, 107–109.

59. Benjamin Swalin, *Hard Circus Road*, 110–114 (quotations on 112 and 114). For an account of Kutschinski, see Curtis R. Craver, Jr., *The History of Music at North Carolina State University* (Raleigh: Department of Music, North Carolina State University, 2000).

60. Benjamin Swalin, *Hard Circus Road*, 150; *Times* (Shreveport, LA), December 4, 2011.

61. *Daily Times-News*, November 17, 1970; *Statesville Record and Landmark*, November 21, 1970; Jimmy J. Gilmore, interview with the authors, October 25, 2017, Raleigh.

62. Benjamin Swalin, *Hard Circus Road*, 150.

63. Pearsall, "North Carolina Symphony Orchestra," 231–233.

64. *Asheville Citizen-Times*, May 14, 1954.

65. *Greensboro Daily News*, May 6, 1957.

66. *Asheville Citizen-Times*, April 26, 1967.

67. Maxine Swalin, *An Ear to Myself*, 89.

68. Sharon Faulkner, "My Trip to the Symphony," and Donald Boswell, "My Trip to the Symphony," March 1963, Newspaper Clipping File and Reviews 1963, North Carolina Symphony Society Records, State Archives.

69. Hugh Partridge, interview with the authors, October 18, 2017, Cary, NC.

70. Maxine Swalin, *An Ear to Myself*, 101.

71. *Ibid.*, 92.

72. *News and Observer*, May 11, 1963.

73. Benjamin Swalin, *Hard Circus Road*, 92; Paul Gorski, interview with the authors, November 8, 2017, Raleigh.

74. *Daily Tar Heel*, November 19, 1970; *Statesville Record and Landmark*, November 21, 1970.

75. *News Journal* (Wilmington, DE), July 15, 1976; *San Antonio Express*, August 27, 1976; *Los Angeles Times*, May 6, 1977.

76. Associated Press, in *Lubbock* (TX) *Avalanche-Journal*, September 28, 1976.

77. Maxine Swalin, *An Ear to Myself*, 103, 107.

78. *Statesville Record and Landmark*, July 25, 1962.

79. Maxine Swalin, *An Ear to Myself*, 119–120.

80. Maxine Swalin to Virginia Bennie, September 10, 1968, Correspondence 1968, North Carolina Symphony Society Records, State Archives.

81. *Nashville* (NC) *Graphic*, May 14, 2015.

82. "Beginning a New Quarter-Century" ([North Carolina Symphony Society, 1970]), copy in private collection.

83. Gilmore interview.

84. D. Mitropoulos to Benjamin Swalin, April 23, 1940, Folder 55 (1940–1988), Series 3: Correspondence 1932–1993, Swalin Papers, Southern Historical Collection.

85. North Carolina Symphony Society contract with violinist Paul Gorski, October 19, 1962, private collection. For an explanation of North Carolina's right-to-work law, see Wiley J. Williams, "Right-to-Work Law," in Powell, *Encyclopedia of North Carolina*, 973–974. Most musicians with the North Carolina Symphony were then and are presently members of the American Federation of Musicians.

86. J. Carlyle Sitterson to Benjamin Swalin, June 22, 1967, Folder 55 (1940–1988), Series 3, Swalin Papers, Southern Historical Collection.

Chapter 5

1. Gilmore, "Long Road Home," 36–37.

2. Benjamin Swalin to Schuyler Chapin, November 28, 1975, Folder 55 (1940–1988), Series 3, Swalin Papers, Southern Historical Collection.

3. Gilmore interview; Maxine Swalin, *An Ear to Myself*, 136; Executive Committee Meeting, April 22, 1972, Minutes of the North Carolina Symphony Society and Its Committees 1940–1973 (microfilm), Records of the North Carolina Department of Cultural Resources, State Archives.

4. Executive Committee Meeting, April 22, 1972, Minutes of the North Carolina Symphony Society, State Archives.

5. *Ibid.*

6. Executive Committee Meeting, October 3, 1972, Minutes of the North Carolina Symphony Society, State Archives.

7. *Ibid.*

8. *Statesville Record and Landmark*, October 7, 1972; *Daily Tar Heel*, October 9, 1972;

Daily Times-News, January 4, 1977; *Robesonian*, November 20, 1977; *Savannah Morning News*, October 21, 2004.

9. *High Point Enterprise*, February 4, 1973.

10. *Asheville Citizen-Times*, December 3, 1972.

11. John Gosling to Benjamin Swalin, October 31, 1972, and Swalin to Gosling, November 18, 1972, Folder 243 (Gosling, John, 1972–1986 and undated), Series 4, Swalin Papers, Southern Historical Collection.

12. Albert and Susan Jenkins, interview with the authors, November 14, 2017, Raleigh.

13. Copy of Executive Committee Meeting Minutes, North Carolina Symphony Society, December 5, 1974, Folder 222 (Executive Committee: Reports and Minutes 1971–1982), Series 4, Swalin Papers, Southern Historical Collection. See also Valerie Niemi to Benjamin Swalin, June 28, 1973, and Margaret Flower to Swalin, May 7, 1973, Folder 242 (Gosling, John, 1972–1986 and undated), Series 4, Swalin Papers, Southern Historical Collection.

14. Benjamin Swalin to Garry de Leon, September 26, 1979, Folder 55 (1940–1988), Series 3, Swalin Papers, Southern Historical Collection.

15. Annual Meeting of the North Carolina Symphony Society, November 30, 1972, Minutes of the North Carolina Symphony Society, State Archives.

16. Executive Committee Meeting, February 7, 1973, Minutes of the North Carolina Symphony Society, State Archives.

17. Benjamin Swalin to Hamilton C. Horton, January 15, 1973, Folder 232 (Forced Retirement: Correspondence 1972–1977 and undated), Series 4, Swalin Papers, Southern Historical Collection.

18. Benjamin Swalin to Governor James E. Holshouser, April 18, 1973, Folder 232 (Forced Retirement: Correspondence 1972–1977 and undated), Series 4, Swalin Papers, Southern Historical Collection.

19. Benjamin Swalin to Mrs. H. L. Hodgkins, Jr., February 15, 1973, Folder 232 (Forced Retirement: Correspondence 1972–1977 and undated), Series 4, Swalin Papers, Southern Historical Collection.

20. Executive Committee Meeting, April 28, 1973, Minutes of the North Carolina Symphony Society, State Archives.

21. Board of Trustees Meeting, May 29, 1973, Minutes of the North Carolina Symphony Society, State Archives.

22. *Ibid.*

23. George E. Norman, Jr., to Lieutenant Governor James B. Hunt, Jr., July 16, 1973, Folder 232 (Forced Retirement: Correspondence 1972–1977 and undated), Series 4, Swalin Papers, Southern Historical Collection.

24. Phil J. Kirk, Jr., to Benjamin Swalin, July 9, 1973, Folder 232 (Forced Retirement: Correspondence 1972–1977 and undated), Series 4, Swalin Papers, Southern Historical Collection.

25. Benjamin Swalin to Schuyler Chapin, November 28, 1975, Folder 55 (1940–1988), Series 3, Swalin Papers, Southern Historical Collection.

26. Mercer Doty to Benjamin Swalin, July 8, 1975, and Swalin to Doty, July 10, 1975, Folder 55 (1940–1988), Series 3, Swalin Papers, Southern Historical Collection; *High Point Enterprise*, May 3, 1974.

27. *Daily Tar Heel*, April 30, 1974.

28. Thomas McGuire to Benjamin Swalin, February 17, 1981, Folder 55 (1940–1988), Series 3, Swalin Papers, Southern Historical Collection.

29. Johnsie Burnham to C. C. Hope, Jr., November 4, 1972, Folder 232 (Forced Retirement: Correspondence 1972–1977 and undated), Series 4, Swalin Papers, Southern Historical Collection.

30. R. O. Huffman to C. C. Hope, Jr., November 21, 1972, Folder 232 (Forced Retirement: Correspondence 1972–1977 and undated), Series 4, Swalin Papers, Southern Historical Collection.

31. *Asheville Citizen-Times*, June 19, 1976.

32. Maxine and Benjamin Swalin to Dear Friends, July 22, 1977, Folder 232 (Forced Retirement: Correspondence 1972–1977 and undated), Series 4, Swalin Papers, Southern Historical Collection.

33. Benjamin Swalin to Karel Netoliscka, September 29, 1979, Folder 55 (1940–1988), Series 3, and Swalin to Hamilton Horton, January 15, 1973, Folder 232 (Forced Retirement: Correspondence 1972–1977 and undated), Series 4, Swalin Papers, Southern Historical Collection.

34. Maxine and Benjamin Swalin to Dear Friends, July 22, 1977, Folder 232 (Forced Retirement: Correspondence 1972–1977 and undated), Series 4, Swalin Papers, Southern Historical Collection.

35. Maxine Swalin to John Morgan, November 17, 1980, Folder 55 (1940–1988), Series 3, Swalin Papers, Southern Historical Collection.

36. Maxine Swalin to Mr. and Mrs. Blank, September 14, 1981, Folder 55 (1940–1988), Series 3, Swalin Papers, Southern Historical Collection.

37. Maxine Swalin, *An Ear to Myself*, 107–108.

38. UNC Libraries, "Swalin, Benjamin Franklin," *NCpedia*; Maxine Swalin, *An Ear to Myself*, 138.

39. North Carolina Symphony, "Swalin, Maxine McMahon [Martha Maxine]" (2009; 2017), *NCpedia*, https://www.ncpedia.org/swalin-maxine.

40. Humber, "North Carolina Symphony," 33; John W. Lambert, "Dr. Ben, Fondly Remembered, & Maxine, Warmly Embraced," *CVNC*, October 13, 2002, https://cvnc.org/article.cfm?articleId=4771.

41. *Daily Tar Heel*, February 13, 1973.

42. *Asheville Citizen-Times*, December 9, 1973.

43. *Rocky Mount* (NC) *Telegram*, February 17, 1974.

44. "Robert K. Anderson, Associate Principal," North Carolina Symphony, https://www.ncsymphony.org/about-us/robert-k-anderson/.

45. *Rocky Mount Telegram*, April 24, 1977.

46. *North Carolina Symphony 1978–1979 Concert Schedule* (brochure); *Robesonian*, October 25, 1974; *Rocky Mount Telegram*, May 13, 1973, April 24, 1977.

47. *Rocky Mount Telegram*, May 13, 1973.

48. *North Carolina Symphony 28th Annual Tour, 1972–73 Season* (program); *Robesonian*, October 25, 1974.

49. Diane Trap, "Mattiwilda Dobbs (b. 1925)" (last edited 2016), *New Georgia Encyclopedia*, www.georgiaencyclopedia.org/articles/arts-culture/mattiwilda-dobbs-b-1925; *Washington Post*, December 10, 2015; *Robesonian*, October 25, 1974.

50. *Rocky Mount Telegram*, February 9, 1975.

51. "Cynthia Clarey" (2000), LA Phil, https://www.laphil.com/search/?q=cynthia+clarey.

52. *New York Times*, August 27, 2002; *Robesonian*, October 25, 1974; Nicolas Slonimsky, *Baker's Biographical Dictionary of Twentieth-Century Classical Musicians*, ed. Laura Kuhn (New York: Schirmer, 1997), 1471.

53. "Watts, Andre (1946–)," *Online Encyclopedia*, BlackPast.org, www.blackpast.org/aah/watts-andre-1946; Slonimsky, *Biographical Dictionary of Twentieth-Century Musicians*, 1473; *High Point Enterprise*, January 20, 1976; "75 Things to Know about the North Carolina Symphony," *Opus Magazine*, Fall 2006, 31.

54. *New York Times*, April 5, 1990.

55. *Rocky Mount Telegram*, June 11, 1976.

56. *Ibid.*, May 13, 1973.

57. *Daily Times-News*, January 10, 1974.

58. *Daily Tar Heel*, January 16, 1974.

59. *Asheville Citizen-Times*, December 18, 1977.

60. *Ibid.*

61. "North Carolina State University, Friends of the College Records, 1959–1994" (2012), Collection Guides, NCSU Libraries, https://www.lib.ncsu.edu/findingaids/ua018_001.

62. *Daily Times-News*, January 5, 1977.

63. *Rocky Mount Telegram*, April 24, 1977; *Asheville Citizen-Times*, March 18, 1979; *Statesman-Journal* (Salem, OR), June 1, 1980.

64. James E. Ogle, Jr., telephone interview with the authors, March 9, 2018, Boise, ID.

65. *Rocky Mount Telegram*, April 24, 1977.

66. Catherine W. Bishir and Michael T. Southern, *A Guide to the Historic Architecture of Piedmont North Carolina* (Chapel Hill: University of North Carolina Press, 2003), 114.

67. *News and Observer*, December 15, 1977.

68. Gilmore, "Long Road Home," 38–39.

69. *News and Observer*, March 6, 1977.

70. *New York Times*, March 8, 1977.

71. Armistead Jones Maupin, "North Carolina Museum of Art," in Powell, *Encyclopedia of North Carolina*, 821–823.

72. Catherine A. Whittenburg, "North Carolina School of the Arts," in Powell, *Encyclopedia of North Carolina*, 829–830.

73. *New York Times*, March 8, 1977.

74. *News and Observer*, March 10, 1977.

75. *Ibid.*

76. *New York Times*, March 12, 1977.

77. *Ibid.*, February 27, 1977.

78. *News and Observer*, March 10, 1977.

79. Gilmore, "Long Road Home," 39.

80. *Asheville Citizen-Times*, October 20, 1978.

Chapter 6

1. Budget of North Carolina Symphony Society 1972–1973, copy in Folder 230 (Fiscal 1970–1979), Series 4, Swalin Papers, Southern Historical Collection.

2. Henry L. Bridgers, State Auditor, to Charles F. Coira, Jr., Chairman of the Board, North Carolina Symphony Society, with copy of Department of State Auditor's Report of Fiscal Year Ending June 30, 1973, Folder 229 (Fiscal 1970–1979), Series 4, Swalin Papers, Southern Historical Collection.

3. North Carolina Fiscal Research Division to Hamilton C. Horton, October 14, 1974, copy in Folder 229 (Fiscal 1970–1979), Series 4, Swalin Papers, Southern Historical Collection.

4. Copy of Executive Committee Meeting Minutes, North Carolina Symphony Society, December 5, 1974, Folder 222 (Executive Committee: Reports and Minutes 1971–1982), Series 4, Swalin Papers, Southern Historical Collection.

5. Gilmore, "Long Road Home," 87; Weddle interview.

6. "An Act to Appropriate Supplemental Funds for the North Carolina Symphony," Senate Bill 552, General Assembly of North Carolina Session 1979, copy in Folder 229 (Fiscal 1970–1979), Series 4, Swalin Papers, Southern Historical Collection.

7. *Statesville Record and Landmark*, September 18, 1976.

8. Gilmore, "Long Road Home," 37–39; Weddle interview.

9. John Gosling to George E. Norman, Jr., May 25, 1979, Folder 242 (Gosling, John, 1972–1986 and undated), Series 4, Swalin Papers, Southern Historical Collection.

10. Gilmore, "Long Road Home," 37–39; Weddle interview.

11. *North Carolina Symphony: A Major Symphony in 50 States* (1979–1980 flyer).

12. *News and Observer*, January 18, 1981.

13. "History," Bear Valley Music Festival, https://www.bearvalleymusicfestival.org/about-2/.

14. *Index-Journal* (Greenwood, SC), November 22, 1990.

15. *Savannah Morning News*, October 21, 2004.

16. *News and Observer*, April 25, 1982.

17. *News and Observer*, as printed in the *Asheville Citizen-Times*, May 10, 1980.

18. *Asheville Citizen-Times*, March 16, 1980.

19. Gilmore, "Long Road Home," 39.

20. "Artistic Director," Article 14.000, 1980–1983 Master Contract, North Carolina Symphony Society and Musicians Association Local 500, American Federation of Musicians, July 1980, transcript in private collection.

21. *Courier-Journal* (Louisville, KY), September 17, 1983, April 20, 2007.

22. Slonimsky, *Biographical Dictionary of Twentieth-Century Musicians*, 1275; *Courier-Journal*, September 17, 1983, April 20, 2007; *Cincinnati Enquirer*, August 9, 1987; *Central New Jersey Home News* (New Brunswick), May 3, 1994; *Daily Record* (Morristown, NJ), May 17, 1996; *Indianapolis Star*, March 14, 2003; "In Memoriam: Lawrence Leighton Smith, Past Music Director of Yale Philharmonia" (obituary), October 25, 2013, Announcements, Yale School of Music, http://music.yale.edu/2013/10/25/memoriam-lawrence-leighton-smith-music-director-yale-philharmonia-1995-2004/.

23. *News and Observer*, June 26, 1981.

24. Gilmore, "Long Road Home," 40.

25. *News and Observer*, July 2, 1981.

26. *Ibid.*, July 16, 26, 1981.

27. *Asheville Citizen-Times*, September 27, 1981.

28. *Sydney* (AU) *Morning Herald*, November 3, 2008.

29. *Spectator* (Raleigh), October 29, 1981.

30. *News and Observer*, September 2, 1981.

31. *Ibid.*, September 22, 1981.

32. Thomas H. McGuire, interview with the authors, January 13, 2018, Raleigh.

33. Gilmore, "Long Road Home," 39.

34. John R. Lambert, Jr., to Mrs. Faircloth and Mr. McGuire, May 14, 1982, and Nancy N. Lambert, John W. Lambert, and John R. Lambert, Jr., to Nancy B. Faircloth, May 18, 1982, copies in private collection; Jenkins interview.

35. *News and Observer*, May 8, 1982.

36. John W. Lambert to Nancy B. Faircloth, May 6, 1982, and to Senators and House Members, May 27, 1982, copies in private collection.

37. *Raleigh Times*, May 5, 6, 1982.

38. *Ibid.*, May 6, 1982.

39. *Rocky Mount Telegram*, April 16, 1982.

40. *Spectator*, May 6, 1982. Lambert wrote under the pen name Morris L. Wilson.

41. *Asheville Citizen-Times*, May 4, 1982.

42. *Sydney Morning Herald*, November 3, 2008.

43. "Gerhardt Zimmermann, Conductor," *Prabook*, https://prabook.com/web/gerhardt.zimmermann/384813; Chris Peters, "Celebrated Conductor Gerhardt Zimmermann Reflects on Time at UI, Influential Teacher He'll Honor," *Iowa Now*, April 4, 2017, University of Iowa, https://now.uiowa.edu/2017/04/celebrated-conductor-gerhardt-zimmermann; *Chicago Tribune*, April 14, 1973.

44. *Asheville Citizen-Times*, May 4, 1982.

45. Gilmore, "Long Road Home," 40–41; Maxine Swalin, *An Ear to Myself*, 135.

46. *Daily Tar Heel*, September 17, 1982.

47. *Ibid.*, October 22, 1982.

48. *Asheville Citizen-Times*, November 5, 1982.

49. Gilmore, "Long Road Home," 41; *Music: It's What We Do. The North Carolina Symphony 97–98* (program book), vii.

50. *The North Carolina Symphony: The 1983–84 Raleigh Concert Season* (flyer).

51. *1983–84 Young People's Series, The North Carolina Symphony* (flyer).

52. *News and Observer*, March 20, 1983.

53. *Chicago Tribune*, July 7, 1983.

54. *Music: It's What We Do*, vii.

55. Gilmore, "Long Road Home," 40.

56. *Asheville Citizen-Times*, December 2, 1984.

57. McGuire interview; *News and Observer*, October 27, 2017; Gilmore, "Long Road Home," 41, 43.

58. "Charity Begins at Home," *1991 Renovation Awards*, reprinted from *Commercial Renovation*, October 1991, [2, 4], copy in private collection.

59. *New York Times*, October 2, 1987, April 6, 2013; "Happy Anniversary," *New York*, September 21, 1987, 94.

60. Gilmore, "Long Road Home," 43; *Robert Ward Celebration: A Seventieth Birthday Concert Tour. The North Carolina Symphony* (1987) (program).

61. "Pops in the Park," The History of Capitol Broadcasting Company, http://history.capitolbroadcasting.com/programs/entertainment-shows/pops-in-the-park/; Gilmore, "Long Road Home," 41–42.

62. "Michael Jinbo, Music Director and Conductor," Nittany Valley Symphony, http://www.nvs.org/about-nvs/; William Henry Curry, interview with the authors, May 31, 2018, Raleigh; "William Henry Curry, Conductor," Opera Musica, https://www.operamusica.com/artist/william-henry-curry/#biography; Carter B. Gregory, "William Henry Curry, Conductor, Composer," February 2015 Honorees, *The Heritage Calendar: Celebrating the North Carolina African-American Experience*, https://ncheritagecalendar.com/honorees/william-henry-curry-2/; *Sun Journal* (New Bern, NC), March 2, 2016 (quotation).

63. Sherri Holmes, "William Henry Curry: The Life of an African American Conductor," November 25, 2014, Triangle Friends of African American Arts, http://www.africanamericanarts.org/music1.

64. *New York Times*, February 24, 2001.

65. *News and Observer*, February 18, 2001; "Memorial Auditorium," "Fletcher Opera Theater," "Kennedy Theatre," Duke Energy Center for the Performing Arts, www.dukeenergycenterraleigh.com.

66. Diane Lea, "Raleigh's Miracle on South Street," *Metro Magazine*, January/February 2001, 26–27.

67. William Murray of USITT to Irvin A. Pearce, December 12, 2001, private collection; Lea, "Raleigh's Miracle on South Street," 27.

68. *News and Observer*, January 9, 2002.

69. "Richard R. Hoffert," Chorus America, https://www.chorusamerica.org/conf2012/richard-r-hoffert; Richard R. Hoffert, interview with the authors, February 9, 2018, Chapel Hill; *News and Observer*, February 18, 2001.

70. Gilmore, "Long Road Home," 43–44; "Richard R. Hoffert," Chorus America.

71. "David Chambless Worters Named President and CEO for the Van Cliburn Foundation," *D Magazine*, September 1, 2010, https://www.dmagazine.com/arts-entertainment/2010/09/van-cliburn-foundation-names-david-chambless-worters-president-and-ceo/.

72. *North Carolina Symphony 2000–01 Season: Experience the Music* (program book), iii.

73. Gilmore, "Long Road Home," 44.

74. *North Carolina Symphony 2000–01 Season*, iv.

75. *New York Times*, February 24, 2001.

76. *North Carolina Symphony Gala Opening, Meymandi Concert Hall, BTI Center for the Performing Arts, February 21, 2001* (program), 7.

77. *New York Times*, February 24, 2001; *News and Observer*, February 22, 2001.

78. *News and Observer*, February 18, 2001.

79. Jimmy Gilmore, "A Musician's Eye View," in *In Celebration: Gerhardt Zimmermann and the North Carolina Symphony, 1982–2003* ([Raleigh: North Carolina Symphony, 2003]), [14–15].

80. Peters, "Celebrated Conductor Gerhardt Zimmermann Reflects on Time at UI."

81. Gerhardt Zimmermann, "Brief History of the North Carolina Symphony," in *In Celebration*, [16].

82. *North Carolina Symphony 2002–2003 Season: Nine Great Guest Conductors* (brochure), 1–9 (quotation on 1).

83. "Gerhardt Zimmermann, Music Director," Canton Symphony Orchestra, https://www.cantonsymphony.org/people-of-canton-symphony/gerhardt-zimmermann-music-director/; "Gerhardt Zimmermann," Butler School of Music, College of Fine Arts, University of Texas at Austin, https://music.utexas.edu/about/people/zimmermann-gerhardt.

Chapter 7

1. *Rocky Mount Telegram,* January 15, 2004.

2. David Worters, interview with the authors, May 1, 2018, Raleigh.

3. Worters interview; Marvin J. Ward, "The Parade of the Guests at the NCS," *CVNC,* April 22, 2003, https://cvnc.org/article.cfm?articleId=4107; *North Carolina Symphony Jan.– May 2004 Concerts: Magnificent Music* (program book). Dates of the conductors' appearances were supplied to Worters and the authors by Sue Guenther, assistant to the CEO of the North Carolina Symphony.

4. *North Carolina Symphony Sept.–Jan. 2004–05 Concerts: We're Creating America's Next Great Orchestra* (program book), iv.

5. *Chicago Tribune,* July 25, 2002.

6. *North Carolina Symphony Sept.–Jan. 2004–05 Concerts.*

7. *North Carolina Symphony February–May 2006 Concerts* (program book).

8. *North Carolina Symphony 75th Anniversary: Celebrate with Us! September 2006– January 2007 Concerts* (program book).

9. *North Carolina Symphony 75th Anniversary. Schubert's Farewell: The Miraculous Final Year, Program Guide, November 2006* (flyer), [2].

10. *Asheville Citizen-Times,* November 25, 2006.

11. Roy C. Dicks, "Grant Llewellyn's Decade with the N.C. Symphony: The Honeymoon Continues," *Classical Voice North America: Journal of the Music Critics Association of North America,* September 30, 2013, https://classicalvoiceamerica.org/2013/09/30/grant-llewellyns-decade-with-the-n-c-symphony-the-honeymoon-continues/.

12. *Ibid.*

13. *Ibid.*

14. *Asheville Citizen-Times,* January 30, 2007.

15. *North Carolina Symphony 75th Anniversary September 2006–January 2007 Concerts,* xxxii.

16. *Winston-Salem Journal,* May 11, 2010.

17. "Sandi Macdonald, President & Chief Executive Officer, North Carolina Symphony," Leadership, North Carolina Department of Natural and Cultural Resources, https://www.ncdcr.gov/about/leadership/sandi-macdonald; "Sandi M. A. Macdonald" (vita, rev. June 2018), copy in private collection; Sandi Macdonald, interview with the authors, June 27, 2018, Raleigh.

18. Nicholas Joubard, "Grant Llewellyn," Hazard Chase, http://www.hazardchase.co.uk/artists/grant-llewellyn/.

19. *North Carolina Symphony Jan.–May 2004 Concerts,* 71–72, 77.

20. Chelsea Tipton II, "2017–18 Biography," Chelsea Tipton II, Conductor, chelseatipton.com/2017–2018-biography.html.

21. "Thomas Wilkins," Omaha Symphony, https://www.omahasymphony.org/about/music-director.

22. "Carolyn Kuan," Carolyn Kuan, Conductor, http://www.carolynkuan.com/biography.html.

23. *North Carolina Symphony 75th Anniversary September 2006–January 2007 Concerts,* vii; "Joan Landry, Arlington Philharmonic Orchestra Music Director," The Philharmonic Society of Arlington, Massachusetts, psarlington.org/orchestra-conductors/.

24. "Bio," Sarah Hicks, Conductor, www.sarahhicksconductor.com/web/bio.aspx.

25. North Carolina Symphony, *Report to the Community, 2017* (brochure); Macdonald interview; North Carolina Symphony, *Vision 2020: Excellence, Community, Financial Stability* ([2017]) (leaflet).

26. *News and Observer*, May 6, 2018.

27. *North Carolina Symphony 2018–19 Season* (brochure), [4].

28. *News and Observer*, May 11, 2017.

Selected Bibliography

The bibliography is arranged by category because the authors used a variety of types of materials in preparing this study. Other than major reference works, most online sources consulted for biographical information and cited in the notes are not included here.

Primary Sources

MANUSCRIPT COLLECTIONS

Bunker, Joffre, Collection. Private Collections. State Archives, North Carolina Office of Archives and History, Raleigh.

Minutes of the North Carolina Symphony Society and Its Committees, 1940–1973 (microfilm). Records of the North Carolina Department of Cultural Resources. State Archives, North Carolina Office of Archives and History, Raleigh.

North Carolina Symphony Society Records. State Archives, North Carolina Office of Archives and History, Raleigh.

Scales, Alfred Moore, Papers. Private Collections. State Archives, North Carolina Office of Archives and History, Raleigh.

Swalin, Benjamin F. and Maxine M., Papers. Southern Historical Collection. Wilson Library, University of North Carolina at Chapel Hill.

PUBLISHED DOCUMENTS AND MEMOIRS

Byrd, William. *Histories of the Dividing Line betwixt Virginia and North Carolina.* New York: Dover, 1967.

Ferencz, George J., ed. *"The Broadway Sound": The Autobiography and Selected Essays of Robert Russell Bennett.* Rochester, NY: University of Rochester Press, 1999.

Gilmore, Jimmy J. "The Long Road Home: A Musician's Story." *Opus Magazine,* Fall 2006, 32–45.

Jefferson, Thomas. *Writings.* Edited by Merrill D. Peterson. New York: Library of America, 1984.

Lemmon, Sarah McCulloh, ed. *The Pettigrew Papers.* 2 vols. Raleigh: North Carolina Office of Archives and History, 1971–1988.

Mencken, H. L. "The Sahara of the Bozart." In *The American Scene: A Reader,* edited by Huntington Cairns, 157–168. New York: Alfred A. Knopf, 1977.

Powell, William S., ed. *The Correspondence of William Tryon and Selected Papers.* 2 vols. Raleigh: North Carolina Office of Archives and History, 1980–1981.

Still, William Grant. *My Life, My Words: The Autobiography of William Grant Still, American Master Composer*. Flagstaff, AZ: Master-Player Library, 2011.
Swalin, Benjamin. *Hard Circus Road: The Odyssey of the North Carolina Symphony*. Raleigh: North Carolina Symphony Society, 1987.
Swalin, Maxine. *Coming of Age in North Carolina's Fifth Century*. Pt. 1, 3–10. Chapel Hill: North Caroliniana Society, 2003.
_____. *An Ear to Myself*. Chapel Hill: by the author, 1996.

Newspapers

Asheville Advocate.
Asheville Citizen-Times.
Bee (Danville, VA).
Brooklyn (NY) *Daily Eagle.*
Brookville (PA) *Republican.*
Buffalo (NY) *Daily Courier.*
Central New Jersey Home News (New Brunswick).
Chapel Hill Weekly.
Chicago Tribune.
Cincinnati Enquirer.
Courier-Journal (Louisville, KY).
Daily Record (Morristown, NJ).
Daily Tar Heel (Chapel Hill).
Daily Times-News (Burlington, NC).
Democrat and Chronicle (Rochester, NY).
Durham Herald.
Greensboro Daily News.
High Point (NC) *Enterprise.*
Index-Journal (Greenwood, SC).
Indianapolis Star.
Iredell Morning News (Statesville, NC).
Lancaster (OH) *Eagle-Gazette.*
Los Angeles Times.
Lubbock (TX) *Avalanche-Journal.*
Nashville (NC) *Graphic.*
New York Times.
News and Observer (Raleigh).
News Journal (Wilmington, DE).
News of Orange County (Hillsborough, NC).
Ottawa (ON) *Journal.*
Raleigh Register.
Raleigh Times.
Robesonian (Lumberton, NC).
Rocky Mount (NC) *Telegram.*
San Antonio Express.
Savannah Morning News.
Spectator (Raleigh).
Star Tribune (Minneapolis).
State Chronicle (Raleigh).
Statesman-Journal (Salem, OR).
Statesville (NC) *Record and Landmark.*
Sun Journal (New Bern, NC).
Sydney (AU) *Morning Herald.*
Times (Shreveport, LA).

Waco (TX) *News-Tribune.*
Washington Post.
Willmar (MN) *Tribune.*
Winston-Salem Journal.

North Carolina Symphony Publications

North Carolina Symphony 28th Annual Tour, 1972–73 Season. Program.
North Carolina Symphony 1978–1979 Concert Schedule. Brochure.
North Carolina Symphony: A Major Symphony in 50 States. 1979–1980 flyer.
The North Carolina Symphony: The 1983–84 Raleigh Concert Season. Flyer.
1983–84 Young People's Series, the North Carolina Symphony. Flyer.
Robert Ward Celebration: A Seventieth Birthday Concert Tour. The North Carolina Symphony. 1987. Program.
Music: It's What We Do. The North Carolina Symphony 97–98. Program book.
North Carolina Symphony 2000–01 Season: Experience the Music. Program book.
North Carolina Symphony Gala Opening, Meymandi Concert Hall, BTI Center for the Performing Arts, February 21, 2001. Program.
North Carolina Symphony 2002–2003 Season: Nine Great Guest Conductors. Brochure.
North Carolina Symphony Jan.–May 2004 Concerts: Magnificent Music. Program book.
North Carolina Symphony Sept.–Jan. 2004–05 Concerts: We're Creating America's Next Great Orchestra. Program book.
North Carolina Symphony February–May 2006 Concerts. Program book.
North Carolina Symphony 75th Anniversary: Celebrate with Us! September 2006–January 2007 Concerts. Program book.
North Carolina Symphony 75th Anniversary. Schubert's Farewell: The Miraculous Final Year, Program Guide, November 2006. Flyer.
North Carolina Symphony. *Report to the Community, 2017.* Brochure.
North Carolina Symphony. *Vision 2020: Excellence, Community, Financial Stability.* [2017]. Leaflet.
North Carolina Symphony 2018–19 Season. Brochure.

Private Collections

Dicks, Roy C.
Gilmore, Jimmy J.
Gorski, Paul.
Jenkins, Albert and Susan.
Pearce, Irvin A.

Interviews with the Authors

Curry, William Henry. May 31, 2018. Raleigh.
Gilmore, Jimmy J. October 25, 2017. Raleigh.
Gorski, Paul. November 8, 2017. Raleigh.
Hoffert, Richard R. February 9, 2018. Chapel Hill.
Jenkins, Albert and Susan. November 14, 2017. Raleigh.
Macdonald, Sandi. June 27, 2018. Raleigh.
McGuire, Thomas H. January 13, 2018. Raleigh.
Ogle, James E., Jr. By telephone. March 9, 2018. Boise, ID.
Partridge, Hugh. October 18, 2017. Cary, NC.
Simonetti, Vincent F. December 19, 2017. Durham.
Weddle, Ronald. December 21, 2017. Raleigh.
Worters, David. May 1, 2018. Raleigh.

Secondary Sources

BOOKS

Ayers, Edward L. *The Promise of the New South: Life After Reconstruction.* New York: Oxford University Press, 1992.

Bisher, Catherine W., and Michael T. Southern. *A Guide to the Historic Architecture of Piedmont North Carolina.* Chapel Hill: University of North Carolina Press, 2003.

Brook, David Louis Sterrett. *A Lasting Gift of Heritage: A History of the North Carolina Society for the Preservation of Antiquities, 1939–1974.* Raleigh: North Carolina Office of Archives and History, 1997.

Coulter, E. Merton. *The South during Reconstruction, 1865–1877.* Baton Rouge: Louisiana State University Press, 1947.

Craver, Curtis R., Jr. *The History of Music at North Carolina State University.* Raleigh: Department of Music, North Carolina State University, 2000.

Crawford, Richard. *America's Musical Life: A History.* New York: W. W. Norton, 2001.

De Lorenzo, Leonardo. *My Complete Story of the Flute: The Instrument, the Performers, the Music.* Rev. ed. Lubbock: Texas Tech University Press, 1992.

Eaton, Clement. *The Growth of Southern Civilization, 1790–1860.* New York: Harper and Row, 1961.

_____. *The Waning of the Old South Civilization, 1860–1880.* Athens: University of Georgia Press, 1968.

Ekirch, A. Roger. *"Poor Carolina": Politics and Society in Colonial North Carolina.* Chapel Hill: University of North Carolina Press, 1981.

Fountain, Maxine Eleanor Taylor, ed. *Enthusiasts All: A Story of the Impact Made by the North Carolina Federation of Music Clubs upon the State of North Carolina, 1917–1974.* Chapel Hill: Creative Printers, 1974.

Gabin, Jane S. *A Living Minstrelsy: The Poetry and Music of Sidney Lanier.* Macon, GA: Mercer University Press, 1985.

Gragg, Rod. *Covered with Glory: The 26th North Carolina Infantry at the Battle of Gettysburg.* New York: HarperCollins, 2000.

Hall, Harry H. *A Johnny Reb Band from Salem: The Pride of Tarheelia.* Raleigh: North Carolina Office of Archives and History, 2006.

Hobson, Fred C. *Serpent in Eden: H. L. Mencken and the South.* Chapel Hill: University of North Carolina Press, 1974.

Humber, John L. "The North Carolina Symphony, the People's Orchestra: A Brief History." Pt. 3 of Maxine Swalin, *Coming of Age in North Carolina's Fifth Century,* 23–34. Chapel Hill: North Caroliniana Society, 2003.

In Celebration: Gerhardt Zimmermann and the North Carolina Symphony, 1982–2003. [Raleigh: North Carolina Symphony, 2003].

Johnson, Guion Griffis. *Ante-bellum North Carolina: A Social History.* Chapel Hill: University of North Carolina Press, 1937.

Kennedy, David M. *Freedom from Fear: The American People in Depression and War, 1929–1945.* New York: Oxford University Press, 1999.

Link, William A. *North Carolina: Change and Tradition in a Southern State.* Wheeling, IL: Harlan Davidson, 2009.

Malone, Bill C., and David Stricklin. *Southern Music/American Music.* Rev. ed. Lexington: University Press of Kentucky, 2003.

Malone, Dumas. *Jefferson and the Rights of Man.* Boston: Little, Brown, 1951.

_____. *Jefferson the Virginian.* Boston: Little, Brown, 1948.

Massey, Mary Elizabeth. *Refugee Life in the Confederacy.* Baton Rouge: Louisiana State University Press, 1964.

Mitchell, Charles P. *The Great Composers Portrayed on Film, 1913 through 2002.* Jefferson, NC: McFarland, 2004.

Mobley, Joe A. *Pamlico County: A Brief History*. Raleigh: North Carolina Office of Archives and History, 1991.

_____. *Raleigh, North Carolina: A Brief History*. Charleston, SC: History Press, 2009.

_____. *Weary of War: Life on the Confederate Home Front*. Westport, CT: Praeger, 2008.

Mueller, John H. *The American Symphony Orchestra: A Social History of Musical Taste*. Bloomington: Indiana University Press, 1951.

Murray, Elizabeth Reid, and K. Todd Johnson. *Wake: Capital County of North Carolina*. 2 vols. Raleigh: Capital Publishing and Wake County, 1983–2008.

Price, William S., Jr. *"There Ought to Be a Bill of Rights": North Carolina Enters a New Nation*. Raleigh: North Carolina Office of Archives and History, 1991.

Smith, Margaret Supplee, and Emily Herring Wilson. *North Carolina Women Making History*. Chapel Hill: University of North Carolina Press, 1999.

Southern, Eileen. *The Music of Black Americans: A History*. New York: W. W. Norton, 1971.

Story, Rosalyn M. *And So I Sing: African-American Divas of Opera and Concert*. New York: Warner, 1990.

Struble, John Warthen. *The History of American Classical Music*. New York: Facts on File, 1995.

Tucker, Glenn. *Zeb Vance: Champion of Personal Freedom*. New York: Bobbs-Merrill, 1965.

Watson, Alan D. *Wilmington, North Carolina, to 1861*. Jefferson, NC: McFarland, 2003.

Wegner, Ansley Herring. *History for All the People: One Hundred Years of Public History in North Carolina*. Raleigh: North Carolina Office of Archives and History, 2003.

Wiley, Bell Irvin. *The Life of Johnny Reb: The Common Soldier of the Confederacy*. Baton Rouge: Louisiana State University Press, 2004.

Wilson, Clyde N. *Carolina Cavalier: The Life of James Johnston Pettigrew*. Athens: University of Georgia Press, 1990.

Woodward, C. Vann. *Origins of the New South, 1877–1913*. Baton Rouge: Louisiana State University Press, 1951.

Articles

Chassler, Sey. "Symphony on Wheels." *Collier's*, February 23, 1952, 30–31.

Dicks, Roy C. "Grant Llewellyn's Decade with the N.C. Symphony: The Honeymoon Continues." *Classical Voice North America: Journal of the Music Critics Association of North America*, September 30, 2013. https://classicalvoiceamerica.org/2013/09/30/grant-llewellyns-decade-with-the-n-c-symphony-the-honeymoon-continues/.

Gilmore, Jimmy J. "Lamar Stringfield: Piper of Dreams." *Opus Magazine*, Fall 2007, 27–30.

"Happy Anniversary." *New York*, September 21, 1987, 94.

Lambert, John W. "Dr. Ben, Fondly Remembered, & Maxine, Warmly Embraced." *CVNC: An Online Arts Journal in North Carolina*, October 13, 2002. https://cvnc.org/article.cfm?articleId=4771.

Lea, Diane. "Raleigh's Miracle on South Street." *Metro Magazine*, January/February 2001, 26–29.

"Maxine McMahon Swalin." *CVNC: An Online Arts Journal in North Carolina*, October 8, 2009. https://www.cvnc.org/article.cfm?articleId=1181.

McCorkle, Donald M. "The *Collegium Musicum Salem*: Its Music, Musicians, and Importance." *North Carolina Historical Review* 33 (October 1956): 483–498.

_____. "The Moravian Contribution to American Music." *Music Library Association* 13 (September 1956): 597–606.

"On the Move." *Time*, May 9, 1949, 69–70.

"Pops in the Park." The History of Capitol Broadcasting Company. http://history.capitol broadcasting.com/programs/entertainment-shows/pops-in-the-park/.

"75 Things to Know about the North Carolina Symphony." *Opus Magazine*, Fall 2006, 30–31.

"Tarheel Symphony." *Newsweek*, June 9, 1952, 86.

Ward, Marvin J. "The Parade of the Guests at the NCS." *CVNC: An Online Arts Journal in North Carolina*, April 22, 2003. https://cvnc.org/article.cfm?articleId=4107.

Theses and Dissertations

Bentley, Christa Anne. "Finding *The Lost Colony* (1937): Paul Green, Symphonic Drama, and the History of a Collaboration." MA thesis, University of North Carolina at Chapel Hill, 2012.
Nelson, Douglas R. "The Life and Works of Lamar Stringfield (1897–1959)." PhD diss., University of North Carolina at Chapel Hill, 1971.
Pearsall, Howard Turner. "The North Carolina Symphony Orchestra from 1932 to 1962: Its Founding, Musical Growth, and Musical Activities." PhD diss., Indiana University, 1969.

Reference Works

Craven, Robert R. *Symphony Orchestras of the United States: Selected Profiles.* New York: Greenwood, 1986.
Dictionary of National Biography. http://www.oxforddnb.com/.
Encyclopedia of Appalachia. http://www.encyclopediaofappalachia.com/entries.php.
Hill, Michael, ed. *Guide to North Carolina Highway Historical Markers.* Raleigh: North Carolina Office of Archives and History, 2001.
Malone, Bill C., ed. *Music.* Vol. 12 of *The New Encyclopedia of Southern Culture*, edited by Charles Reagan Wilson. Chapel Hill: University of North Carolina Press, 2008.
NCpedia. https://www.ncpedia.org.
New Georgia Encyclopedia. www.georgiaencyclopedia.org.
Online Encyclopedia of Significant People and Places in African American History. Black Past.org. www.blackpast.org/view/vignettes.
Powell, William S., ed. *Dictionary of North Carolina Biography.* 6 vols. Chapel Hill: University of North Carolina Press, 1979–1996.
_____. *Encyclopedia of North Carolina.* Chapel Hill: University of North Carolina Press, 2006.
Slonimsky, Nicolas. *Baker's Biographical Dictionary of Twentieth-Century Classical Musicians.* Edited by Laura Kuhn. New York: Schirmer, 1997.

Index